THE
SOPHISTICATED
TRAVELLER

· THE SOPHISTICATED TRAVELLER ·

BELOVED CITIES
·EUROPE·

EDITED BY
A. M. ROSENTHAL & ARTHUR GELB

IN ASSOCIATION WITH
MICHAEL J. LEAHY, NORA KERR
AND THE TRAVEL STAFF OF
THE NEW YORK TIMES

EBURY PRESS 🙿 LONDON

Published in 1986 by Ebury Press
Division of The National Magazine Company Ltd
Colquhoun House 27-37 Broadwick Street
London W1V 1FR

Copyright ©1983, 1984

by The New York Times Syndication Sales Corp.

This edition published by arrangement with Villard Books, A Division of
Random House, Inc.

ISBN 0 85223 513 5 (hardback)
0 85223 548 8 (paperback)

Illustrations by Joe Ciardiello
Cover illustration by Michael Doret

Computerset in Great Britain by ECM Ltd, London

Printed and bound in Great Britain
by Butler & Tanner Ltd, Frome

CONTENTS

ROME AND BEYOND

ATHENS AND BEYOND

INTRODUCTION

Now, we are all travellers. It used to be, and not long ago at all, that only a few kinds of people travelled.

Men and women of substance travelled. The ability to see some of the world imparted not so much pleasure as power, the power of knowledge of the faraway and the arcane.

The very act of travel was a gesture of privilege, which, of course, was pleasure enough to make up for the carriage jouncing over the rutted road or the unspeakable tediousness of weeks at sea.

Adventurers travelled, and always did – the explorers, freebooters, the men-at-arms. They travelled not so much to get to any particular place, but because it was only in some place far away that they knew they could triumph. It is so sadly often easier to overcome the unknown and the exotic than to deal day by day with the familiar and the mundane. What they knew they could not overcome, and where they were known they could not conquer.

And there have always been the truly brave travellers, in search not of gold or power, but of bread and freedom – the migrants – those men and women of great soul who left their lands and their homes, not because of force but simply because they had heard that beyond the oceans there was work to be found and liberty to be breathed.

We are all travellers now, and that is one of the glories of our time. Almost anybody who picks up this book can read it, not as the literature of the unknown, but as remembrance of what was seen yesterday or what will be experienced tomorrow.

Japanese on Fifth Avenue, Indians on the Via Veneto, or Australians in Machu Picchu. The great revolution of travel is not that they are there, but that Americans, Italians or Peruvians are not at all surprised to see them there, and would be quite astonished if all those strange faces were indeed not part of the scenery every day.

The jet age, cut rates, excursions, credit cards have opened travel to everywhere for tens of millions. But travel is still very much an individual act, an individual exhilaration. There are no 'crowds of tourists,' just lots of people moving, seeing, tasting, wondering, thinking, but all one by one, one by one.

At *The New York Times*, travel is part of life and work. The *Times* is a newspaper that takes not simply its city, but its nation and its world as its beat. Its reporters and editors are probably the most travelled journalists in the world.

That is a fact and a boast too. We simply adore the idea of *Times* reporters lurking in Peshawar, riding ponies in Mongolia, Inner and Outer alike, talking Chinese in Peking, Arabic in Damascus and money in Berne. We hug with pleasure the memory that on the same day a few years ago, there were stories from one reporter climbing mountains with a Soviet team and from another jotting down notes in a research submarine off the French coast.

Some of us – correspondents in places like Southeast Asia, Africa or Latin America – are away from our bases, travelling, sixty to ninety per cent of the time. Others spend most of their time in one country – Italy, say, or Japan. There are still others who move from New York and return, or wander about the regions of the United States. Whatever, travel is as much a part of *The Times* as paper and ink. An immobile *Times* would be like a berthed ship – very bulky, but not very interesting.

Good newspapers are full of the sense of travel every day because truly good correspondents – domestic, local or foreign – can evoke the sense of place with a word or phrase. Sometimes it is obvious: 'Dakar is a steam bath with a view.' Often it is unconscious as far as the writer is concerned, and almost imperceptible to the reader.

But if you read a newspaper with enough attention, you will find that over a period of time the dispatches from India are quite different than those from France. In New Delhi people speak with a different rhythm and think with a different mental cadence than they do in Paris. A good correspondent, after a while, develops different lilts in his typewriter – or more exactly his portable computer-transmitter – for different places.

But travel writing is not merely a byproduct of a good story. It is a craft, a talent, in itself. Like most large newspapers, *The Times* has long had a travel department and even a weekly travel section.

It struck us, rather late, that we had not really recognized the scope and joys of travel writing as an end in itself. It struck us that we really ought to pay at least as much attention to travel as to sports or the theatre or the stock exchange. Perhaps a lot more, because travel means more to our own lives and tastes than even plays, bonds, or – forgive us – football.

So we discarded everything we had done before about travel and decided to start fresh in a new weekly travel section. Since we, the editors of the paper, are all travellers, and so are our friends, we decided to put out a section for our most cherished readers, us and people like us in New York or any other city they have had to choose as second best.

We realized to start with that we were not the repository of all travel-writing talent – a cultural shock. Some of the most interesting writers in the world had been turning out travel stories without a newspaper to print them in and doing quite well – Mark Twain, Charles Dickens, Mary Shelley, Henry James, Charles Darwin. Somewhat earlier, Marco Polo and Ptolemy. Somewhat later, André Gide, Aldous Huxley, Edith Wharton. And how about John Steinbeck and Graham Greene?

We were a little late for Ptolemy, even for Steinbeck, but there were others. So we set out to cajole into writing travel stories people who could write well about many things and who found the idea of writing about travel enticing.

We were gratified and grateful at the kind of writers who decided that sitting down and writing about places they had been was exactly what they wanted to do. Saul Bellow wrote for the new section and so did Muriel Spark and Shirley Hazzard and Luigi Barzini and A. E. Hotchner, A. Alvarez and V. S. Pritchett. They are all here in this book, writing on cities beloved to them.

We realized that we had a built-in staff of sophisticated travellers and travel experts – our own correspondents abroad and in the United States. We asked them to make travel writing not an afterthought but a built-in part of their jobs. They did.

And so we are able to put together week after week not a random bunch of pieces written by travel-guide editors, but a thoughtful collection of essays by fine writers and correspondents caught in the act of enjoying themselves. They salted and peppered their work with their findings on matters that mean as much to them as to any traveller – advice on prices, places to shop, what to eat and where.

From the weekly grew another concept – *The Sophisticated Traveller*, a twice-yearly magazine devoted to one or two themes. Then of course came the decision to put out *The Sophisticated Traveller* books.

The idea was to create not yet another basic guide, but a new entity, and we hope a new kind of travel book, based on the weekly section and the semi-annual magazine. There was no issue or section of the magazine called 'Beloved Cities,' but thinking about what had been printed and rereading it, we realized that it was a theme that appeared time and again, week after week.

So we culled them, put them together, ordered special pieces where we thought there was a gap, and the result is a book that we wanted to be thoughtful, entertaining, and as practical as a good pair of walking shoes. We hope it is.

A.M.R. & A.G.

POINTS OF DEPARTURE

Shirley Hazzard

Each year the travellers set out in millions to score and circle the globe – and roaring over seas and continents, weaving through landscapes and towns, scarcely slackening pace in temples, museums and shops, scaling mountains, scouring catacombs, crossing deserts and glaciers; intersecting one another, unseeing, at stations and airports as in some immense and intricate dance.

This act of pilgrimage has become intimidating in many ways. It is a lucky traveller who doesn't suffer through strikes, losses, delays. Enthusiasm falters during the pentitential wait at the airport and before the serried ranks looming in the jumbo, terrible as an army with banners. In these and many other respects, travel has resumed its ancient meaning, of travail. Yet expense and anxiety are evidently discounted as incidental, merely, to one of the supreme and most reliable of pleasures – a human venture charged, even yet, with legendary possibility and high romance.

'We change our skies, not our souls,' Horace cautions. Some souls nevertheless bring with them a capacity for joy, an accessibility to other thoughts and tastes, an ear for other tongues, an eye for other beauty: a readiness. Revelation – so inalienable an element of travel that there is even a luggage of the name – takes multiple and often inward forms. Many a traveller departs in the hope of defining an elusive self or mislaying a burdensome one – of being, literally, carried away. Literature has prepared us to expect the release of new aspects of ourselves in the presence of the fabled and unfamiliar. Simply by looking on given scenes and monuments human beings have been known to become happier and wiser. Travel is an elixir, a talisman: a spell cast by what has long and greatly been, over what briefly and simply is.

Travel, according to the nineteenth century French wayfarer Astolphe de Custine, is a means of visiting other centuries. Imagination goes with us on our journey, a thrilling and beautiful companion. Modern purposefulness gives place to plurality of sensation; explanation is shamed – if not always silenced – by mystery. The traveller simultaneously sheds and receives, and in the very thick of the crowd may still experience the poignant reciprocity of place and person. Even the tourist who only glimpses, from a sealed bus, the Eiffel Tower or the Colosseum, seeks his particle of the holy relic of the world's experience. And how much passion and event have been invested in those famous sights, that they should continue to yield meaning – even to the millionth and most casual eye – with unstinted generosity; assimilating decay itself as an enrichment. (A sceptical young woman of Henry James's invention, who supposes Rome to be spoiled, receives the experienced answer: 'I think not. It has been spoiled so often.')

Thus the world exchanges, annually, its store of contrasts, adventure and refreshment, and almost everyone continues to feel the better for it. That the contrasts are dwindling, that adventure is often frenzied, that the modern onslaught of curiosity may itself be depleting the world's reserves of human interest – these are menaces put out of mind along with other presentiments of Armageddon. The great theatre that Europe has come to constitute for tourists remains a magnet, though the summer show may sometimes offer standing room only. In the Pacific, the prophecies of Herman Melville and Victor Segalen have been fulfilled at Waikiki; and even for the farthest archipelagoes:

> *. . . the satiate year impends*
> *When, wearying of routine resorts,*
> *The pleasure-hunter shall break loose,*
> *Ned, for our Pantheistic ports –*
> Herman Melville, *To Ned*

Despite such evidence, and the airport bookstall's terse announcement that 'Civilization is now in paperback,' the exhaustion of travel's immemorial repository of delights is apparently as unthinkable as the extinction of fossil fuels. The very precariousness and anonymity of contemporary existence, and its acceleration of destruction and change, create a compulsion to seize the moment. The excursion to other centuries – undertaken these days with antibiotics, credit cards and a return ticket to the 1980's – has new urgency and a tinge of valediction. The modern visitor to the past may yet embrace abroad what is déclassé at home – ripeness, grace, ceremony, repose, an acceptance of mortality: waning concepts that may never revisit our planet; while the denizens of ancient places seek, in turn, in newer nations, expansiveness, volatility, an unconcern for and even repudiation of experience. And still others take to the wilderness, for respite from all manifestations of their fellow man. Although the intention of travel is far from non-committal, its commitment is luxuriously selective: relieved of responsibility for the failings he encounters, the traveller can enjoy the haunting quality of the antique without its terror; the poetic emanation of past strivings without their anguish; the energy of the future without its aridity. A condition of the attraction of the unknown is that it remain, in some measure, inscrutable.

The coast of my native land supplied, in my case, a first glimpse of the unknown: in the lights – seen from a deck on the first night of sailing to the Orient – of Australian seaboard towns that lay beyond the range of my landlocked childhood excursions. Those clustered lights gave the first sensation of passing a barrier; they were at once departure and discovery. A five-week journey from Sydney to Japan in the postwar 1940's – in a little, old, durable ship that made one brief stop, in a jungle cove of New Guinea, for water – was a fitting preparation for momentous change. Awakening one dawn of befogged vermilion in the Inland Sea we were faithfully brought to port, and other travels began. I had read Conrad's *Youth*, and lived, then, the closing moments of that story – waking to the East 'so old, so mysterious, resplendent and sombre, living and unchanged, full of danger and promise.'

The East is unchanged no longer; and such rapture is itself said to come only once. In fact I have re-experienced it many times – spending a moonlit night on deck to sight the coast of Crete, the straits of Messina, the cone of Stromboli; setting foot on an unperturbed Europe at Marseilles one September morning; lying off the Cornish coast at sunrise and driving that noon into London through a shambles of blitzed docks. And landing, years later, at Rome one evening in early winter – to mild air, trees in leaf and baskets of violets for sale on the then unlittered and unsullied Spanish steps. I remember a snowbound Epiphany in hills south of Florence; and blue shutters opening, near Carthage, on a turquoise sea; a hillside of narcissus at Volubilis; and the dry summer grass of the Camargue.

Distant lights have retained their power. Time after time, from the transatlantic flight, I have looked out, before sunrise, for the lamps of fishing fleets off Ireland – signals of a life older than memory, perceived from the age of jet propulsion.

I, too, have visited other centuries – in Arcadia itself, in sunbaked towns south of the Atlas and under the colonial arcades of a vanished Hong Kong; have seen old Chinese women hobble on stumps of their bound feet, and the scholars passing, gowned and slippered, along the streets of Asia. I have shared, from Monticello, the nineteenth century vision of America. I have watched French missionary nuns, in white and blue, red parasols aloft above the towering medieval headdress, move unconcerned through tropical rain; and country women, in ceremonial bodices and long skirts, stroll down the quays of Venice.

It is women, more usually, who bear such emblems into other times

— as, last summer at the port of Capri, a trio of handsome matriarchs who stepped ashore from Catanzaro – gold and silver lace over their coiled hair and on their dresses, of *rosso antico*, that swept the ground. By their festive costume they honoured the great occasion of travel: Their restraint, among the modern hubbub, was a form of authority, a stately humility before the wonders of this world.

If, on our travels, we are not precisely surprised by such apparitions, such enchantments, it is because we always dreamed we might see them.

The traveller equipped with even one introduction arrives with a card to play, a possible clue to the mystery. Yet those who have never experienced solitude in a strange and complex place – never arrives in the unknown without credentials, without introductions to the right people, or the wrong ones – have missed an exigent luxury. Never to have made the lonely walk along the Seine or Lugano, or passed those austere evenings on which all the world but oneself has destination and companion, is perhaps never to have felt the full presence of the unfamiliar. It is thus one achieves a slow, indelible intimacy with place, learning to match its moods with one's own. At such times it is as if a destination had awaited us with nearly human expectation and with an exquisite blend of receptivity and detachment.

In this truest spirit of travel forty years ago, an English poet – Henry Read – pondered a city known to him only on the map, Verona, to which he would some day go:

> *The train will bring me perhaps in utter darkness*
> *And drop me where you are blooming, unaware*
> *That a stranger has entered your gates at last*
> *And a new devotion*
> *Is about to attend and haunt you everywhere.*
> From 'A Map of Verona.'

The moment comes: we intersect a history, a long existence, offering it our fresh discovery as regeneration.

PUBLISHER'S NOTE

The Sophisticated Traveller series was originally written, edited and compiled for an American audience and in view of the fact that it is the outstanding quality of the writing that readers will most appreciate, factual information (including prices) remains as in the original American edition. When prices are given they should be taken as a general guide, since inflation and fluctuations in the exchange rates can have a significant effect on costs.

LONDON
AND BEYOND

MY LONDON

V. S. Pritchett

I am not London born, but I have spent a large part of my life as a London perambulator, footing it from the unfashionable south to the north since I was a boy. In those years I felt myself to be a sort of Indian hunter, following a maze of brickish jungle paths from one native village to the next across mysterious frontiers, the most exciting one being the ancient Thames. I grew up kippered by smoke and fog from sulphurous Bermondsey to the lighter mists of high-minded Hampstead, with the tales of my Cockney mother in my head.

There was no skyline in those days: the great splodge of what Henry James called 'the horrible numerosity' was as flat as Venice. The city had no style, he said, only innumerable attempts at style, but, on the whole, it was 'the most possible form of life.'

It is the most livable city that I know. High-rise buildings, the modern prison towers, the brutal postwar strong-point architecture, did not come in until the late 1950's; and London is still the green city of more trees, gardens and grass growing romantically wild than any capital I have ever seen. It is difficult to be more than fifty yards from a tree, when you bear in mind the scrub behind the drab shops or fanciful houses that stare at you. The Londoner is an inveterate gardener. At the back of his mind – and it has more back to it than front – he thinks he is in the country. The blocks of new flats near where I lived now bear the names of the Lake District: Ullswater, Buttermere, Windermere, acclaiming Wordsworth and the Lake poets. In Cherry Garden Street close to the Thames-side wharves there are actually cherry trees. There is rich growing soil around the warehouses.

I am now a North Londoner. I live in an area generally known as Camden Town, near Regent's Park, and can walk, but for the crowds, to Piccadilly in half an hour if I am in form. Yet I live in a house that is surrounded back and front by a jungle of huge plane trees and acacias, so that in spring and summer I can't see the lorries going by to the railway freight depot at the end of the short street; nor can I see the main line to the Midlands and Scotland running behind the large

Victorian villas opposite. Only in the winter can I see the tall houses at the back or even spot what neighbours are doing on their lawns or in their orchard-like gardens. We live in the inner London boscage, which is always sprouting – how healed we felt when miles of willow herb grew at once out of the ruined streets during the last war.

I wake in the morning to the dawn chorus of tropical birds and to the shouts of the hilarious gibbons and the roars of lions at the zoo. They sound like a football crowd. The milk bottle is at the door, left by that sexy folk hero, the London milkman, guaranteeing our national traditions. (What happens at the high-rise blocks of flats, goodness knows. They are the new non-London London. When the planners decided to rob us of gardens, crime increased.)

I am lucky to be living in a private terrace of twenty-two houses with a long communal garden in front: the city is rich in privacies. The Regent's Park terraces are alleged to be late John Nash, with huge windows, yet we are far from being as grand as the 'royal mile' of lordly early Nash mansions of Regent's Park, two minutes away, with their oriental domes and romping classical gods and goddesses.

But consider the irony of my neighbourhood's history and frontier situation. In 1840 the Camden Town area was the boundary of London farmland that had become the city refuse dump when the railway age began. We are an island in a mishmash of railway tracks going to Edinburgh. Our street shakes at the corner because under it are the deep vaults and stables where the horses and the hay, the petrol of the Victorian age, were kept. Until twenty-five years ago, when we were forbidden to burn coal (electric and diesel trains had come in), this was one of the smokiest, most bronchitic areas of London. If you read Dickens's *Dombey and Son*, you will see exactly the ruthless chaos out of which our elegant terrace grew, and why the district is one of London's inner frontiers: we are as much Regent's Park as we are the proletarian Mother Red Cap Tavern. I mention Dickens advisedly: he was the greatest of the London day and night walkers; and when he was a lad and the family were on their beam ends, they lived in poverty in Bayham Street, close by, as his father was marched off to the Marshalsea, the debtors' prison south of the river. When Dickens became famous, he went to live in state in Devonshire Place, just the other side of the park. But in his latter years, when he separated from his wife he planted her in one of the big, substantially middle-class houses whose gardens back onto our own. (And when I say middle-class, think of the troops of London 'skivvies' who carried the coals up five flights of stairs, the cooks, the between-maids and the carriages!)

In the main, Camden Town is a neighbourhood of thousands of little early Victorian houses, some 'going down,' but most now tending to 'go up'. The district still lives for crafts and trade. Turn right at the end of my terrace and you are soon among warehouses of the old kind, the workshops of the dress trades, the huge lorry park for transcontinental lorries. You pass the classic circular piano factory, which is a collector's piece for architects. Pianos are not made there now. Someone round here, a man with exactly my name and initials, was 'in the ivories,' and I used to get calls for quotations a few years back.

You soon feel 'historic' in London districts. The railway clatters: there is a pub called The Locomotive; there is a huge red building of at least a couple of hundred narrow windows, a place built for homeless labourers who want a cheap bed for the night – now no longer cheap – and then you are in the main road for traffic to the North.

Turn to the left from my house and in half a minute you are in a traffic-jammed street of small pubs, shops and cheap cafés. This is the real Camden Town. It must have been plain Cockney until the Irish labourers came in to build the railroads. Now their descendants fill the pubs – the Dublin Castle in honour of Ireland, the Edinburgh Castle for the Scots and Windsor Castle for the English. (Old local boozers still talk of 'going round the Castles.')

The Irish are noticeable because they stand whispering soft-voiced outside the betting shops, confiding a tip to a friend and going off with a bottle in their pockets. When the pubs close in the afternoon there is usually a gathering of Irishmen outside the gentlemen's convenience on the traffic island at the crossroads, where they stand talking for an hour or so. The site is known locally as 'the Emerald Isle.' You can buy all the Irish provincial papers – the Cork *Examiner* and perhaps even the Skibbereen *Eagle* – at the paper shops, now run mainly by Pakistanis or Hindus or Sinhalese who speak a politer and more antique English than we do (it sounds like Welsh).

Not all the Irish talk is about memorable jockeys. My bank manager has a literary turn, and my friend at the pharmacy knows his Joyce and his Yeats better than many an academic. He comes from the Falls Road. He has left Camden Town lately but returns, as he says, for its great amenity: 'the social life.' Competing with the Irish, but in the grocery, fruit and restaurant trades, are the impassioned and enterprising Cypriots and Greeks. And in the afternoon hundreds of Japanese children come out of their school at the corner, which used to be a convent. We have a Japanese hairdresser.

But, that social life. Where do we all meet? At shops and pubs, of course, but mainly in the street market, the melting pot in all inner London districts. It is mostly run by the Cockneys, whose aim in life is to shout and play-act at stalls everywhere between Shoreditch and Soho and beyond: 'You're in England. Stick to the language, carntcher? Speak up! What is it, love?' That final phrase is imposed to heal all wounds. For at the market we are not Mr. or Mrs., Sir or

Madam, or even Mum and Dad, but, in a thick wash of sentiment, 'love,' 'ducks,' 'dear' and 'darling' for the women and 'guv' for the men. We are people who are used to being rained on and jeered at; the street market is the heart of any London village – and town planners dare not do away with it or impose a cross-Channel elegance.

The crowd is thick, you bump into your betters as you shuffle past the stalls from potatoes to apples, from cabbage to pineapples and on to clothes and junk and a few books. Last week I saw the complete works of George Moore stacked on the kerb. We have a sprinkling of professors, editors, theatre people, lawyers, poets and television stars. Just around the corner the winos sit in deep privacy, crammed into the back doors of a cinema. On hot days they will move to the sunny side of the street. Harmless, sad people. A few months ago I saw one of them, a fat woman, trying to roll on top of an old man and tearing at his shirt collar. Not a murder: she was trying, she said to passers-by, 'to give him the kiss of life.' He sat up, thanking her.

We have a fair number of that London specialty, the eccentric. Most of us are reserved and dissimulate in the London way, but the eccentric publicly dramatizes his inner life. Why does that man suddenly open his jacket and display a naked chest tattooed with a nest of serpents? Why does that respectable woman with the dog stamp and shout her way into shops denouncing 'the technological, scientific, communistic-capitalist society' and scream out that 'the blacks, Chinese, Indians, are taking your jobs'? No one takes any notice of her diatribes. We shrug our shoulders; the blacks and the Asians politely smile. Who is that tall, ghostly, rather distinguished lady in long evening dress and satin slippers who once asked me whether I would 'adopt' her because she happened to be 'temporarily short of funds'? Or that man who steers his way through the crowd, arm outstretched, his finger pointing accusingly at all of us? These people are martyrs to compulsion. They are carrying to extremes something present in most Londoners: a suppressed histrionic gift. London, as Dickens observed in his street prowling, is a theatre populated by actors asserting a private extravagance. The desire to be a 'well-known character,' to enlarge modestly a hidden importance, is endemic.

My walking aim is always dead north as far as Regent's Canal (the local segment of the Grand Union Canal) in a devious journey by backways to the 'country' – Regent's Park. I've seen sheep grazing there, heard nightingales, watched the geese and ducks fly over in the evenings. You pass the antique shops, the sex or political pamphlet places, and find yourself by Camden Town's pleasure dome: Camden Lock, the wide stretch of cobbled wharves along the canal. You are suddenly among hundreds of young people dressed, it seems, in fantastic gear concocted from old rugs and throwaway Victorian garb, skirts that drag the dust or are giddily short. Camden Town has its Covent Garden, its Tivoli. It has a 'scene.' This is where the young buy their native-disguises cheap, grow their beards, munch their hot sandwiches as they walk. Here they paint and make jewellery or listen to rock. You can eat well and drink your wine at Le Routier and watch the red and green barges rise in the lock, while the guitarists and singers perform outside.

Here at Paddy Walker's (he is a local hero for leading the drive to preserve this neighbourhood) you get your tickets for those long canal trips where you eat on board, eastbound to the London Docks, westbound through the park, past Little Venice and miles out into real country, beyond London, remembering that before the railway the canals were the winding highways of England. The wine flows; once out in the country the madcaps tip off their clothes and swim naked alongside the boat. London pleasures are hearty without ceasing to be demure.

For the perambulator, there is another hidden pleasure. You can get onto the townpath at the lock and walk – past the backways of houses and gardens, past a man fishing from his kitchen window, eventually past the zoo, the pleasure boats and the fleets of ducks, and on to the outer solitudes of Regent's Park and the exotic golden dome of the Arab mosque. You have crossed a new frontier. For myself this is the loveliest of our vast parks. You can row, even sail on its lake, circle the island where the strange birds nest, take part in the Sunday morning promenade along its bank. In spring there are seas of crocuses, daffodils and tulips; the trees are immense. Occasionally an eagle may have escaped from the zoo and settled high in the trees. 'Pore thing,' the sentimental Londoner says.

On the wide stretches of grass the kite-flyers are tugging away. In the summer, the couples are cuddling and thick on the ground, the dogs racing round them. If you are a profound Londoner you go into Queen Mary's Garden, the most specialized and botanically erudite in London. It is an education in the gardening aspect of the London mind. A man who doesn't know his roses, the rare plants of his rockeries or how to plant that extraordinary goulash, the English herbaceous border on the grand scale, who doesn't know what to do with a trellis or a rustic bridge, who cannot accurately name a tree – such a man is very peculiar to us.

In Regent's Park you see for once the full expanse of the London sky. It is not a postcard sky. It may be sad or leaden, it may be superb, but it is never hard. There will be slight, worrying, even pathetic breaks in it. By the evening there will perhaps be a reassuring, even seductive mist, which appeals to the Londoner's dislike of seeing things too clearly. Or, more likely in this changeable climate of spinning foreign winds, there will be one of those blowing and ballooning skies of sailor blue and toppling white clouds that make us feel London and even the whole of the British Isles is a ship rocking off the coast of Europe. For London is the captain's bridge of a ship of seedy traders, crewed by impecunious pirates and hamish actors longing to 'get out,' collar the spoils and smuggle them home, and then to disappear into some private spot where they can moralize at leisure.

LONDON WALKS

Paul Goldberger

It is the serenity of it all that is so startling – the ability of the place, no matter how frantic the moment, to seem so right and so comforting. London is far too big and far too busy to be called tranquil, but it is ordered in a way that New York is not; it has a certain way of looking that speaks of self-assurance. It is a city full of change and growth, yet nothing seems to shake its basic solidity – mediocre skyscrapers may damage its physical fabric but they do not break it; increasing amounts of traffic make the process of moving about slower but somehow not uglier, as in so many other cities. This is probably the least shrill large city on earth, and in that lies a key to its essence.

It is no accident that in London the taxis are black and the beloved double-decker buses red, that telephone booths look like tiny red conservatories and the names of streets are marked on large, clear plaques. It is of such consistent and carefully wrought details that civilized cities are made.

London is full of surprises, but they are the good kind of surprises – the sudden view of the tower of Big Ben from the front of Buckingham Palace back through the leafy richness of St. James's Park, or the privacy of the St. George's (Hanover Square) Gardens, hidden in the middle of a Mayfair block. These are very different kinds of surprises from the realization that there is almost no place to sit down on the entire length of Madison Avenue.

London does not look like Paris, or New York, or Rome or Tokyo, and it looks only somewhat like other cities in Britain. It sprawls in a way that, horrifying as this may seem, makes it not altogether unlike Los Angeles: both cities cover vast areas, both have older central business districts that are now occupied largely by their financial communities, and in both the rich seem to prefer living in the western segments while the eastern sections are left to the poor. But there the resemblance ends, for Los Angeles is essentially a single burst of twentieth century energy coming from a central source, while London is a complex web of separate villages, spun together over centuries of growth.

The London we see today is essentially a city of the eighteenth and nineteenth centuries. Though it is rich in buildings that came before – Westminster Abbey, after all, was started in 1220, and Sir Christopher Wren, London's best-known architect, did most of his work in the late seventeenth century – the streetscape, the block-after-block of buildings we think of as characteristic of London, for the most part came later. And while there are plenty of new, or relatively new, buildings in London, the architects of the twentieth century have had nowhere near the impact on the total form of their city that their colleagues in New York have had. Despite their presence in considerable quantity, modern buildings here tend to poke up awkwardly, as if caught poorly dressed at a gathering to which they had not been invited.

The metaphor is not as frivolous as it may seem – this city is a gathering of sorts, a gathering of buildings that do seem to spring from common impulses. There is a commitment throughout London to an orderly relationship between buildings, to modest scale, to open space amid urban density. This is a crowded city but it is not a tall city; the sky is always visible. Squares and streets are lined with buildings that, though they may have been built over time, clearly seem intended to belong with each other – one rarely senses, as occurs so often in New York and even in Paris, that a town house or an office building erected half a century later than its neighbours seems destined to engage in permanent battle with its surroundings.

The huge size of this city is perhaps its only drawback as a walkers' place: one must travel by Underground or by bus or car to begin a walk, and there is a lot of territory to cover. But everything else about London makes it ideal – the reasonable scale, the relative quiet, the lively yet never wild rhythms of the façades. Curiously, though the pattern of streets is random and complex, the sense of order is so much greater than it is in Cartesian Manhattan – a reminder, perhaps, that a feeling of order comes from subtle things.

The three walks below are highly personal and by no means exhaustive. Each covers a somewhat different portion of central London, and thus gives a somewhat different sense of the city. Together they do not make up all of London, which a hundred walks could not do. While each has its share of significant architecture, this is by no means a tour of London's famous buildings. The Houses of Parliament and St. Paul's can be visited on their own; it is more a sense of the city that is the goal. Each walk begins at a conveniently located tube stop.

MAYFAIR ELEGANCE

Mayfair is well-to-do London, a neighbourhood that is often spoken of as an equivalent to the Upper East Side of Manhattan. It is really more like

Manhattan's East Fifties, however, for it is at the edge of several commercial districts, and its fine eighteenth century houses have been largely taken over by the needs of commerce. But the essence of a good neighbourhood remains – there is a pleasing mix of commercial and residential uses still, and eighteenth and nineteenth century London co-exist here with considerably grace and even beauty.

Begin at the Green Park tube stop along Piccadilly, the great street that links Piccadilly Circus with Hyde Park Corner, and walk west past Half Moon Street to White Horse Street. Turn right and walk up to **Shepherd Market**, a hidden oasis of shops and restaurants that feels like a mews masquerading as a village square. It is here, in a commercial development by an architect, Edward Shepherd, that Mayfair began in 1735; today it survives as a hideaway. With its antique and fabric shops it has become a touch precious, but the presence, at least by day, of vegetable sellers hawking their wares from the back of a lorry brings some balance.

Leave the tiny square by the left, then turn right and pass through an archway to Curzon Street. This is the 'real' Mayfair, as opposed to the original one, a mix of old and new buildings, few of them remarkable but all to some degree elegant, and all distinguished by a pleasing, compatible scale. Turn left on Curzon Street, then right on Chesterfield Street; here Mayfair becomes quieter, more serene and more all of a piece – all of a Georgian piece, in fact.

It becomes quieter still as Chesterfield Street ends at Charles Street – here is one of the few sections of Mayfair that still feels residential. Walk to the left: the street narrows at the end to accommodate a large tree in an old yard, a reminder that this was not a section laid out on a planner's draughting table, but one that grew ad hoc. There are some fine houses on this street, with a hint of English whimsy – No. 26 has a bust of Nero over the lintel of its front door.

Double back down Charles Street for a block to Chesterfield Hill and turn left. This residential block calls to mind Beekman Place in New York; it is quiet and self-consciously pretty. Stay on Chesterfield Hill past Hay's Mews and Hill Street, and turn left at South Street. Just after the sumptuous orange-brick apartment house at No. 51 South Street turn right and slip down the path into **St. George's** (Hanover Square) **Gardens**, usually called St. George's Gardens, an exquisitely landscaped public space, different from other such in that it is bordered directly by buildings and not by streets. There are trees and benches and wide lawns, and a wonderful sense of being outdoors and yet indoors and private at the same time; it is as if Manhattan's Turtle Bay Gardens could be reached from the street.

St. George's Gardens has the added virtue of an unusual shape, making it seem full of hidden alcoves and cul-de-sacs. Walk through it and exit to the left; this will put you in front of a public library dating from 1894, one of those brick-and-stone Tudor-Renaissance mixes that is particularly characteristic of Victorian London.

Turn right at the corner onto South Audley Street, one of Mayfair's finest shopping streets. It is classic late Victorian genteel London, lined with warm red- and orange-brick and terracotta buildings that are far more inviting, really, than their cooler Parisian counterparts of stone.

This block contains a fine mix of shops, from **Purdey & Sons**, the legendary gunsmiths, to a little local food shop of considerable panache. The next corner is Mount Street, and the intersection of South Audley Street and Mount Street is pure nineteenth century Mayfair, just as Charles Street and Chesterfield Hill were pure eighteenth century Mayfair. Worth special note is the complex of shops with three floors above that fills the entire block of South Audley Street and the **Grosvenor Chapel** and **Mount Street**. It is a glorious rhythm of Victorian stone; the long façade on Mount Street brings life and vibrancy and yet utter dignity to a street of otherwise unexceptional shops.

Turn right on Mount Street to explore this building for its full length, then let the gracefully curving façade of the **Connaught Hotel** swing you around to the left onto Carlos Place. The Connaught, with its flower-bedecked white entry porch, is at once welcoming and imposing; like the South Audley Street building, it is a fine example of nineteenth century red brickwork yielding a building of considerable luxury and ease. The curve of the façade is a reminder of how easily even monumental buildings in this city often work into a larger urban fabric; Carlos Place is a short street with a bend at its end, and both the Connaught and the apartment building across the street at No. 1 Carlos Place express the curve gracefully.

Walk up Carlos Place into **Grosvenor Square**, one of London's most famous – and dullest – squares. It is a flat lawn, notable largely for the quality of its maintenance. (Would there ever be such a clean square in New York, or such gentle signs as these, which do not order us to keep off the grass, but merely urge us to 'Keep to the Paths to Avoid Unnecessary Wear to the Grass Area'? It is in such gestures that London reveals its character.)

The one thing of note on Grosvenor Square is Eero Saarinen's **American Embassy** at the west end. This Portland Stone façade of overscaled window frames tries hard to be modern and yet to be respectful of its surroundings; it is moderately successful, but it is hard not to feel that it is an overachiever, a building that just tries too hard. Its enormous cast and gilded aluminium eagle – Saarinen wanted an even bigger one – was at least as controversial as the building when it was new, but it now seems to have settled into comfortable middle age. Walk back across the square to head east on Brook Street, which runs across the north end of Grosvenor Square. Here, commercial Mayfair comes back with a vengeance, and there is a mix of eighteenth, nineteenth and twentieth century buildings.

At the corner of Davies Street is **Claridge's**, surely London's most famous hotel; it is a nineteenth century pile of red brick given an Art Deco overlay, bigger and less pure than the Connaught, but a rather glorious hybrid nonetheless. The entry hall feels like a mix of old London and a Central Park West apartment-house lobby, and there is a hauteur unlike the warmth of the Connaught's interior.

Turn right on Bond Street, a mix of elegant and not-so-elegant shops;

despite its reputation, this is not the Faubourg St. Honoré or even Rodeo Drive. Though the architecture on upper floors is often superb, clumsy renovations at ground level have given the street a more garish look than one might expect. Turn right at Grafton Street, at **Asprey's**, the renowned jeweller, and make a fast left again on Albemarle Street, past the dull and oh-so-proper façade of Corinthian columns on the Royal Institution of Great Britain. On the right is the group of old houses that have been thrown together to constitute **Brown's**, the celebrated hotel that aspires to mix homeliness with luxury.

Just beyond Brown's and on the other side of the street is the **Royal Arcade**, one of London's many covered, off-street rows of shops (the most famous, the Burlington Arcade, is just to the east off Piccadilly, and others are on the other side of Piccadilly). This is a small arcade, but a handsome one, with a pleasing skylit ceiling and an even rhythm of glass fronts; all of these London arcades serve as valuable reminders that successful merchandising need not mean a street of loud and contrasting shopfronts.

Continue down Albemarle Street back to Piccadilly, where you can again pick up the Green Park tube; on the way give a glance to the **National Westminster Bank** on the northwest corner of Albemarle Street and Piccadilly, a rather nice, inventive piece of 1927 classicism by W. Curtis-Green, where Doric columns and arches and Ionic columns and setbacks combine into an unusual and lively pattern. And if you have not already been exhausted by luxury hotels, look at the **Ritz** of 1906 by Mewes & Davis on the other side of Piccadilly. It is a building that uses such French elements as a mansard roof and an arcade like that of the Rue de Rivoli, and gives them a tone of English solidity.

JOHN NASH'S LONDON

Regent Street to Regent's Park is the London of John Nash, the favoured architect of the Prince Regent in the early years of the nineteenth century. We can only be grateful, for Nash was practising at a time of much growth for London, and his splendid designs left a mark on the city that, in its way, was broader than that of Wren. Most important, Nash's instinct was what we today would call urbanistic – he saw buildings as parts of greater wholes, and he was as concerned with creating a coherent and handsome totality as with making individual monuments.

Nowhere is Nash's legacy more clear than in the stretch of London from Carlton House Terrace at the edge of St. James's Park up to **Regent's Park**. Nash laid out Regent's Park itself, on lands owned by the crown, and then created Regent Street as a road to tie the park to Westminster in central London – and, not incidentally, to create a grand route between the Prince Regent's town house and the villa he planned for Regent's Park. It was urban planning of a majestic sort, its scale prefiguring Haussmann's boulevards in Paris – but Nash's design was altogether English.

Begin at **Carlton House Terrace**, which faces St. James's Park along the Mall. (The nearest Underground station is Charing Cross; walk across Trafalgar Square and through Admiralty Arch to reach the Mall.)

This was the last of Nash's many terraces, or groups of town houses tied together by a common monumental façade; it was finished in 1833. The terrace is of stucco, painted a warm off-white, with a Corinthian colonnade tying together a row of houses set back on a wide terrace, itself set on a base of Tuscan columns. It has a warm colour, not unlike that of vanilla ice cream, and it calls to mind the splendid rows and crescents of houses in nearby Belgravia. But Nash is a bit lusher than Belgravia: his work is at once grandly formal and highly energetic. There is classical propriety here, but the pleasure of a stage set as well.

The terraced setbacks reflect the rise of the land as it moves north, and gives the houses a noble distance, rare indeed for city residences. In the midst of the two sections of the terrace is a wide staircase leading up to the monumental Duke of York's Column and to Waterloo Place, the lower end of Nash's Regent Street.

Walk up the stairs and look straight ahead – you can see only as far as Piccadilly Circus, but you are at the beginning of one of the greatest urban axes anywhere, and the road, unseen, curves its way for a far greater distance. From here on it is all a vision of classical order, altered, added to and jumbled over the years, but still powerful.

Walk on into **Waterloo Place**, the square framed by the fine classicism of the **Athenaeum Club** on the west side (by Decimus Burton, 1829) and by Nash's own (1827) **Institute of Directors**, formerly the United Service Club, on the east. The next four blocks are Lower Regent Street, leading to Piccadilly Circus. The vista is closed by Sir Reginald Blomfield's French classical building with a triple-arched base completed in the 1920's; it replaced original Nash buildings. Along the way you will pass the temple-fronted **Haymarket Theatre** on the right, a Nash design of 1821.

The road runs right into **Piccadilly Circus**, a swirling pinwheel of traffic, its centre marked by a statue of Eros about which traffic glides. One senses here, as one does not in, say, Times Square in New York, a kind of movement: this is not so much a centre point as a whirlwind, a place that pulls us in, whisks us about and sends us out again.

Now Regent Street begins its greater drama. It leaves Piccadilly Circus not by moving straight out, as it came in, but by sweeping out in a curve to the northwest. This section, called the **Quadrant** (it is in fact a quarter of a circle), is Nash's finest gesture, and though his original buildings lining it were all gone by 1927, the power of his plan remains. The Quadrant is the most commercial section of Regent Street, and it is lined with rather heavy classicizing buildings from the 1920's, respectful of Nash's plan though not nearly as graceful as his smaller originals.

As Regent Street crosses Oxford Street, Nash's next bit of urbanistic genius becomes visible – his **All Souls**, Langham Place, church of 1825, about which more in a moment. First, take a brief detour two blocks to the right just above Oxford Street to **All Saints**, Margaret Street, William Butterfield's church of 1859. Crammed into this mass of patterned brickwork is every bit of the passion and power the Gothic Revival dreamed of. This is not a discreet church, it is an explosive one. All Souls,

Langham Place, is different. It uses a rounded portico and a rounded spire to move the eye (and the traffic) neatly around a bend. Here, Regent Street must move a bit to the west to hook into Portland Place, a noble street laid out in 1774 by the Adam brothers; since it was already there, so close to his route, Nash realized that it made sense to join his Regent Street to it. But existing buildings made it impossible for the streets to run directly into each other, so Langham Place and the church came into being to turn an awkward corner into a moment of urban delight.

Just beyond All Souls is the headquarters of the British Broadcasting Corporation, one of London's few works in the style we might call Bureaucratic Art Deco, and then we are on Portland Place, a wide street that is now a mix of eighteenth century remnants and twentieth century additions. No. 75 Portland Place is an Adam house, a good hint of the eighteenth century grandeur that this street once had. But Portland Place – and the Regent Street axis – ends in a burst of Nashian grandeur with **Park Crescent**, a pair of curving rows of town houses that frame the entrance to Regent's Park.

Park Crescent dates from 1822; like all of Nash's town-house groupings, this is both dignified and vibrant, its lines taut, its rhythms alive. From here you can enter the park itself or skirt up the edges to see some more of the eleven terraces (most, but not all, by Nash) that line it – among them Park Square East and Park Square West, of 1825, and the monumental Cumberland Terrace on the east side of the park, of 1828. Cumberland is probably Nash's masterpiece, among the greatest groupings of classical town houses anywhere.

Regent's Park tube station will take you back.

A DICKENSIAN CORNER
Spitalfields is another world – not the elegant London of John Nash or Robert Adam, but something more like the chaotic and messy London of Charles Dickens. Spitalfields is an old commercial quarter in East London, known in part for the presence there long ago of Jack the Ripper, but also for the market that still forms its centre-piece. If Spitalfields resembles anything, it is the Lower East Side of Manhattan; there is that same kind of physical density, the same sense that this is a place that has been the incubator for generations of immigrants.

Take the tube to Aldgate East, and walk up Commercial Street, past a harsh, Neo-Brutalist high-rise urban renewal project that is all too typical of postwar British architecture. But nineteenth century commercial buildings quickly surround you. Turn right into Fashion Street for a look at a curious grouping of industrial buildings – a group of structures one can only call Moorish Victorian on the south side, more conventional brick factories on the north. Old hanging signs advertise leather garments and textiles, the manufacture and sale of which are still a major industry here.

Return to Commercial Street and stop next at Spitalfields' monument, one of the greatest churches in all of England – **Christ Church**, of 1729, by Nicholas Hawksmoor, at the corner of Fournier Street. Hawksmoor had a long apprenticeship with Wren, but their buildings could not be more dissimilar. Where Wren's architecture is cool and precise, Hawksmoor's is vivid and emotional. His brand of English Baroque is eccentric and altogether personal, and nowhere is it better shown than here.

The façade of the church is a startling mix of arches and columns that mount upward like a triumphant fanfare; there is a huge tower, wildly overscaled, leading up to a spire and an immense entry portico that shelters a tiny door, barely bigger than the bases of the columns. Hawksmoor's genius was such that the effect of all of this is not to intimidate, but to empower; the church seems to say, 'Come in. I will ennoble you.' Christ Church is now in derelict condition, but that almost heightens the drama. Restoration has begun and is expected to be completed in the near future. The interior, as powerful as the exterior, can be visited during the annual music festival in early June, and at other times by appointment: call Jonathan Balkind of the Friends of Christ Church, Spitalfields at 586 0079.

Cross Commercial Street and walk a block or two down Brushfield Street to get the best view of Hawksmoor's monumental façade, as well as for a look at the old buildings of the sprawling Spitalfields Market that line Brushfield Street off Commercial Street. Walk back to Commercial Street, then down Fournier Street beside the church; you will pass the Jack the Ripper Pub, commemorating Spitalfields' most infamous denizen, and you will find yourself in the midst of a warren of three- and four-storey brick buildings, some with their original eighteenth century weavers' garrets, others plain. Turn left on Brick Lane and left again on Hanbury Street, which will take you to Commercial Street.

Back on Commercial Street there is a four-storey brick building at the corner of Folgate Street that is a particularly handsome piece of English eclecticism, a mix of Flemish and Italianate and Romanesque details; it is now converted into flats, and is a pioneer work in the gentrification of Spitalfields. And if you turn down Folgate Street to No. 18, there is another kind of gentrification – an eighteenth century house restored so authentically by its American owner, Dennis Severs, that it has only candles for light and open fires for heat. (Mr. Severs permits visits by appointment: telephone 247 4013.)

Return down Commercial Street to the Aldgate East tube station.

WHERE BLOOMSBURY FLOWERED

Quentin Bell

Bloomsbury. Where is it? What is it? It is by no means easy to answer these questions as precisely as one could wish. Look at a large-scale map of London showing the West Central District and there you will easily discover a big block representing the British museum. With this near its base, you may describe a quadrilateral bounded on one side by Tottenham Court Road, the other side by Euston Road, on a third by Gray's Inn Road and finally, less neatly, New Oxford Street and Theobalds Road. That more or less is Bloomsbury.

Within it you may find some little oblong islands: Gordon Square, Tavistock Square, Bedford Square and Brunswick Square. Apart from Brunswick Square, which has been brutalized by bombs and builders, they are still very pleasant places in which to wander; the houses have a certain tall Victorian grace about them, the square gardens are easeful to eyes distressed by the shoddiness of Tottenham Court Road. Here and there you may find blue plaques set up by the County Council to commemorate the inhabitants and, if you linger by the railings in front of 46 Gordon Square, you may reflect that something happened here that changed the mores of the twentieth century.

There are dozens of books to tell you all about it, if you don't already know. Can I summarize their contents in a few sentences? Of course not; but I can try, thus: Bloomsbury began in 1905, when a group of young men from Cambridge began coming to No. 46 to air and to expand their ideas. Of these the most celebrated today are Lytton Strachey, Maynard Keynes and Leonard Woolf (in the early years it was Strachey who took the lead); they met painters and people concerned with painting: Roger Fry, Duncan Grant and Clive Bell. They also met the two Miss Stephens, Virginia and Vanessa, and met them on terms of such equality that all the barriers that then divided the sexes were forgotten, all taboos were discarded, and the outrageous ideas of Cambridge were freely discussed in the quiet squares of Bloomsbury.

Bloomsbury grew, some of its members vanished, others became celebrities; twenty years later it had changed almost out of recognition, but, geographically, it remained attached to its first centre. All along the northeast – that is, the Tavistock Square side of Gordon Square – there were colonies of Bells or Stracheys, coming and going, but never going very far; and there were many who, without being exactly berries of the old Bloom, established themselves there. Keynes took over No. 46; there were Stracheys at 41 and more Stracheys at 51; Clive Bell and later Arthur Waley were at 50; E. M. Forster was in Brunswick Square, Leonard and Virginia Woolf at 52 Tavistock Square and Roger Fry between them in Bernard Street.

I must confess that there were so many residents and they wandered so much that I cannot be sure who was where. The traveller must therefore use his or her imagination and picture that area in the 1920's filled to bursting with people old and young who wrote or painted or were in some way connected with the arts, who played tennis in the square, who flocked each summer to see Diaghilev's ballets and, as it now seems, had a very happy time of it. He must use his imagination also in thinking of those earliest years of Bloomsbury, when the four children of the late Sir Leslie Stephen set up house at No. 46 and in so doing shocked their respectable relations.

You might not think it now, but at that time Bloomsbury was thought to be a shabby, sleazy, meretricious sort of place, much too far from the discreet elegance of Kensington, the district whence they came. I suspect that it was precisely that distance that recommended Gordon Square; it represented a break with the too insistent past; it was a place where new ideas could be discussed in a new way, where a new kind of novel or a new kind of biography could be planned, a new kind of painting imported from Paris.

But friendship rather than ideas was always the cohesive force in Bloomsbury; these young people never moved far from each other, and when, after her sister's marriage, Virginia Stephen moved beyond the true frontiers of Bloomsbury and settled in Bernard Shaw's former house in Fitzroy Square (it is a pretty square worth visiting), she was still within comfortable walking distance.

When you have visited Gordon Square, Tavistock Square, Fitzroy Square and perhaps Bedford Square – No. 44 was the home of that remarkable woman Lady Ottoline Morrell – you will have seen all those Bloomsbury sites that it is still a pleasure to inspect. You may reflect that you have seen nothing but façades; if you were to enter you would, I think, find no trace of the peculiar people who once inhabited those houses. If you desire a closer view you must travel about fifty miles in a southerly direction. Go then to Lewes and thence to Firle, as Virginia Stephen did in 1911.

Being a civilized visitor you will drive slowly into Firle. You may even hesitate before entering the village, for there on your left is the entrance to a noble park in which stands Firle Place, the home of that General Gage who lost a continent at Lexington. But your present business is in the village itself, a place still so quiet, so very soporific, that one feels that the inhabitants might lose a continent by pure inattention.

There, amid houses that seem to have slept side by side for centuries, you will find one very ugly modern villa named Little Talland House by Virginia, who came there seeking the peace and quiet that she needed in order to write her first novel, *The Voyage Out*. She came, surely, to the right address and, as she said, 'being inside the house I don't have to look at it.' Nevertheless she felt the urge to move and in 1911, before she married Leonard Woolfe, they discovered Asheham.

It is an easy walk from Firle; you pass along the foothills of the South Downs. They loom grand and dizzy above you to a height – but let us not be specific, for if I told you how few feet separate Firle Beacon, our loftiest summit, from sea level you might laugh. The landscape implores you in its quiet way to suspend your disbelief in its grandeur. Oddly enough, the plea is answered: The water meadows are becomingly flat and the hills, although sheep may safely graze upon them, still somehow have the air of being, as an eighteenth century writer put it, 'a range of horrid mountains.' You may also walk upon them – it is the pleasantest walking surface in all the world – or you may drive and cover the distance in a few minutes.

But whatever you do, don't arrive. If you come by road a peremptory notice will tell you to go away; and although Asheham House still stands and looks beautiful and feels haunted, that lovely valley, it must be said to our abiding shame, has been utterly ruined by the callous operations of modern industry. Never mind, go on past Asheham and cross the little River Ouse; if you are a pedestrian the distance is short; if you are a crow it is no way at all to Monks House at Rodmell, whither the Woolfs removed in 1919.

Here our nation has made some amends (not without American aid) and on certain days the house will be open to you. You will find a Bloomsbury interior with furniture and pictures well worth a visit. Also you may visit the beautiful garden, which is again receiving that affectionate care that Leonard Woolf bestowed on it for half a century, and in the garden the summer house in which, escaping from the too exciting life of London, Virginia Woolf wrote.

Virginia had her own ideas about interior decoration and although she sometimes feared that the painters at Charleston – her sister Vanessa and her friend Duncan Grant – laughed at her, still she liked not only to import their works but to express her own ideas. Thus we find not only intermingled tiled work and pictures by Bell and Grant, but also the paintings of some mute, inglorious Douanier Rousseau of the Sussex countryside that had taken her fancy, the coloured glass- and shell-work that always delighted her. She once obtained the blue glowing jar from a local chemist's shop.

And, of course, books, books everywhere. At one time they became so numerous that they were stacked all the way up the stairs so that one picked one's way with difficulty from the ground floor up. The new rooms were added almost haphazardly as novels provided the funds for them: One bathroom resulted from *Mrs. Dalloway*; an outside bedroom was the fruit of *The Years*.

Monks House may give you a taste for that peculiar style of decoration that Bloomsbury derived from English post-impressionism, and you may perhaps sharpen your appetite by looking at the interior of Berwick Church, which within its discreetly English fabric contains great murals by Duncan Grant and Vanessa Bell. These exuberantly display the colour and the reckless gaiety of Italy, a lively joy that some critics may find too worldly but that can please – even a large wall painting depicting the wise and foolish virgins painted by the writer of this article, altogether a very odd monument indeed, but one that results very naturally from the close proximity of Charleston Farm House. These, however, are, so to speak, preliminaries. Monks House is, essentially, a monument to unseen things, the local habitation of a talent that adorned and enriched our language rather than a shrine for the art historian.

The same may be said of Tilton, although it did at one time contain an astonishing collection that included works by Delacroix, Ingres, Braque, Matisse, Picasso and Cézanne, but is now a private house. Tilton, which is in the parish of Firle and very close to Charleston, of which more hereafter, was the home of Maynard Keynes. He came there after marrying Lydia Lopokova of the Russian Ballet.

The house itself is not particularly interesting and the pictures have gone elsewhere. Nothing seems to remain. But I fancy that there are still old men at the BarleyMow or the Rose and Crown who could tell stories about the Squire of Tilton, that strange mixture of agricultural innocence and business acumen, of his odd sayings and doings, which once amazed the neighbourhood, and above all of Lady Keynes, whose charm, vivacity and unaccountable manners brought to that quiet Sussex neighbourhood a bizarre and intoxicating whiff of old Russia. There must still be some who saw her disguised – sometimes as an impoverished aviator, sometimes as an aged moujik – and some perhaps who came across her reciting Pushkin on the Downs or lying naked in the raspberry bed.

Here again we have a monument to unseen things, to the memory of a remarkable man and his remarkable wife; but if we seek those more tangible records of the past that are kept upon plaster, wood or canvas, in clay or in stone, then we must look to Charleston, although it is a little uncertain what we shall find. Charleston is not now a visible shrine, it is a promise, a magnificent but still conditional promise.

Charleston Farm, Firle, not to be confused – as it so frequently and tiresomely is – with Charleston Manor, belongs to a trust that hopes to give it to the public. When and if that does happen the public will have a rare treat; in fact it will have something more, a kind of document, the visible testimony to a way of life led by some very remarkable people, a way of life that has vanished utterly, the lair of an aesthetic creature that is now extinct.

It is a beautiful but not at all a grand house, a place where books were written and pictures painted, a very lived-in place. For half a century Duncan Grant, Vanessa Bell and some other artists painted and repainted the walls and furniture, made mosaics, designed curtains and chair covers, imported all kinds of lovely junk, peopled the garden with sculpture, converted more and more rooms into studios so that this, going on from year to year and largely uninfluenced by the passing fashions of the art world, resulted in something for which it is hard to find a convenient word, a shabby, comfortable, serenely decorated home of a most unusual kind.

It was Leonard and Virginia Woolf who first discovered the place. A very odd ménage consisting of Vanessa Bell, her children, and Duncan Grant and David Garnett, was then looking for somewhere to live. It settled at Charleston for the duration of the war (this was in 1916) and at once began to decorate the walls. Presently they found that they could not bear to leave it. Other people turned up, notably Clive Bell and Maynard Keynes, and one may still see the room where Keynes wrote his first politically explosive book, *The Economic Consequences of the Peace*. Then guests began to arrive in droves and Charleston, like Monks House, became a rural outpost of Bloomsbury.

Something perhaps of the English genius for compromise shows in the odd mixture of order and disorder that occurs almost everywhere. In the room that finally became Duncan Grant's bedroom, the original intention, a most orderly and balanced design, is still visible. The two doors and the fireplace were united in one scheme, and the bold embroidered work made from Duncan Grant's drawings fitted in well enough, as did the carpet, designed, if I remember correctly, by Vanessa Bell. But then, almost by chance, a canvas still unframed, a translation of Raphael's *St. Catharine* in the National Gallery, was popped above the fireplace; it holds its position beautifully.

Then, as though tempting fate, Duncan Grant added a gaudy beadwork early nineteenth century prie-dieu. 'No, Duncan, it's really too vulgar,' said Clive Bell, and indeed by rights it should have wrecked everything. But it didn't. In the exceptionally beautiful morning light of Charleston it looks perfectly in place. Just how these aesthetic accommodations have been arrived at I do not understand.

Duncan Grant was the last inhabitant; he died in 1978 at the age of ninety-three. I think that most people would say that by then Bloomsbury had for a very long time been extinct, but certainly with him it expired completely.

The question arose, what was to be done about the house? To let it perish, to see it transformed by unsympathetic hands seemed impossible; some kind of effort had to be made to save what could be saved. Committees met, manifestos were drawn up and rather to our surprise a great many people began to offer help. Alas, though rich in enthusiasm, they were rich in nothing else. Even so, quite a lot of money was raised. A great deal more is still needed, but there was enough to buy the house from its landlord and to replace a roof. The fabric and decorations are being carefully restored.

We are trying to save a scrap of the past; for Bloomsbury belongs to history now. It can still inspire admiration and deep dislike and perhaps will always do so; certainly our descendants will want to know what it was like, what it was all about. And because the 'Bloomsburys' themselves were painters and decorators living as much by the brush as by the pen, this little last surviving evidence of their life-style, this extraordinarily eloquent deposit of evidence, would be worth preserving even though it were without any intrinsic merit.

The traveller wandering through those London squares and carrying perhaps one of Virginia Woolf's many evocations of her beloved city, visiting the real, the geographical, Bloomsbury, is certainly not wasting his time. But there is more, or may be, in 'Little Bloomsbury by the Sea.' He may open the front door, walk into the sitting room and, with an astonishing intimacy, come face-to-face with the past.

– LONDON –
AN EYE FOR ART

John Russell

When I think of the London art world in which I lived for many years it is in terms of hearing, as much as of sight. I remember the wingbeat of the fat, spoiled pigeons that lumber in and out of the portico of the National Gallery in Trafalgar Square. I remember the immemorial wheeze of the elevator that goes up to the Courtauld Galleries in Woburn Place. I remember the cry of the seagulls that on windy days are blown inland as far as the Tate Gallery. And I remember the sound of the human voice as it is thrown back upon us when we walk across the courtyard of the Royal Academy in Piccadilly.

Irrelevant, you may say. But memory leads its own life. If it were a matter of listing the most important works of art in the London area, almost everyone would come up with the same kind of list. What is interesting in this context is not what any intelligent person can work out from the guidebooks. The great things choose themselves. Beginning with the Elgin Marbles in the British Museum, it would be easy to go on to the Michelangelo tondo in the Royal Academy, the Piero della Francesca *Baptism* in the National Gallery, the Giovanni Pisano head of the prophet Haggai from the cathedral façade in Siena in the Victoria and Albert Museum, the Titian *Perseus and Andromeda* in the Wallace Collection, the Velásquez in the Wellington Museum at Apsley House, the Rembrandt self-portrait in Kenwood House and the Rubens ceiling in the Banqueting House in Whitehall.

But a list is a notional, disembodied thing. It takes a special temperament to work steadily and decisively according to a pre-arranged plan. This is a matter in which a master plan should be cut loosely, like a poacher's overcoat. So I propose on this occasion to leave the great national institutions to themselves, saying only that mouthful for mouthful and dollar for dollar the restaurant in the basement of the Tate Gallery is one of the best in London. (That goes for the wine list, too.)

Art historians have no trouble separating a work of art from its environment. A picture for them is a picture, regardless of whether it hangs in the operating room of a third-rate hospital in an Italian market town or on the walls of a ducal country house in Scotland. But for most other people, what we see and where we see it are inseparable, and all the more so if we happen to see it when there is nobody else around.

For that reason a special charm attaches to places that not too many people go to. The Banqueting House in Whitehall, for instance, is by Inigo Jones, one of the greatest English architects of his day. It is the house from which King Charles I stepped forth for his execution in 1649. The ceiling by Rubens may well be the most important single commission ever carried out in England by a major artist. Anyone with a good eye and a sense of history must be overwhelmed by the combination of these things. But when you step into that majestic space you are as likely as not to be the only person there.

You won't be elbowed aside by the crowd at Apsley House, either. But No. 1 Piccadilly – its official address, and one in which the first Duke of Wellington delighted – is not only a town house of the first order. It is the repository of many of the paintings, sculptures, works of art and pieces of furniture that came Wellington's way when he was the greatest soldier in Europe. Canova's heroic portrait of Napoleon would be impressive anywhere, but at the foot of Wellington's staircase it has a particular savour.

If you are interested in other people's houses and you like them to be as complete as possible, don't miss Sir John Soane's Museum in Lincoln's Inn Fields. Soane (1753–1837) was the foremost English architect of his day. He made money himself, he married a rich wife, and he figured quite rightly that if he built his own house and filled it with the paintings and sculptures and other works of art that he most liked people would be glad to come and see it. The house and its collections are still there, intact, and they are one of the great semisecret pleasures in London.

London is still rich in complete environments of that sort. Walking into the forecourt of the Royal Academy of Arts in Piccadilly, for instance, we instinctively adjust our tread to what remains one of the noblest of metropolitan spaces. If our business takes us into the academy's private offices we shall find room after room that could come straight from a great English country house in the late eighteenth century. Fires blaze in the open hearth. Fine furniture is taken for granted. The telephone looks ridiculous.

When it comes to the dealers' galleries, something of that same continuity still lingers here and there. Thomas Agnew & Sons have been at the Piccadilly end of Old Bond Street for more than 150 years, for instance. In the nineteenth century Sir William Agnew would bid at auction for the National Gallery, and in our own day Sir Geoffrey Agnew still stalks into Christie's and Sotheby's and performs just the same service. (With a little more panache, however. It was not in the nineteenth century that Agnew's van waited outside Christie's, with television cameras at the ready, to whisk a much coveted painting directly from the sale room to the National Gallery after Agnew's had outbid its rivals.)

P. and D. Colnaghi's, just across the street from Agnew's was quite recently the same unmistakable firm that Lord Byron, the poet of liberty, and William Hazlitt, the best of all English essayists, had been happy to drop into. Colnaghi's for generations was a kind of club, a coffee house that happened not to serve coffee but was open to everyone with a serious interest in art. In the last few years it has changed hands and had identity troubles, but I live in hopes of its recovery. Meanwhile the Old Master drawing fancier will find very good things just a few yards away at Baskett & Day, at 173 New Bond Street.

Sometimes an older gallery takes a new lease on life when a younger generation takes over and the prime subject matter of the gallery coincides with a decisive shift in taste. This is what happened at the Fine Art Society on New Bond Street when people began to think that late Victorian and Edwardian painting and sculpture was not a joke.

The Fine Art Society had then, and has still, a delightfully old-fashioned set of rooms, with a white balustraded staircase, a fine top-lit back room and a faint and inexplicable marine air to the whole building. We feel as if we are on a pleasure steamer, built in the 1880's, that is about to set sail on halcyon seas.

At this point I must attempt to dismiss a spectre that has ruined many a first visit to the London art world. American visitors often think that the dealers' galleries in London are intimidating. 'We go in,' they say, 'and people look us up and down without saying a word. We feel unwelcome, and we go out again and wish that we'd never left home.'

This point of view is based on a misreading both of the English character and of the geography of the London dealer's gallery. Human relations in England are rooted in tolerance, discretion and a reluctance to pry. Dealers' galleries in London are mostly small – some would be unbearable, from an English point of view, if everyone had to pass the time of day with everyone else. Besides, salesmanship as such is rather frowned on in London, where the elegant thing is to pretend that commerce does not exist and that the visitor has done the dealer a kindness by dropping in.

Nonchalance can be carried very far, in this context. Peter Wilson, until 1979 chairman of Sotheby's and the main architect of its postwar prosperities, was a master of that particular ploy. To see him ambling through his auction rooms you would think that he was an undergraduate who had just cut a lecture. As for his opposite number, I. O. Chance, chairman of Christie's until 1974, he could make even the most tiresome intruder feel that he was about to be pressed into uncorking a particularly good bottle of wine.

Members of the London art trade rarely or never press hard for a sale. Eagerness, on the part of one famous veteran, was manifested merely in a very slight reddening of the earlobes. Another had a yawn that could be heard through six feet of concrete.

Even among the younger generation, folkways of this sort may still be found. Anthony d'Offay is generally rated as one of the two or three best dealers in London, but if you try to price a picture in his gallery, he is likely to bow his head in grief. 'I'm terribly sorry,' he will say, 'but that one's not for sale.' Mr. d'Offay has two separate galleries in Dering Street, which is a very small street on the right as you walk up to the north end of New Bond Street. One is devoted to the English art of the last eighty or so years, and the other to the international avant-garde. Both are well worth a visit.

In the contemporary field, Mr. d'Offay's most conspicuous rivals are Leslie Waddington and Kasmin, both of whom have galleries on Cork Street, which runs parallel to and a little to the east of Bond Street. They have nothing in common, beyond an attitude to business that is more overtly positive than is traditional in London.

The Waddington Gallery is clean, light and white. Many of the best British painters and sculptors of the day show there, and the hidden stock of modern masters is such that Leslie Waddington can slip a landscape by Cézanne into a late summer anthology and not even give it pride of place.

If the Waddington Gallery is versatility made visible, Kasmin (who is universally addressed as 'Kas,' by the way, and never uses his first name) has quite another style. Now affiliated with Knoedler's in New York, his gallery bears Knoedler's name and from time to time shows Knoedler artists. But somewhere within that trim little room is the ghost of the London art world as it was in the 1960's. Kasmin in those days held breakthrough exhibitions of Anthony Caro, David Hockney and others, and to a remarkable degree those artists have remained loyal to him.

Cork Street had for many years been the single most beguiling street of its size in London, where art is concerned, and it still has that character, thanks in part to a certain amount of coming and going among the galleries. A recent arrival is a gallery run by Nicola Jacobs as a haven for younger painters, and her roster includes Derek Southall, arguably the best English landscape painter of his generation. The Redfern Gallery, Browse & Darby and the Piccadilly Gallery are also well worth a visit.

Even the most vigorous gallerygoer is overtaken in time by dreams of a very good lunch. If you want to have one in a place that has good art on the walls, I recommend Langan's Brasserie in Stratton Street, just off Piccadilly and hard by the Ritz Hotel. Peter Langan has collected art and collected artists ever since he first opened a London restaurant in the mid-1960's.

The subject of one of the more incisive of David Hockney's portrait etchings, he soon filled his first (and still existing) restaurant – Odin's on Devonshire Street – with a collection of paintings that was eclectic to the point of delirium. He continues to double back and forth between his kitchen and the auction rooms. His Brasserie, which is not outrageously expensive, continues the tradition of new art and innovative food.

It would be quite unfair to suggest that the Bond Street area is the only one in which good dealers' galleries can be found. It would also be unfair to suggest that I have named all the good ones in the Bond Street area. Lists are tedious to read, and I have left out galleries – Gimpel Fils, for one, and the Juda Rowan Gallery, for another – that have long had a dedicated American following. Immediately south of Piccadilly there are galleries that have a no less devoted constituency. The Heim Gallery on Jermyn Street is a great place for European Old Master sculpture. Hazlitt, Gooden and Fox on Bury Street have first-rate Old Master drawings and paintings. Just across the road is the London headquarters of the formidable consortium of international art dealers called Artemis, which sometimes has exhibitions of the highest quality. Fischer Fine Art on King Street, St. James's, has a personal choice of mainly figurative painting that takes in parts of Europe not often covered elsewhere. In Mason's Yard, Matthiesen Fine Art has lately brought back to London a name long famous in the Old Master trade. If you can afford to lunch at Wilton's at 55 Jermyn Street – and not everyone can – you will get the best plain English food in London.

And there are whole other quarters that I have not mentioned – toward Sloane Square, just west of Tottenham Court Road, and hard by the British Museum. But London in this context is a labyrinth, and this particular Theseus has run out of thread.

MUSEUMS

Admission is free at most of London's great art institutions. Many are closed Christmas Eve, Christmas Day, Boxing Day, New Year's Day, Good Friday and bank holidays.

The British Museum, Great Russell Street; open weekdays 10 am to 5 pm, Sunday 2.30 pm to 6 pm. (636 1555)

The National Gallery, in Trafalgar Square; weekdays 10 am to 6 pm, Sunday 2 pm to 6 pm. (839 3321)

The Victoria and Albert Museum, on Cromwell Road in South Kensington; Monday through Thursday and Saturday, 10 am to 5.50 pm, Sunday 2.30 pm to 5.50 pm, closed Friday. Voluntary fee for admission. (589 6371)

The Wellington Museum, Apsley House, Hyde Park Corner; Tuesday through Thursday and Saturday, 10 am to 5.50 pm, Sunday 2.30 pm to 5.50 pm, closed Monday and Friday. (499 5676)

Kenwood House (Iveagh Bequest), on Hampstead Lane; daily 10 am to 5 pm (or until dusk), April through September, 10 am to 7 pm. (348 1256)

The Courtauld Galleries, Woburn Square; weekdays 10 am to 5 pm, Sunday 2 pm to 5 pm. There is an entrance fee of $1.50. (580 1015)

Sir John Soane's Museum, 13 Lincoln's Inn Fields; Tuesday through Saturday, 10 am to 5 pm, closed Sunday and Monday. (405 2107)

The Wallace Collection, Herford House, Manchester Square; weekdays 10 am to 5 pm, Sunday 2 pm to 5 pm. (935 0687)

The Tate Gallery, Millbank; weekdays 10 am to 6 pm. Sunday 2 pm to 6 pm. (821 1313)

The Royal Academy of Arts, Piccadilly; daily 10 am to 6 pm. Admission fees vary with the exhibit. (734 9052)

The Banqueting House, Whitehall; Tuesday through Saturday, 10 am to 5 pm, Sunday 2 pm to 5 pm, closed Monday. Admission, about 75 cents for adults, half price for children.

GALLERIES

Most dealers' galleries are open Monday through Friday from about 10 am to 5.30 pm. Although most are closed on Saturday afternoon, some close all day. What follows is a by no means exhaustive list of galleries.

Anthony d'Offay's Galleries, 9 Dering Street (629 1578) and 23 Dering Street (499 4695) specialize in twentieth century English art and the international avant-garde.

Gimpel Fils, 30 Davies Street, has contemporary paintings and sculptures (493 2488).

Sotheby Parke Bernet, 34 and 35 New Bond Street, the auction house (493 8080).

The Fine Art Society Ltd., 148 New Bond Street, specializes in Victorian and Edwardian painting and sculpture (629 5116).

The Juda Rowan Gallery, 11 Tottenham Mews, has contemporary painters and sculpture (637 5517).

Nicola Jacobs, 9 Cork Street, specializes in the works of younger painters (437 3868).

The Piccadilly Gallery, 16 Cork Street, has contemporary art with a special accent on the Symbolists (629 2875 or 499 4632).

Browse & Darby, 19 Cork Street, has some contemporary works, as well as nineteenth century French and English paintings (734 7984).

The Redfern Gallery, 20 Cork Street, has contemporary (but not avant-garde) paintings (734 1732 or 734 0578).

Knoedler, 22 Cork Street, has such contemporary British pain ters and sculptors as Hockney and Caro (439 1096).

The Waddington Galleries, Ltd., 10/12 Cork Street, features a broad spectrum of contemporary British art (439 1866).

Baskett & Day, 173 New Bond Street, is strong on Old Master drawings (629 2991 or 493 7569).

P. and D. Colnaghi and Co. Ltd., 14 Old Bond Street, is a venerable institution that has recently changed hands (491 7408).

Thomas Agnew & Sons, Ltd., 43 Old Bond Street, displays major Old Masters and acts as agent for the National Gallery (629 6176).

Hazlitt, Gooden and Fox Ltd., 38 Bury Street, is strong in French nineteenth century drawings and Old Master paintings (930 6422).

The Heim Gallery (London) Ltd., 59 Jermyn Street, specializes in European Old Masters – paintings and sculpture (493 0688).

Artemis Fine Arts (U.K.) Ltd., 15 Duke Street, is a consortium of international dealers (930 8733).

Christie Manson and Woods, Ltd., 8 King Street, is another one of London's great auction houses (839 9060).

Fischer Fine Art, 30 King Street, has mainly figurative nine teenth and twentieth century works from all over Europe (839 3942).

Matthiesen Fine Arts Ltd., 7 Mason's Yard, off Duke Street, has Old Master paintings (930 2437).

SCARLET AND GOLD ON PARADE

John de St. Jorre

The changing of the Queen's Guard at Buckingham Palace is still the best military pageant in Europe. And it's free. The ceremony, however, is not just a show for tourists. It is full of historical echoes and symbolizes the continuing importance of the monarchy as an institution and the affection Britons feel for their Queen.

Moreover, the Guards themselves are simultaneously dedicated practitioners of the military parade, to which they bring the expertise of a Broadway musical, and a superbly disciplined force of fighting men exchanging their scarlet tunics for flak jackets or parachute smocks with the easy rhythm of their marching step. Within twenty-four hours of marching up and down outside Buckingham Palace, they can be found in full battle gear patrolling the mean streets of Northern Ireland, and they were represented in the conflict with Argentina over the Falklands.

The changing of the Guard and the much larger pageant of Trooping the Colour, held every June to celebrate the Queen's birthday, underline the special position the Guards hold in the British Army and in the society itself. The five regiments of Foot Guards and two regiments of cavalry that form the Household Division, known collectively as the Guards, came into existence over three hundred years ago as bodyguards of the monarch.

They have fought in every major encounter in Britain's numerous wars and their regimental roll-calls are a litany of famous Britons. They are a unique part of British history, having outlived all their European rivals (the Russian Guards, the famous Prussian regiments, Napoleon's Imperial Guard and so on), and have earned the title of the world's oldest continuous military formation.

By simply being there, the Guards evoke the glory and the pathos of the past in the way that a painting or piece or architecture sometimes does. Their daily presence is a reminder of the great commanders and great battles of history, of Marlborough and Blenheim, of Wellington and Waterloo, of the retreat to Corunna, the bloody mêlées in the Crimea, the slaughterhouse on the Somme and the dark days of Dunkirk.

There are in fact several different Guard changes that take place daily in London, but the ceremony in the forecourt of Buckingham Palace is the most elaborate and the most fun to watch. Unfortunately, pressed up against the tall iron railings that surround the Palace is not the ideal way to view anything, but there is no real alternative.

The ceremony begins at 11.30 am daily in summer and every other day in winter. Arrive, if you can, at least half an hour before. The best positions are, I think, a few yards to the left or to the right of the Centre Gate. This places you close to the band and also allows you to move quickly to the entrance to watch the Guards march off, accompanied by the band, when the show is over.

Another possibility is to place yourself on the steps of the Victoria Memorial, 'the wedding cake' in Guards' jargon, which commands the road leading up to the Centre Gate. This position has the advantage of height – you will be able to see over the heads of the mob packed againt the railings – but you will be farther from the action. It is, however, ideal for those who want to capture the panorama on film or exercise their telephoto lens.

A preliminary ceremony takes place in Friary Court at St. James's Palace half an hour before the main event. Here the section of the Guard that has been on duty at St. James's Palace forms up, is inspected and, led by the fifes and drums and carrying the regimental colours, marches off to join the Buckingham Palace detachment.

It is worth watching because it is a small and intimate ceremony that the public can observe at close range, its vision uncluttered by the bars that get in the way outside Buckingham Palace. (You can also have a close look at the sentries, who are similarly unprotected.) The disadvantage is that the best positions will have been taken at Buckingham Palace by the time you and the St. James's detachment arrive.

What happens during the actual ceremony may seem baffling to the uninitiated. But all that really goes on is one group of soldiers handing over their guard duty to another, albeit in a rather ponderous military way. What makes it charming is the music, the bright uniforms, the hoarse cries of command and the seemingly magical way in which each individual moves himself and his rifle in perfect unison with everyone else.

The old Guard, composed of the now reunited St. James's and Buckingham Palace detachments, forms up on your left as you face the Palace. At 11.30 am precisely, the new Guard, led by the band – usually forty-five musicians strong – marches in and stands on the right, facing the old Guard. After being aligned by the drill sergeant, the new Guard advances in slow time to the slow march of the regiment mounting guard that day.

The two main units present arms to each other and the captain of the old Guard hands over a brass key, made especially for the purpose by Messrs. Chubb, royal key- and safe-makers, to the captain of the new Guard. The act is purely symbolic: the key fits nothing and opens nothing. The captains disappear into the Palace via what is somewhat arcanely known at the Privy Purse Door, the ensigns (second lieutenants) march up and down with their respective regimental colours and the senior NCO's go to the guardroom to receive their orders. New sentries – whose job is largely ceremonial, since the actual protection of the Palace is primarily a police responsibility – are posted.

During this interlude, which lasts about thirty minutes, the band plays a medley of tunes, many from well-known musicals, which have been selected by the captains of the two Guards. Sometimes there is the added bonus of a pipe band – the bagpipes of the Scots Guards or the Irish Guards – taking it in turn to perform with the regular band. At 12.05 the band re-forms with the two Guards. The old Guard, preceded by the band and corps of drums, slow marches out of the Centre Gate. Once clear of the gate they wheel right and break into quick time. The St. James's Palace detachment of the new Guard waits until the old Guard has gone, then marches off down the Mall while the Buckingham Palace detachment disappears into the guardroom, leaving two sentries in their boxes. At 12.09 the ceremony is over.

The Guard-changing ceremony at Horse Guards in Whitehall is a much simpler affair, but worth looking at because it is done on horseback. It is mounted alternately by the two cavalry regiments – the Life Guards, distinguished by their white plumes and scarlet tunics, and the Blues and Royals in red plumes and blue tunics – that together comprise the Household Cavalry.

There is also a ceremony at the Tower of London every midday when the court is in residence at Buckingham Palace, a scaled-down version of the Palace show. The Guards should not, of course, be confused with the Yeomen Warders, that venerable body of retired servicemen dressed in their Elizabethan uniforms who look after the Tower and who are often called Beefeaters.

A few tricks of the trade: the different regiments of Foot Guards can be recognized by the plumes in their bearskins (skins of the male bear for NCO's and enlisted men; female bearskins for the officers) and the arrangement of the buttons down the front of their tunics. The Grenadier Guards have a white plume on the left of the bearskin and evenly spaced buttons; the Coldstreams a red plume on the right and buttons in pairs; the Scots no plume and buttons in threes; the Irish a blue plume on the right and buttons in fours; and finally the Welsh with a green and white plume on the left and buttons in fives.

When the Queen is in residence at Buckingham Palace the royal standard flies over the buildings; when she is away the flagpole is bare.

If you have always wondered how the two sentries synchronize their movements without apparently looking at each other, signals are transmitted by tapping the rifle butt on the ground with the senior man (always on your right as you peer through the railings) taking the initiative.

The Guards' ceremonial role is taken very seriously. The British Tourist Authority and the Foreign and Commonwealth Office would like to see more of it – the first for boosting the tourist trade, and the second to please visiting foreign dignitaries. But there are many critics too who say that it is an enormously expensive way of providing free entertainment, besides which it ties up roughly a tenth of the entire British infantry during the summer months.

There are few people, however, who want it stopped altogether. The thump of the drum, the skirl of the pipes, that marvellous rhythmic swagger of the men in scarlet, and the glitter and jingling of the cavalry have become so much a part of the British way of life that it would be hard to imagine a time when they were no longer changing the Guard at Buckingham Palace.

THE CONNAUGHT

Rona Jaffe

When my English publishers invited me to come to London to help launch their paperback edition of my novel *Class Reunion*, I was delighted that they put me up at the Connaught Hotel. I had heard of the Connaught for years, but had never stayed there, and I wanted to see why a hotel could be such a legend that it does not even have to advertise, and must turn away more people than it can accept.

Like all big cities, London has become a mixture of the old and the new, but in Carlos Place, Mayfair, where the Connaught is located, time stops. The little buildings on the street look like a setting for *Upstairs, Downstairs*, and the hotel itself is quite small: a narrow block wide, seven stories high. It is old and elegant, but homely. You do not feel you are entering a hotel but that you are visiting the home of a rich friend.

You walk through a cosy little entrance into a small lobby with dark wood-panelled walls, Oriental rugs, upholstered antique chairs and a magnificent staircase so wide you could easily lie across it. The staircase is of dark wood, made quiet by a patterned carpet bordered in brass, with enormous well-polished dark wood banisters. To the right is the desk where you sign in and a small lift; to the left is the desk of the hall porter, who wears a navy-blue tailcoat. From him you get your key, mail, newspapers, or anything else you want. The Connaught can house 140 guests and has a staff of 280. When it is not full there can be three staff members for each guest. This is definitely the home of a very rich friend.

I arrived about 10 o'clock at night, and no sooner had my bags been brought to my room than the housekeeper appeared to ask if there was anything I wanted. This was one of the few times in twenty years of staying at hotels when I did not have to ask for more hangers. And these were not the ubiquitous hateful hangers of flimsy plastic or splintery wood with the top part permanently attached to the closet so the guests will not steal them – they were removable, of smooth, heavy wood, and there was even a rack full of shirred satin ones for sweaters and dresses. You know immediately that no one who stays at the Connaught ever steals anything – if he expects to be let back in. My room was pleasant and cheerful, with yellow and white wallpaper in a small subtle pattern, two single beds together on one delicate king-size brass headboard, two night tables with reading lamps, a small antique secretary filled with elegant stationery, a colour television set, two armchairs, ample closet space, enough mirrors and light, a little vase of fresh flowers on the dressing table and a wall of windows overlooking a quiet side street. It was not a large room, but all this furniture did not make it feel crowded.

The tiled bathroom was roomy – a good third the size of the bedroom – with a huge bath, plump little cakes of expensive scented soap, packets of bubble bath, lots of thick bathsheet-size towels on a towel warmer, and one of those European hand-held showers to wash your hair. Besides all this, there also was a small room with a standard shower in it.

My bed had been turned down for me. The sheets were white linen. On subsequent nights I found my night-gown, robe and slippers put out for me, and in the daytime my suitcase and clutter were put neatly into one of the closets. You can also leave your shoes outside your door at night to be polished and returned at dawn.

One evening I pulled a cord, which was over the bath and looked like one of those unrolling clothes lines, and a maid dashed in. It turned out to be a signal cord for use in case I needed something while I was in my bath. A doctor? A towel? A Martini? My back scrubbed? My mind reeled with possibilities.

As soon as the housekeeper left on that first night, the phone rang. It was the hall porter, introducing himself and asking if there was anything I needed. Would I like newspapers delivered in the morning? He suggested *The Times* of London and *The International Herald Tribune*. There is a service kitchen on every floor, so if I were ever hungry he could bring me something. I told him that one morning I would need breakfast at 5.30 because I had an early appointment. He was apologetic and a bit dismayed – not because of the request, but because the fresh bread and rolls are not delivered that early. 'I'll have to make you toast with yesterday's bread,' he said. 'I hope you don't mind.' I had to assure him three times that I really could eat yesterday's bread.

Every night I ordered breakfast for the next morning and a wake-up call. Both the call and the breakfast came on time to the minute. The latter arrived on a table with a cloth, a beautiful flowered china breakfast set, the butter in little scalloped slices nestled in ice, the jam in covered jam jars with spoons, fresh orange juice. The medium-boiled egg (three minutes, the hall porter suggested) was perfect. You can press a button for someone to take the dishes away.

There is a breakfast menu in the room with prices, but until you check out you never see a bill, never have to sign anything or add up a tip. Would your rich friend give you a bill in his home?

Within twenty-four hours everyone who worked in the hotel addressed me by name. They knew where I was. I got a phone call; they found me in a dining room, even when I forgot to tell them I would be there.

The night after my arrival, a Sunday, I was to have dinner with my publisher. He had been disappointed at not being able to get a reservation in one of the hotel's two dining rooms, but I called from my room and a table was arranged. I knew from staying at other good hotels that a few tables always are saved for hotel guests, especially on Sunday nights, when few restaurants are open. What makes the Connaught special is that once you have reserved a table it is your table, even if you arrive at 6 pm and stay until midnight. No one hovers around hinting that you leave before the next sitting. There is only one sitting at the Connaught.

There are several public rooms in the lobby where you can have drinks or tea, meet a friend, write letters, or just read the paper. The bar is a series of inviting little wood-panelled rooms, one with a fireplace. I met my publisher in the bar, and while we were having drinks a maitre d' brought menus so we could look at them at our leisure. We ordered food and wine and had another drink. Then the maitre d' reappeared to say our table was ready in the Restaurant, the more formal of the two dining rooms, any time we wanted it.

We entered and took our seats at a crimson corner banquette. The room was quietly sumptuous, with cream-coloured walls, a blue and yellow carpet and crystal lighting fixtures. We started our meal with smoked Scotch salmon and quail eggs with caviar. Then I had grilled fresh Dover sole and my companion had a seafood stew with shrimps and lobster in a wine sauce. We chose desserts from a large trolley laden with every temptingly fattening thing you can think of as well as fresh fruit. I had a delicious bread-and-butter pudding. With coffee came a plate of sugar-glazed grapes and orange slices, candies and strawberries dipped in chocolate, a festive finish for a festive meal.

As I was the guest at dinner, there was a bill, which had to be asked for. It appeared and was paid while I was in the ladies' room. When, on a subsequent night, I was the hostess, there was no bill, nor was there one the morning I had coffee in the lounge. As I hate to spend money and find a big bill gives me indigestion at the end of a good meal, I found this infinitely relaxing. However, you are not apt to get a total shock when you check out, since the prices are on the menu. The food is as expensive as in an expensive New York restaurant.

Some people claim the hotel's other dining room, the Grill, has better food than the Restaurant, or even different food, but both are supplied from the same kitchen and the main differences are of size and décor. The Grill is a smaller, less formal room. The walls are painted in a rich green, as is the ceiling, which has mouldings tipped with gold; there is a blue and yellow scrolled carpet and from the ceiling hang bronze lights with gold shades.

When I had dinner in the Grill with my agent, I again chose smoked Scotch salmon and Dover sole and they were just as good as the Restaurant's. My agent chose roast beef and Yorkshire pudding, which was the speciality that night and was wheeled around on a trolley for our inspection. I had trifle – another outrageously caloric dessert – and she had fresh fruit with cream. The same dish of sugar-glazed fruit and candies came with the coffee.

We sat and talked at our corner table for hours and no one hurried us. One thing I noticed about both the dining rooms and the upstairs rooms is that everything is laid out for privacy. You can talk in peace at your table, and you never seem to see the other guests who are staying on your floor when you leave your room. Yet at the same time the atmosphere is cosy.

If you like your room, you will always get it again when you come back, or you will at least get the same room on a different floor. I was there in March and I saw guests leaving and saying to the staff, 'Goodbye, see you in September.' I could see why it is so hard to get in when people come back again and again and make reservations months in advance.

For a business traveller, as I was, the hotel is perfect because you can have everything you need and it is always on time, and because you are so pampered that you can unwind immediately at the end of the day. For a vacationer it is perfect because the hotel is a holiday in itself. I would be completely content just to stay there for a week and never leave, but most vacationers would want to see London.

A good place to start is Mount Street, right around the corner from the hotel, with its antique shops, and the charming little Mount Street Gardens, through which you can walk to the Farm Street Church, where Evelyn Waugh was received into the Catholic faith. Carlos Place, incidentally, is tucked between Grosvenor Square, home of the United States Embassy, and Berkeley Square, and Park Lane and Piccadilly are just a few minutes' walk away.

After three days and four nights at the Connaught I had to start a hectic three-day publicity tour of five cities in England and Scotland, so I left one of my suitcases in the care of the hall porter until my return. It was waiting safe and sound when I came back and was whisked right up to me. I knew it would be. After all, at some moment I had not detected, the hotel had stopped being the home of a rich friend and had become my home.

LODGING FOR THE NIGHT: SMALL AND STYLISH

Donald Goddard

There seems little point in enduring the boredom of international air travel only to succumb to the monotony of international hotels more or less indistinguishable from their sister establishments in Syracuse and Milwaukee. That is why many visitors to London, in growing revolt against conveyor-belt holidays assembled by tour packagers, are happily discovering or returning to the city's small hotels of character.

This is not to suggest, of course, that London's big hotels are all entirely lacking in character, although most of the newer ones are. Visitors who like, and can afford, the full traditional treatment will not be disappointed with Claridge's, for example, which continues to resist the trend toward the motel-anonymous school of hotel-keeping with superb disdain, simply refusing to accept inflation, staffing problems or declining expectations on the part of the public as excuses for lowering standards. If Claridge's is full, there will be few complaints from those who fall back on the Berkeley (despite its air of luxurious boredom), the Ritz (despite disturbing hints of a 'marketing policy'), Grosvenor House, the Savoy, the Dorchester or even the Hyde Park. But this is the easy way out – all it takes is money. For those prepared to take the trouble to seek them out, there are scores of smaller hotels in London aspiring to comparable standards of excellence on a less grandiose scale.

The only problem for those who have not yet found a home away from home is how to choose one of character and individuality from the hundreds of places listed in the standard guidebooks. If a small hotel is taken to mean one of less than a hundred rooms but offering all or most of the services expected of a larger establishment (or, if not, some compensating advantage), then the choice in London is wide enough for a theoretically perfect match between visitors who know what they like, however quirky, and an equally quirky hotelier who knows what they like – be it friendliness, comfort, personal attention, peace and quiet, charm, haute cuisine, refinement of décor, location, atmosphere or some combination of these, plus just plain caring about a guest's sense of well-being.

The following fourteen smaller hotels each provide something out of the ordinary and, except for people who really should have stayed at home, will add considerably to the pleasures of a visit to London.

Small does not necessarily mean cheap, of course. No list would be complete without the **Connaught** – but, as the old joke goes, if you have to ask how much it costs you Connaught afford to stay there. The hotel is so beset by would-be patrons hungering for a bed with status that its management actually pleads with the media not to mention it. Luxurious in a restrained, English manner and blessed with a notable restaurant, the Connaught is a haven for the privileged few, but some of its ninety rooms are on the poky side, and as excess demand is not always a spur to impeccable service, those turned away may find an alternative Connaught of their own at the **Stafford Hotel** in St. James's Place.

The Stafford's location is, if anything, better, and its restaurant and cellar at least as good and in the same classic tradition although the two young managers do admit they are down to their last five bottles of '61 Cheval Blanc (at about $200 apiece).

Tucked away peacefully in a cul-de-sac between St. James's Street and Green Park, the hotel exudes an Edwardian serenity, with one of the prettiest lounges in London for afternoon tea, and sixty-five bedrooms or suites, all different, and furnished in unaggressive good taste. The Stafford rewards its old friends with membership in 'The Better 'ole Club', and both old friends and new with the attentions of Louis Croset, who has presided over the bar for thirty-two years and claims to have exported the first dry martini to the United States. (The Better 'ole Club is named for the sandbagged trench dugout of World War I that preserved Bruce Bairnsfather's immortal cartoon character Ole Bill for posterity.) The very small, very select membership (fifty-one at the last count) can drink, if it wants to, in a replica of Ole Bill's Better 'ole constructed in a corner of the hotel's extensive cellarage.

Failing the Stafford, not fifty yards away, in a gaslit courtyard off St. James's Place, is **Duke's Hotel**, built originally to provide a London address for the younger sons of the nobility, and a hotel since 1908. Declining gently over the years in this convenient backwater, Dukes was bought in 1976 by a former patron in the oil business, who appears since then to have applied the revenues from at least one well to doing the place up. Aiming for opulence rather than flash in the forty-one bedrooms and fourteen suites, he has even replaced the plastic toilet seats with warmer wooden ones. But when the management deliberately broke with tradition after refurbishing the second floor by omitting to replace the old ducal nameplates previously affixed to the doors, the regulars responded as though they had been offered a bed without sheets.

Tradition can be a powerful factor in the hotel business, as three generations of Gorings will testify. **The Goring Hotel**, situated between Buckingham Palace and Victoria Station, was built in 1910 by the grandfather of the present resident director, George Goring, who still makes a point of sleeping in every one of its one hundred rooms and suites (when unoccupied, of course) to make sure 'they are as comfortable as they look.'

In this, the first hotel in the world, so it is claimed, to provide steam heat and a private bath with every room, shoes left outside the door will not only still be there in the morning but brilliantly polished as well. It has its own private garden, a generosity of space now rare, and a ratio of staff to bedrooms three times the national average.

For many people, location is not a critical factor, as two of the most fashionable hotels in the city have proved. **The Portobello**, near the antiques market in Notting Hill, and **Blakes**, buried in probably the ugliest street of South Kensington, are both remembered in taxi drivers' prayers because guests can go nowhere without them, and yet each has a devoted international clientele. Launched at the start of the 1970's from the common ground of no previous experience in the hotel business, a desire to cater to a self-indulgent generation without pomp or mock-humility, and a passionate interest in interior design, the two hotels have since moved in opposite directions without changing course.

Blakes, masterminded by the beautiful former actress Anouska Hempel, has grown bigger, lusher and more exotic in décor, encouraging (and encouraged by) the patronage of the fashionable film and media crowd, plus a touch of the rag trade, while the Portobello, managed since it opened by the glamorous Eva Lofstad, has shrunk from thirty-two rooms to twenty-five (to provide more space and comfort for fewer guests), is steadily replacing its modern furniture with antiques, and is much favoured by working celebrities who really do want to be left alone.

Blakes is a full-service hotel, with an almost paralyzingly smart restaurant sometimes patronized by royalty; the Portobello, still staffed as a matter of policy by local people with no previous experience, so as to avoid 'bad habits' picked up in lesser hotels, is run like a private house, without porters or room service, but with a reception desk as efficient as any in London, and a bar-restaurant that serves good, simple, inventive meals twenty-four hours a day.

For some, the décor at Blakes may seem self-conscious and studied, perhaps lacking in humour. For others, the décor at the Portobello may seem low-key and casual, if occasionally bizarre – its Round Room, for example, features a canopied, circular bed in a round bay window overlooking Stanley Gardens, and a mighty Wurlitzer of a bathtub and shower with enough exposed piping and brass taps to please a ship's engineer. But for those too tired, or too uninterested, to keep up with the latest trends in decorative thought, the answer may well be **Number 16**.

Unimpressed with London's small hotels as they were then, Michael Watson left the brewery trade in 1970 to show the world how they should be run, at Number 16 Sumner Place, South Kensington. Since then, he has succeeded well enough to spread out into Numbers 15 and 17 as well, and today can offer a choice of twenty-five rooms at competitive rates in one of the most elegant terraces of early Victorian town houses in London.

Number 16 is for those who prefer to eat out, for there is no restaurant; who are fit enough to cope with stairs to the upper floors, for there is no elevator; who can be trusted to help themselves at the bar, for there is no barman (guests are asked to sign chits for their drinks); and who generally value fresh flowers, fine furniture and quiet domestic efficiency.

Equally unhotel-like is the newly opened **L'Hôtel** at 28 Basil Street, a mere croissant's throw from Harrods. Frenchified by Margaret and David Levin, who own the Capital Hotel a few doors up the street, its twelve rooms have been furnished as though by a Gallic Laura Ashley in pine and country-style fabrics, with touches of brass and Art Nouveau, notably in the working fireplaces. Again, there is no restaurant, unless one counts the Metro, a trendy new wine bar in the basement, but the Capital offers – at a price – some of the best French food to be had in London, and at a shorter distance than usually separates the restaurant of a big hotel from its bedrooms.

Indeed, the **Capital** itself qualifies as one of the capital's most comfortable small hotels, with sixty rooms furnished regardless of expense in a spirit of international five-star neutrality, a style as likely to be found in Bangkok and Baton Rouge as Basil Street. Just right for those who take comfort in the familiar when travelling abroad, the hotel offers unfamiliar standards of courtesy and personal attention, maintaining a register of its client's likes and dislikes, for example, that extends to including such details as the preferred wattage of bedside reading lamps.

On the other hand, those who enjoy at least a touch of local colour may hanker after something a little less cosmopolitan, even leaning, perhaps, toward a traditional English establishment, an endangered species nowadays, but still lingering on in parts of Kensington, around Sloane Street, and along the Pimlico borders of Belgravia.

Of these, the **Wilbraham** is among the hardiest – robustly independent, eclectically furnished, slightly old-fashioned, and proud of it. Having catered for years to the not-so-well-off middle class up from the country, and its New England and Midwestern cousins, the management foresees no change more radical than the provision of a few more private baths for its fifty rooms, many of which are reminiscent of those one stayed in as a child when visiting a maiden aunt. Publishers and musicians in particular find this endearing. When the Orlando String Quartet found none of its four rooms large enough for them all to work in, Auntie Wilbraham let them practise in the bar.

Such a thing is unlikely to happen at the **Ebury Court**, however, which must be one of the last bastions of true English gentility. Presided over since 1938 by Mrs. Diana Topham, whose velvet calm evidently charms her staff as well as the guests, for most of them have worked there for years, the hotel somehow expects those who enter to lower their voices, offering thirty-eight pleasantly furnished rooms 'for people to come and have a rest.' They may also drink if they wish, although, in the interests of decorum, the bar is open only to members of the Ebury Court Club, and hotel residents must ask the porter to serve them. (Temporary club membership can sometimes be arranged, however, for suitable applicants, screened by the secretary, who happens to be Mr. Topham, lately retired from the legal profession.) The regular membership consists of local people who prefer to drink with their own kind rather than with just anybody, and people up from the country or from overseas who share the same clannish outlook.

No such impediment, however, will keep the thirsty from refreshment at the **Gore** – another decidedly dead-on English hotel, whose owners, Brian and Aminge Dale-Thomas, are still having to disappoint guests who stayed there in the 1950's and 1960's and look forward to the kind of Tudor-style banquet and revelry, complete with bosomy serving wenches and mildly licentious carryings-on, for which the Gore was then famous.

The last of these was held years ago, but visitors ready to exchange mock-Merrie England for a warm, friendly hotel at a reasonable price will be anything but disappointed with the improvements wrought since by Brian Dale-Thomas, a do-it-yourself hotelier now nearing the end of his seven-year programme of renovating and adding baths to the fifty-nine rooms. One of them, Room 101, is where the banquets were held. Very suitable for family occupation, therefore, it comes complete with beamed ceiling, linen fold panelling, minstrel's gallery (doubling as a sleeping loft for the kids), a four-poster bed, and a chastity belt.

Budget-conscious families may also appreciate the **Elizabeth Hotel** on Eccleston Square, behind Victoria Station. Intended, in the proprietor's words, for 'people who want to sleep in quiet, clean, comfortable accommodations at a moderate price', the Elizabeth's twenty-four rooms include several with private bath, television and refrigerator that will sleep four for under $20 a head, including a full English breakfast. Though otherwise fairly basic, the hotel stands out like the Ritz among the usual run of flophouse bed-and-breakfast joints that infest the streets around London's principal railway stations. Its guests are even entitled to use the private gardens and tennis court of Eccleston Square, the Pimlico cousin of stately Belgrave Square, both having been built early in the nineteenth century by Thomas Cubitt.

But in the end the choice of a small hotel, blending atmosphere, comfort, character and price in just the right proportions, is such an individual matter that any selection from the hundreds to be found in London is bound to be arbitrary and invidious. The result is still the product of personal preference, so that those attempting to offer advice are probably obliged to declare their own favourites as a benchmark.

Very well, then. For style, the Portobello. For self-indulgence, the Stafford. And for general, day-in, day-out dependability, **Durrants**. Not just for its splendid position, behind the Wallace Collection and near Baker Street. Not just because it always looks inviting, or because the Millers, who own it, are putting the rooms back to something like the way they were before a misguided attack of 'modernization' in the sixties and seventies. For most of its two-hundred-year history, Durrants has quietly served a quiet circle of regular visitors – senior medical men, in more recent times, and those having business with the BBC – the sort of people who simply would not go back if they were not quietly satisfied.

Other hotels may have classier restaurants, or more up-to-date décors, or smarter reputations, but Durrants somehow catches some of the essential 'feel' of London as it coexists with the modern world. How? Perhaps because Charles Miller, at ninety-four, still drops in occasionally to keep an eye on things.

THE GRAND OLD SPA OF BATH

Jan Morris

Something strange, startling but perfectly proper was happening within the first century Roman spa buildings in Bath when I strolled in after dinner recently. The rock group Spandau Ballet was making a video recording, and while flames blazed and smoked on lamp-brackets all around, the lead singer mimed his lyrics into the camera as he wandered lovelorn around the colonnade. Floating across the surface of the Great Bath, an almost entirely naked lady, strewn with real red roses and veiled over the face in black, lay flat on her back upon an inflatable bed, misted about by the rising vapours of Aquae Sulis, the immemorial Waters of Sul.

Perfectly proper, not only because the Romans who built the pool would surely have loved it, but because Bath, a middle-sized city in the English county of Avon, is presently enjoying an unmistakable reju-venation – or perhaps a return to form, for its civic purpose has traditionally been recreation of one sort or another: recreation of the body, by means of its curative springs; recreation of the spirit by means of art and music, good food and congenial pastimes, sometimes snobbish satisfactions and the sheer restorative presence of one of Europe's most beautiful townscapes.

In recent years changing medical fashion allowed Bath's spa, its original raison d'être, to fall into disuse, and with it there went some of the city's sense of purpose, and some of its glamour too. Now there are plans to revive it in the grandest style, with new hotels, new treatment centres and a new international clientele of the poshest and most profitable kind. And at the same time Bath, on and off one of the most fashionable cities in England, is becoming distinctly smart again in its own right, and is perceptibly returning to the condition of high spirits and good living, not altogether unmixed with effrontery, that God obviously meant for it in the first place.

This is an inspiriting process to watch. You might call it, all in all, the Youthing of Bath. Like Venice, Bath is rather an obfuscatory city and it is sometimes hard to put a finger on the causes, or even the exact symptoms, of this new mood. The city has always had its ups and downs. If the Romans made it one of their principal transalpine resorts, the Dark Ages left it grimly derelict. If Beau Nash, the eighteenth century entrepreneur, packed the nobility into its halls and salons, by the beginning of our own century the city had acquired a reputation for seedy gentility, and only a few gouty, arthritic or rheumatic familiars were to be seen taking the waters in its palm-decked Pump Room above the Roman baths.

Vivacity does not come naturally to the place. Its setting, in a bowl in the hills above the Avon River, is picturesque but soporific. Some people suggest that the fumes of the hot springs drift invisibly about its streets, dulling all responses. The climate is nothing to write home about. Jane Austen detested the city, and the poet Alexander Pope, who often used to stay at a friend's house on the hills above, subscribed to the drifting-fumes theory, and thought coming downtown was like entering a sulphurous pit.

So the liveliness has to be injected, and this makes it a cyclical city, rather like a manic depressive – brilliant and abject in successive moments, or successive centuries, according to the availability of talent and enterprise. Fortunately, the structure of Bath as we know it today is, by and large, the product of its heydays. The Roman remains that provide a stunning fulcrum for the town are clearly the work of a terrifically confident era – wonderful constructions, some of the most exciting Roman relics anywhere, and still throwing up new discoveries year by year as the archaeologists labour away beneath the modern city streets. And all around that extraordinary core, in graceful squares and intricate pedestrian alleys, in terraces and crescents up the surrounding hills, in villas and churches and on a lovely old bridge with shops upon it, extends the Bath of the Georgian decades, the greatest single architectural monument to that age's sprightly and resilient elegance.

It is lucky for us, too, that Bath is so evidently now entering another of its optimistic periods. Not so long ago these magnificent legacies of the past were sadly neglected, and the city stood above its river lifeless and disheartened, as though the great world had forgotten it. Today everything seems to be happening. It is more a sensation, perhaps, than an actual event. But wherever you look, there seems to be initiative or restoration, and even on one of those despondent mornings, when Pope's pit seems more than usually pitlike, the grey is greyer than ever and the drizzle looks never likely to stop, somehow you feel the old place stirring with new life and bounciness.

People are vague, when you ask them why it is, but for a start the city has never been in better physical state. Since the drear days of the curtain-wall 1960's, when they began insidiously knocking down the lesser Georgian streets to make way for trendy shopping precincts, there has been a merciful change of heart or policy. Nothing less than a few tons of explosive can ever rid us of the ghastly hotel erected by the city's own official architect upon one of its finest sites – a proper bureaucrat of a building, attended as by some sycophantic clerk by the ventilation tower of an underground car park. Nothing so terrible, though, has happened since. On the contrary, thousands of nice old houses have been unobtrusively modernized, and assiduous stone-cleaning has given the place a new clarity – changing its prevailing colour, at least when the sun is shining, from that hangdog grey monochrome almost to gold.

Then many an outmoded building, not so long ago destined for certain demolition, has been found a useful new function. For example, the Octagon, a curious eighteenth century chapel tucked away behind the city's main shopping street, has been rescued from oblivion to become the Royal Photographic Society's National Centre of Photography. A dowdy old department store, once the very epitome of auntly Bath, has emerged as the raciest of antique markets. A half-derelict warehouse at the river's edge has become a charming group of apartments (bang opposite that unspeakable hotel, to which it offers a perpetual reproach).

Happiest of all for my own tastes, a splendid future is opening for the former Green Park railway station, a well-known hulk that had been standing dilapidated and forlorn for ages. It has been restored to life with majestic care and is being used partly as a supermarket and partly for the benefit of the community for such events as concerts. It is a fine thing to see its high-vaulted roof repainted once again, its handsome atrium cleared of rubble at last, its girders relieved of their ancient filth, and the whole great building gradually made spick, span and ready for almost anything, I suppose, except perhaps trains.

The more sensual pleasures are being revivified too. Bath is, of course, a pleasure city above all else. There is very little industry, and it is only proper that the great speciality of Bath's municipal authorities is the care of gardens: They are always winning Britain-in-Bloom contests, or prizes from L'Entente Florale, and the parks that infiltrate the centre of the town, the flower-baskets that dominate its pedestrian alleys, deliberately announce that this is a place meant above all to be enjoyed.

Today the nature of its hedonism is shifting. Fast new trains, plus a motorway, bring ever more visitors down from London, and the city is busily adjusting to more metropolitan tastes. Many of its restaurants, for instance, are adopting new idioms. Some, of course, are the kind that swallow and regurgitate a fresh idiom every season, but even those rooted most firmly in the city seem to be gearing up for new times – even the Hole-in-the-Wall, perhaps the best-known English restaurant outside London, has turned itself into something unfamiliar in these islands, a 'restaurant with rooms' in the French manner. As for the hotels, they are primping themselves all over town. The latest to achieve gossip-column attention is the Royal Crescent, the central building in the proudest of all the Georgian terraces, which used to be just the place to retire when your husband the dear vicar passed on, but is now seldom out of the glossies for long.

The city has always been a place of music. The Bath Festival, which happens in the summer, has long been one of Europe's most urbane, but is supplemented now by concerts all the time: pop stars in the Sports Centre beside the river, recitalists at musical weekends, jazz in pubs, brass bands in gardens, diligent buskers (rock, folk or Mozart) in the covered arcades downtown. Why, the very Pump Room Trio itself, the most beloved of all Bath's ensembles, seems to be evolving a new image. When I went in the other morning to listen to its music over my coffee and Bath bun, I found that it no longer confined itself to 'Rosemarie' and 'Oklahoma!' but dashed off pieces that even the fondest Pump Room habitué could scarcely tap a toe to.

And when I walked over to the Theatre Royal, a trifle apprehensively by now, to see what was happening there, I got another kind of shock. This is one of England's oldest theatres, full of theatrical lore and mannerism, David Garrick to John Gielgud, red plush and gilded pillar to statutory in-house ghost. But venturing through the stage door I found the whole of it ripped out – all that gold and velvet gone, all the chandeliers removed, stage, auditorium, crush bar and all. They have since completed the rebuilding of the whole thing within its original walls, just as it was but with modern equipment. It now provides a West of England stage for London's controversial National Theatre, the Royal Ballet and other travelling presentations as well as local productions.

How were they raising the money? I asked, voicing a doubt that had been nagging me throughout my tour of this impetuous new Bath, apparently so heedless of recession or cash flow. By loans, I was told, by gifts, by official grants, by the sale of advertising, by sponsorship, and by marketing pincushions made from the seat covers of the very box haunted by the Grey Lady of the Theatre Royal – suffused, they added, offering one delicately to my nostrils, with a few drops of her celebrated jasmine scent.

Well, this really is a different Bath, almost unrecognizable, one would think, to the retired valetudinarians and clerygmen's relics of old. And it will all be capped, they say, when the new spa plan comes to fruition. All they need for that is $30 million or so, which a consortium of British, French and Italian interests is now trying to raise. If they succeed, the city will certainly be entering one of the most fruitful of all its productive cycles, and acquiring another and dazzling identity: a modern Carlsbad perhaps – or, for that matter, a truly modern Bath.

Such a refulfilment will only be, after all, honouring the original destiny of this place. Even before the Romans, we are told, Celts and their animals wallowed gratefully in Bath's soothing ooze, and ever since visitors have managed to combine Taking the Waters with Living It Up.

As it ironically happens, the hot springs, which have been solacing people here for at least two thousand years, have chosen this particular moment to infect themselves with a microbe, making themselves temporarily unfit for human use. Bath is in no mood, though, to be deterred by mere bugs. The little rascals, I am assured, will soon be eliminated, and they certainly did not seem to worry the lady of the pool at Spandau Ballet's performance that night, or spoil her historical symbolism. When her job was done she shook off her roses and veil and stepped out of the steam-hazed Aquae Sulis, in all the fullness of her glory, as to the Roman manner born.

TELEPHONE NUMBERS are all on the **Bath** exchange.

GETTING THERE
Train: Hourly service from Paddington Station. Fast trains take an hour and ten minutes, slow ones an hour and a half.
  Car: From London, Bath is 106 miles away via the M4 Motorway. The drive takes about two hours.
  Bus: Service every two hours. The trip takes three hours.

GETTING AROUND
Information Centre, in Abbey Church Yard, is open from 10 am to 5 pm (phone 62831). It supplies a list of private guides who take tourists around the city. If all the places of interest in Bath and the surrounding district are to be visited, at least two or three days are needed.

HOTELS
The Royal Crescent Hotel (phone 319090), $90 to $200, has log fires, antique furniture, impeccable service and fine food. Rooms at the rear overlook gardens; those at the front have views of the Crescent. The hotel also has a Palladian villa on the grounds with eight luxury rooms, four of which can be combined to make two suites. The suites cost $360 a night.
  The Beaufort Hotel, Walcot Street (phone 63411), $68 or $77 (breakfast $5.50 or $7.65), is a fairly modern place. The best rooms are at the rear, overlooking the river and hills.
  The Francis Hotel, Queen Square (phone 24257), is a traditional establishment, $72 to $80 (breakfast $8). The quietest rooms are at the rear; those in front have the best view.
  Lansdown Grove Hotel, Lansdown Road (phone 315891), $66. Rooms in the wings overlooking gardens are best.

RESTAURANTS

Prices quoted are for a typical meal for two including tax and tip.

Hole-in-the-Wall, George Street (phone 25242), about $55 with aperitif and wine. A speciality is guinea fowl marinated in wine. Closed Sunday, except to guests of the hotel, which offers accommodations, including continental breakfast, for $60 to $75.

Ainslies, 12 Pierrepont Street (phone 61745), $43 with aperitif and wine. One speciality is lamb's kidneys with port, cream and red currant jelly. Closed Sunday lunch.

Beaujolais, 5 Chapel Row (phone 23417), $39 with house wine and brandy. Renowned for onion soup and fish dishes. Closed Sunday.

K-T's, Grand Parade (phone 61946), $12 without drinks. Charcoal grilled specialities.

SIGHTSEEING

Roman Baths, Roman Museum and Pump Room, open 9 am to 6 pm; adults $2 (phone 61111). The baths are fed by the only hot springs in the country. The centrepiece of the museum is a gilt-bronze head of the goddess Minerva, found on the site.

Bath Abbey, famous for its traceried stone chantry chapel. Open 9 am to dusk; a small donation is requested.

Assembly Rooms open 9 am to 6 pm, include the **Museum of Costume** ($1.80), devoted to the history of fashion.

Carriage Museum, in Circus Mews open 10 am to 5 pm, Monday through Saturday, adults about $1.20 (phone 25175), has the finest collection of horse-drawn carriages in the country, which may be booked for trips around the city.

No. 1 Royal Crescent, open 11 am to 5 pm, Tuesday through Saturday, and 2 am to 5 pm Sundays; adults 90 cents (phone 28126), a Georgian house maintained as a museum, with a library, drawing room, dining room and bedroom furnished with authentic eighteenth century furniture.

Camden Works Museum, Julian Road, open 2 pm to 5 pm, closed Fridays; admission $1 (phone 318348), contains the complete stock in trade of John Bowler, a Victorian brass founder and engineer. There is an ironmonger's shop, a re-creation of Mr. Bowler's office, a pattern shop where brass patterns were made and a foundry.

Holbourne Museum, Great Pulteney Street, open 11 am to 5 pm, Monday through Saturday, 2.30 pm to 6 pm on Sunday; adults $1 (phone 66669), has two notable portraits by Gainsborough, who lived in Bath; collections of eighteenth century china, porcelain and silver; and a crafts study centre.

National Centre of Photography, in Milsom Street, open 10 am to 4.45 pm, Monday through Saturday; adults $1.80 (phone 62841), also houses the headquarters of the Royal Photographic Society. Its exhibits trace the history of photography from the earliest days.

American Museum, two miles from the city centre at Claverton Manor, open from the last week in March to the end of October, 2 pm to

5 pm, closed Mondays; adults $2.70 (phone 60503), is the only museum of its kind outside the United States. There are eighteen rooms furnished with American pieces that date from the mid seventeenth to the mid nineteenth centuries, a display of hand-made quilts and folk art.

ANNUAL EVENTS

Late May-Early June: Bath Festival, one of the premier music festivals in England, with more than forty concerts, mainly in the Guildhall, Assembly Rooms and Abbey. Tickets are from $1.80 to $18. The box office number is 63362.

Late May: Contemporary Art Fair, Assembly Rooms, with exhibitions from leading British and European galleries. Adults $1.80; children 45 cents.

Early July: Floral Festival, with parks, shops and offices providing displays of flowers. Free.

— John Beaven

SOME QUINTESSENTIAL BRITISH GARDENS

Ronald Blythe

The great gardens of Britain are spellbinding achievements, as majestic, in their way, as any cathedral. Once through their gates, and their scale, colour, scents, learning and harmony lay hold of you. You walk and think and look – and are changed.

How was it done? I ask myself during compulsive excursions to Bodnant Gardens in Wales, or Stourhead in Wiltshire, or Hidcote Manor in Gloucestershire. How did this ravishing bringing together – of lawns and lakes, flower beds, terraces, trees, shrubberies, walks, views and walls – come to happen? And why should it be so satisfying? It is, I suppose, because such gardens reveal a truly heroic pursuit of pleasure.

There is pride in a great garden. For centuries, those who lived in castles and palaces and manors woke up each morning to the delights of the world as they had contrived it, and not at all as it was outside their parks. When Xenophon was shown the garden of King Cyrus, he made a note of its Persian name – a 'Paradise.' Britain's finest gardens offer a pick of many paradises. Each is the result of its owner's determination to lay out a notion of heaven in full view of his own house.

An exploration of Britain's great gardens should begin in London. I myself, were I mapping out a tour, would include parks, botanical gardens and other public grounds, for their affinities of grandeur and confidence. Thus Regent's Park and that not-to-be-missed corner known as Queen Mary's Garden. And the forty acres of Buckingham Palace's garden – although only those who attend the Queen's vast summer parties ever get a glimpse of it.

To discover the epicentre of Britain's gardens, both stately and homely, one must go to Kew, to the Royal Botanic Gardens there. This is the heart of the horticultural matter. Once the Duke of Kent's home, it has long been a garden beyond compare; a day there must not be missed. Although it has a long history, the feeling of Kew is forever one of the flowering present. The seasonal blooming is unforgettably abundant – the Kew bluebells, for example, are so multitudinous that they appear to stain sky and land for miles with their blueness.

Kew is Britain's collector and processor of all botanical intelligence. Plants from all over the world are brought here to be understood, protected, propagated and preserved. It is a library and a laboratory, and also a garden in the most perfect sense. Sir William Chambers's pagoda guards its mysteries, and I never see it without realizing that I am in for a few hours of garden enlightenment of the most exciting kind.

Kew Gardens leads naturally to the Royal Horticultural Society and its irresistible shop window, the Chelsea Flower Show. The show, more than sixty years old, takes place at the Royal Hospital, Chelsea, the munificent shelter that Charles II founded for his old soldiers. The buildings date from the late eighteenth century. Held in mid-May, when these islands are at their botanical best, the Chelsea Flower Show is a nurseryman's trade fair, attended by every devoted gardener from the monarch down.

The Queen visits the show on a day of such exclusivity that it is a mark of one's standing in horticultural circles to be there at the same time. Then the rest of us rush in to gasp and stare, to succumb yet again to the Chelsea magic. By some annual miracle, every kind of garden imaginable has been transported to the bank of the Thames and set up under gleaming marquees – not just floral and vegetable displays but fountains, pavilions, rocks and pools. But the thing that is most admired is what might be called the perfection of the species: the biggest and best, the brightest or most subtly coloured peonies, begonias, delphiniums, pelargoniums and, of course, roses, each as glorious as nature and inspired gardening can make them.

And there is another sight worth seeing at the Chelsea Show, the spectacle of British gardeners en masse. Even I, who am so familiar with these plant-obsessed people, find myself enthralled by them. Their voices and weathered faces, along with the bruised grass, the wine, the tea, the scents of canvas and of flowers, are all a part of what makes Chelsea unique. There is a great sense of continuity in these shows and, at the same time, an equally powerful feeling of change.

Gardens last, often for centuries, but they are never static. Outside London, one of my favourite gardens is the one that Sir Eric Savill made for King George VI in Windsor Great Park, shortly after World War II. It is one of the last to be designed and planted in the grand manner, but many visitors to Windsor never see it because it lies more than three miles from the castle itself. The garden is actually a series of woodland gardens incorporated in the ancient park, just off the Staines Road.

These gardens are so big and their trees – many of which must have seen Elizabeth I hunting beneath them – are so superb that you feel as though you have discovered a new country. With their meandering mown walks and flower-packed verges, they are a triumph of informality.

Other gardens around London provide a contrast to Savill's carefully cultivated disorder. If you are in a formal mood, you might wish to visit Hampton Court with its calm stylized hedges and twisting Tudor ornaments. Or Osterley Park House, with its vast greensward and Doric temple, its stately cedars of Lebanon and its air of classical deliberation in all things. To understand such proud gardening best, you need to stand on the steps of the house. The beeches and maples don't rustle here. They quote the Latin poets.

But the most popular garden in Britain is one whose creator did all she could to see that it would never qualify for the big league. Sissinghurst is a village in Kent, near Maidstone. A mile or two on its outskirts there stands a tall, pinnacled gateway, and it may without exaggeration be said that, for anyone with a spark of gardening passion in him, this gateway is the entrance to ten acres of bliss. The story is recent and romantic.

In 1930, the poet Vita Sackville-West, hero-heroine of Virginia Woolf's *Orlando*, purchased what was then little more than a clutter of semi-derelict buildings and some stagnant grounds and began to put down a statement about her own life, set out in botanical terms. Her intention as she confessed in book after book, was private, to make a world for herself. Yet from the very start, because of what she accomplished here and because of the way she described it in some of the best gardening journalism ever written, Sissinghurst soon began to influence gardens everywhere. By cultivating her own plot, Vita Sackville-West helped to transform the art of British gardening.

The most famous thing to see at Sissinghurst is the White Garden. Vita Sackville-West had early begun to contemplate such a notion: 'It is amusing to make one-colour gardens . . . For my own part, I am trying to make a grey, green and white garden . . . I visualize the white trumpets of dozens of Regale lilies, grown three years ago from seed, coming up through the grey of southernwood and artemisia and cotton-lavender, with grey-and-white edging plants such as Dianthus "Mrs. Sinkins" and the silvery mats of Stachys lanata, more familiar and so much nicer under its English names of Rabbits' Ears or Saviour's Flannel . . . There will be white pansies and white peonies, and white irises with their grey leaves . . . I cannot help hoping that the great ghostly barn-owl will sweep silently across a pale garden, next summer, in the twilight – the pale garden that I am now planting, under the first flakes of snow.'

Vita Sackville-West died twenty years ago, but she continues to dominate her garden. Her tall figure, dressed in twin-set and pearls, breeches and boots ('Lady Chatterley above the waist and the gamekeeper below,' as the wits said), her earth-stained hands and cigarette holder, seem to be as securely held here as the soaring creepers on the walls. 'Once of the noble land/I dared to pull the organ stops,' she wrote in a poem. Sissinghurst is the result.

In my own corner of England, there is Oxburgh Hall, Swaffham (Norfolk), with its ornamental parterre, through which paths run like embroidery, and Melford Hall, Sudbury (Suffolk), with its Tudor-brick architecture that reaches its climax in a sixteenth century garden pavilion. Queen Elizabeth I was here received by five hundred men dressed in velvet. Blickling Hall, Aylsham (Norfolk), is a rural palace to which a garden lends a grand view. There is an orangery and, where the moat used to be, a mass of old English roses, among them a rare rose called the Duchess of Portland that is the ancestor of all our modern roses. Blickling is the handsome remnant of the traditional English formal garden, of which the garden of Montacute House, Yeovil (Somerset), is the peak. The lawns, the symmetrically cut yews, the Spanish chestnuts and the series of gardens that open from each other like rooms have here survived an elaborate Victorian remodelling. It is the enduring strength of this earlier formality – the triumphant union of architecture and growing things – that makes Montacute so memorable.

Stourhead (Wiltshire) is to gardening art what Mozart is to music. It was created by Henry Hoare and his descendants, Georgian bankers and garden geniuses, during the eighteenth century, when, under the influence of the classical landscapes the poets and painters invented, gardens spread themselves widely into the surrounding countryside, taking in rivers, hills and vistas. Stourhead has everything – exotics, native plants, a setting of unimaginable loveliness, rare birds, walks to suit every mood from morbidity to ecstasy, statues, bridges, temples and urns and a constant series of surprises and wonders. Now nearing its two-hundredth year, Stourhead is to be seen at its mature best. It supports to a convincing degree that Chinese philosopher-gardener who said, 'If you would be happy for a week, take a wife: if you would be happy for a month, kill a pig: but if you would be happy for ever, plant a garden.'

Other examples of the garden as high art are Anglesey Abbey (Cambridgeshire), a romantic creation designed between the wars by Lord Fairhaven; Bodnant (near Colwyn Bay, Wales), from whose many terraces one can see the mountains of Snowdonia and where one is engulfed by the rich planting scheme, the waterfalls and dense foliage; Wakehurst Place and Petworth House (Sussex), and Lanhydrock (Cornwall), which Thomas Hardy borrowed for the mansion in the novel based upon his own courtship, *A Pair of Blue Eyes*. Both Bodnant and Lanhydrock are places to see rhododendrons at their mightiest, as well as spring flowers in amazing quantity.

There is not a county in Britain without its great gardens, and never a time when more people enjoyed them. I sometimes think of them as contemporary versions of the old healing wells and shrines, for their influence is noticeably beneficial. Looking at people who are looking at gardens proves it.

The garden I myself revisit constantly is the botanical garden at Cambridge. I love its learnedness; I drop into it on the way to lesser scenes and I am immediately admitted to its mixture of faithfulness, intelligence and novelty. There is always something constant and something newly out. It educates me for such glorious flights of fancy as Wallington (Cumbria), Mount Stewart (County Down, Northern Ireland), Tatton Park (Cheshire), Saltram (Devon). And, particularly, for my own two acres.

FOLLOWING THE FOOTSTEPS OF THE BARD

A. L. Rowse

The chief pleasure of living in an old country – as against the discouragements of the brave new social order – is that it is feet deep in associations, historical, literary, and visual, for those that have eyes to see. And actually there is much more in existence of the England that William Shakespeare knew than people realize.

We should begin with his native Stratford-upon-Avon, except that it is so well known that we need say little about it. One important thing: It is little short of a miracle that so much of Shakespeare's hometown would remain recognizable to him, if he were to return to it today: river, meadows, the great church where he was baptized and lies buried, streets, quite a number of Elizabethan houses, including his birthplace. Then Sir Hugh Clopton's old stone bridge that carried that ambitious actor-poet over the river and along the road to London – to the theatre, all that exciting busy life and eventual, universal fame.

Again, there is actually more of Shakespeare's London, and the places he knew there, available for us to see than we may realize. Take Southwark Cathedral, which he knew familiarly, for it is next door to where stood the Globe Theatre where he worked, and he lived for a time there in that parish. In his day the big church was known as St. Mary Overy – i.e., over the water. The interior was dominated by the monument of the medieval poet John Gower, which we can still see as Shakespeare did. But people have not drawn the obvious conclusion from the fact that *Pericles* is dominated by John Gower, who speaks the Chorus between the acts. The story of the play came from Gower's *Confessio Amantis* – and, behold, the old poet lies there still with his book plain to see.

As to Shakespeare, we may rightly apply Thomas Hardy's line to him: 'He was one who used to notice such things.' From all his work, sonnets and plays alike, we see that he had an attentive eye for monuments, ancient brasses, the ruins of monasteries – 'bare ruined choirs, where late the sweet birds sang' – as he went about the country. Southwark Cathedral has a stone to mark where his youngest brother, another actor, Edmund Shakespeare, was buried.

Farther along the South Bank, opposite Westminster, stands Lambeth Palace, still the residence of the Archbishops of Canterbury. Redbrick Lollards' Tower, which had been used as prison for their precursors, the Lollards, stands up well overlooking the Thames by Lambeth Bridge.

Opposite are Westminster and Whitehall. Nothing of Whitehall Palace – where his plays were frequently performed – remains, except some of the vaults and undercrofts. But St. James's Palace, which Henry VIII built, is still there with its fine clock-tower gateway and north front of red brick much as Shakespeare knew it; it was then in the fields.

Westminster Abbey is all there, with the eighteenth century addition of the towers, and we can study the monuments – any number of them – that he knew, some of them going grandly up in his time. We have the splendid medieval effigies of Richard II, along with the famous portrait, and of Henry V, about both of whom the observant actor was to write plays. Henry VII's chapel has the grandest Renaissance monuments to that king, his wife, Elizabeth of York, and his mother the Lady Margaret, ultimate heiress of John of Gaunt, whom we remember from the plays.

It was a regular thing in Shakespeare's day to make the tour of the tombs of Westminster Abbey. In 1601 we find Sir Walter Raleigh engaged in showing the famous Marshal Biron, over from France, around them. (Shakespeare had used that name, Berowne, for himself in *Love's Labour's Lost*.) Not long after the two noble pillared four-posters were going up for Elizabeth I and Mary Queen of Scots, made by Maximillian Colt and Cornelius Cure of the workshops in Southwark – Johnson's there was to provide Shakespeare's own bust at Stratford. Nearby in the Abbey is the urn containing the bones of the poor little princes murdered in the Tower, discovered two centuries later at the foot of a staircase.

Two more of the Abbey monuments touch Shakespeare more closely. The biggest there is that of Lord Chamberlain Hunsdon, first cousin of Elizabeth I, and patron of Shakespeare's company – who had for his young mistress Emilia Bassano, the half-Italian musical lady who was unanswerably the Dark Lady of the sonnets. In the chapel of St. Edmund is the tomb of Sir William Harvey – who is no less unanswerably the 'Mr. W.H.' of Thorp's dedication of the sonnets, not Shakespeare's.

We can follow Shakespeare around Elizabethan London, what remains of it, rather better than we think. First and foremost, we cannot miss the Tower of London, which appears so often in the history plays. It is essentially unchanged; the only thing missing from his time is the little palace annex, where the monarchs resided for some days before their coronations. Everything else is there – the cell where Henry VI was murdered the night of Richard of Gloucester's visit, as we know. Those Yorkists were a bloody lot, and Shakespeare knew quite well what was what about them.

We know that in the later 1590's Shakespeare was lodging in the parish of St. Helen, Bishopsgate. The church he knew is still there, with the fine Renaissance monument put up in 1579 to Sir Thomas Gresham, the great financier of the age. In 1608 a monument was put up to Richard Staper, the well-known merchant of the Levant Company who was a client of Simon Forman and appears in his Case Books. And next year one to Sir John and Lady Spencer, ancestors of our Lady Diana, the young Princess of Wales. In fact, a good many monuments Shakespeare would have known, or that were put up in his time, remain even when the churches have been rebuilt. But one grand medieval church still stands, St. Bartholomew's Priory, Smithfield, as he would have known it; as also the little medieval church of St. Ethelburga in his Bishopsgate parish.

We have little in the way of secular buildings to go on, but we do have the splendid great Middle Temple Hall in which *Twelfth Night* was performed – the young lawyer John Manningham records seeing it on Candlemas night, February 2, 1602. Fronting Holborn we find a row of (rather restored) Elizabethan houses; but the interesting thing is that they are on the property of Shakespeare's patron, Southampton House.

Out into the country! – beyond the Roman Wall, near a corner of which he lived after 1600, when he lodged with the Mountjoys in Silver Street, obliterated in the German Blitz.

Let us go down to Hampshire, where his young patron Southampton's country estate lay. The big house, Titchfield Priory, is all there though in ruins. It was unroofed by Southampton's Portland descendants in the eighteenth century. I cannot forgive them, for they must at the same time have destroyed the archives, where there would have been Shakespeare's letters – though the sonnets are really verse-letters to the patron and friend. In Titchfield church is the magnificent monument to Southampton's grandparents and parents, on which he himself appears as a little boy in armour, kneeling.

We should go on through the New Forest to Beaulieu Abbey, not far away, which was a hunting lodge in Southampton's day. (Now the historic house is inhabited by another descendant, Lord Montagu, of the famous Motor Museum, who has a fine portrait of Shakespeare's Southampton in the house and has public-spiritedly restored the great tomb.)

Again not far away, in Somerset, is lovely Montacute House, of honey-coloured stone, built by a well-known figure in the age – and now it is filled with an overflow from the National Portrait Gallery of figures who pranced then upon the stage of public life: Sir Walter Raleigh; his opponent, the Earl of Essex, to whose following Shakespeare was affiliated through his patron, Southampton; the Cecils (of the family still going in our time), who governed the country then under the eye of that glittering old peahen, Queen Elizabeth I. One can see her everywhere still today.

Take the road north to Bath, with its Roman hot baths still in situ. It was the fashionable thing for Elizabethan grandees to crowd thither to take the water for treatment of ailments.

Then let us away, and hurry up through the lovely Cotswold hills, so familiar to him – the ridge usually visible from Stratford down in the Avon valley – to Warwickshire, home territory. The plays are full of references to all this country from the beginning, the *Henry VI* trilogy, onward to the end. All round are the places, towns, villages, hamlets, churches, country houses he knew.

The Shakespeares came into Stratford from woodland Arden country – the Forest of Arden – north of town. Their parish was Snitterfield: there is the church, with the font in which generations of them were baptized.

But there are definite indications that William was prouder of his mother's family, the Ardens, on the border of being gentry. And Mary Arden's house, Wilmcote, exists out there on those endearing slopes, lovingly cared for. As does grander Charlecote, with its Elizabethan gatehouse of diapered brick, still held by the descendants of the Lucy family. In the chapel are the effigies of the Lucy knights he would have known.

And there are still deer in the park. I have no doubt that the ancient tradition about Shakespeare's deer-poaching is true, for all his early plays reveal a perfect fixation on hunting the deer. All young bloods addicted to country sports went in for it. Then there was archery at the butts by the river, between the bridge and the new theatre, and bowls at the inns, one or two of which go back to his time, and coursing the hare on the heaths north of the town – where we still find Clopton House of his time – or out on the Cotswolds to the south.

Follow the road uphill out northwest to Alcester, which still has a street of Elizabethan houses, besides a church with the father of Sir Fulke Greville – Philip Sidney's friend – lying on his tomb. Up the road we come to the Tudor house of the Catholic Throckmortons, Coughton Court, where in the fine room over the gatehouse the women waited for news of their menfolk involved in the sensational Gunpowder Plot of 1605.

And so on across the Cotswolds – churches and orchards all the way, Pershore and Evesham abbeys – or down the Avon to Worcester.

Thither the young William had to journey to the Bishop's Registry for special licence, at the mature age of nineteen, to marry his bride, Anne Hathaway, right quick, a family friend eight and a half years older – and that meant much more in those days. In the cathedral there we can see, as he could, the figure of King John dominating the choir – another subject to write about.

Farther down the Severn, at the southwestern tip of the Cotswolds, we come to rose-red Berkeley Castle, unchanged, where Marlowe's Edward II was murdered; the castle and its site referred to in Shakespeare's *Richard II*.

Coming back home to Stratford we have Coventry, the cathedral city of Warwickshire, Warwick, the county town, with its fine castle intact, and the spectacular ruins of Kenilworth Castle on the way to Birmingham.

Kenilworth had been granted by Elizabeth I to her favourite, the Earl of Leicester. There in 1575 he laid on a week of splendid entertainments for the Queen, with water pageants on the lake that then almost surrounded the castle. That has now gone, and the castle was ruined in our odious Civil War. But one can still go into the courtyard at the great gate, and the practised eye can distinguish the medieval buildings of John of Gaunt and the airy later apartments added by Leicester. Warwick Castle makes a splendid sight, its cliff of a façade rising above the river, its towers dominating the scene for miles around. The contents inside have been mostly dispersed, shamefully quite recently. Shakespeare would have known the superb medieval effigy, in the parish church, of the Earl, who figured so largely in the Hundred Years' War – so much around him spoke to the dramatist's imagination and inspired his work.

The town of Warwick is not spoiled, any more than Stratford is. At the town-end is the old Westgate, with Leicester's charming hospital-almshouses with chapel above.

Before World War II Coventry had much that Shakespeare would recognize: medieval guildhall, etc., and two great Perpendicular churches. The Germans obliterated much of it in the war; only one of the great churches remains, with the shell of the other preserved for a memorial.

Two roads led over Stratford Bridge on to fortune, one of them through Oxford, which Shakespeare knew well. John Aubrey tells us that he knew the wife of the keeper of the Crown tavern only too well – and that the gifted dramatist of the next generation, Sir William Davenant, liked to think that he was a by-blow of William's. The old Golden Cross today incorporates the Crossed Keys, where one day in November 1605 Richard Hakluyt – whose *Principall Navigations* Shakespeare read and made use of – was surprised to find that he had been dining with the Gunpowder conspirators fleeing to their fate.

Mount the staircase to the top of St. Martin's old church tower at nearby Carfax, in the city's centre, and from the top you will see the layout of the old city Shakespeare knew. On the right, southward, Cardinal Wolsey's (of *Henry VIII*) grand front of Christ Church; to the east, the High Street, the main highway to London. On the left, along Cornmarket, are one or two rooms behind later façades that still retain Elizabethan frescoes on the walls, like those in the White Swan at Stratford.

At the end, by the Anglo-Saxon tower of St. Michael's-at-the-Northgate – before the Norman Conquest, think of it! – is the Elizabethan house by Bocardo Prison, where Archbishop Cranmer was kept before being taken around the corner to be burned outside the city wall, in front of Balliol College. That bit of the wall with its bastion remains behind the houses that front here on Broad Street – to Oxonians, 'the Broad.'

The Lord Chamberlain's Company can be partially traced on its tours around the country from entries in numerous town records. In earlier years he toured the country, as he tells us in the sonnets. We know that the company visited such places as Leicester – with its extraordinary Roman forum open to the sky outside the railway station: the place is called Holy Bones, between Castle and Norman church built out of some of the stones. We know that the company visited Bath, Marlborough with its wide street for playing, Canterbury and Dover. So Shakespeare's Cliff at Dover is appropriately named; he had it in mind in *King Lear*, where it appears, the beetling height with the 'dreadful trade' of the samphire gatherers. At Canterbury he would see the resplendent tomb of Richard II's father, the Black Prince, and that of Henry IV, subject of his two finest plays on English history. The effigy shows a stout, rather pudgy, very masculine figure of the king, a marked contrast to his cousin, Richard II, whose throne he took. Jerusalem chamber, in which Henry died, still exists, of course, at the west end of Westminster Abbey.

At Westminster we also have the vast great hall that Richard II built, where all the law courts were congregated in Shakespeare's time – it was part of the royal palace, still technically considered and called so. Farther up the Thames was Richmond Palace, of which fragments only remain. All of Hampton Court is there, of Wolsey's and Henry VIII's building, as well as Wren's additions.

Elizabeth I took a prejudice against the place, because she caught smallpox and was very ill there. She much preferred healthier Windsor Castle on its hill. We can see how well Shakespeare knew Windsor from *The Merry Wives of Windsor*, written for a feast of the Order of the Garter, with all its Windsor lore and the familiar places: the inner and outer wards, Henry VIII's great gate, the Castle Ditch; Frognal and Datchet Mead, where Falstaff was tipped into the Thames; the park with the legendary haunted Herne's Oak where he was publicly exposed.

For a final suggestion: It gives me much pleasure touring round the country to collect in my mind the figures that played their part in Shakespeare's time, not only from the effigies on their tombs but their portraits. Sometimes one learns something significant. At Arbury in Warwickshire are two portraits of Mary Fitton, with auburn hair and grey-blue eyes. That puts paid to the nonsense that she was the Dark Lady – I always knew that that was nonsense on other grounds.

One hardly comes to the end of these treasures and relics, or knows where they may not turn up – one of the joys of touring about the old country with an open eye and an inquiring mind. It often happens to me to know who was living in the old manor house in the Elizabethan age, though I haven't the least idea of the people living there today.

MAKING THE OXBRIDGE CONNECTION: CAMBRIDGE

Christopher S. Wren

In 1209, a group of Oxford students took refuge in Cambridge after clashes with hostile Oxford townsfolk. Some students returned to Oxford when a truce in the feud was called in 1214, but the rest stayed to start what is now Cambridge University.

As at Oxford, the normal academic year runs from early October to mid-June, with three eight-week terms interspersed with generous holidays. All the colleges are open to visitors, although some charge a small admission fee and limit the size of tour groups. The most popular colleges, like King's and Trinity, also close to visitors for several weeks during final examinations in late May and early June.

The train trip to Cambridge from the Liverpool Street Station in London takes a little over an hour, with trains departing usually hourly. If you arrive in Cambridge by rail, take a taxi or a red double-decker bus just across from the station to the town centre two miles away, alighting at the corner of Market and Sidney streets. From there it is a few minutes' walk to the tourist information office on Wheeler Street, which has a friendly, generally informed staff and an up-do-date list of what is happening around Cambridge. There is also a selection of inexpensive or free guide booklets and brochures as well as free walking maps.

The tourist information office offers guided walking tours of the colleges, or you can equip yourself with a guidebook and strike out on your own. Visitors who are staying only a few hours should confine their sightseeing to the colleges along Trinity Street and King's Parade.

If its individual colleges are not quite the architectural masterpieces found at Oxford, Cambridge as a university town is probably the more beautiful, for it retains the atmosphere that Oxford has lost through urban spread and industrialization.

The best place to start is at King's college, arguably the most renowned and beautiful of the Cambridge colleges. From the tourist office, walk past the bustling outdoor stalls of Market Square and continue west to King's Parade. King Henry VI founded the college in

1441 for schoolboys graduating from Eton, which he also founded, hence the royal purple in the scarves that King's College undergraduates wear.

The college is best known for its magnificent cathedral-like chapel, built between 1446 and 1515. It is one of England's finest examples of perpendicular-style Gothic architecture, with the largest, most complete collection of stained glass windows in the world. They cover over ten thousand square feet by one estimate. The roof has extremely delicate lace-like stonework, and the woodwork was carved by Italian craftsmen. Several years ago a large painting by Rubens, *The Adoration of the Magi*, was given to the college, and it stands under the east window. The chapel has a famous boys' choir, known for its Christmas Eve service, 'A Festival of Lessons and Carols.'

After King's College, turn south along King's Parade, perhaps window-shopping – or really shopping – at some of the elegant clothing shops catering more to tourists than students. A good pair of shoes or a Shetland sweater cost less than on London's Regent Street. There is also a colourful array of long woollen scarves and rugby shirts in the colours of individual colleges. In theory, these are reserved for the undergraduates. The Bene't Gallery on King's Parade offers an interesting selection of old and reproduction college and town prints. Off to the left on Bene't Street is St. Bene't Church (short for St. Benedict).

As you continue south along what turns into Trumpington Street, you will encounter Corpus Christi College on your left. Two merchant guilds in medieval Cambridge founded the college in 1352 to house clerical scholars saying mass for the many local plague victims. Its interior court, the oldest in Cambridge to survive virtually unaltered, is reached by walking through the manicured nineteenth century front courtyard. (Across the street, St. Catherine's College displays buildings from the seventeenth and eighteenth centuries, though the college itself dates from 1473.)

Beyond the next intersection of Trumpington and Pembroke streets is Pembroke College on the left, founded in 1347. The Pembroke chapel, completed in 1666, was the first building designed by Sir Christopher Wren, whose numerous other churches include St. Paul's in London. (This writer, according to family tradition, is a descendant of the architect.) Wren's uncle, the Bishop of Ely, commissioned him to build Cambridge's first college chapel in thanksgiving after the bishop was released from eighteen years' imprisonment in the Tower of London under Oliver Cromwell. Across Trumpington Street is Peterhouse College, the oldest at Cambridge, which was established by a previous Bishop of Ely in 1284 with fourteen scholars.

If there's time, continue on to visit the university's Fitzwilliam

Museum. On show are illuminated manuscripts, china from its earliest beginnings, armour from the Middle Ages and archaeological discoveries, especially from ancient Assyria, which is roughly modern Iraq. There is also a valuable music collection.

Back on Silver Street, turn west toward the Cam River. Pause to look at the wooden 'mathematical bridge,' which was built without bolts in 1749 to connect buildings of Queens' College on both sides of the river. According to local tradition, a later generation took the bridge apart to see how it was done and had to resort to bolts to put it back together. The present bridge is a 1902 copy. Queens' College, built in 1448, was named for its two benefactors, the wives of King Henry VI and Edward IV, and has a beautiful cloistered courtyard.

The entrance off the Cam is reserved for students and town residents. To enter the college by its main gate, walk back down Silver Street a few steps to Queens Lane, a small street off to the left. The first court, dating from the fifteenth century, is done in old red brick. Pass through an archway on the farther side and enter Cloister Court.

The timbered gallery of the President's Lodge, forming the upper storey on the north side, was added in 1537. An arched passageway under the sundial on this side leads to Walnut Tree Court with the library and chapel.

Beyond the Cam and Queens' College, turn north on the shady grassy strip between the Cam and Queen's Road along the gardens of a half-dozen Cambridge colleges, known as 'the Backs.' The stroll is loveliest in spring when the first crocuses, snowdrops and daffodils appear, but the views of King's and other colleges are always impressive. Along the river are entrances to smaller gardens reserved for the college masters and fellows, some of which are opened occasionally to the pubic.

After a short walk Carret Hostel Lane leads eastward back to town. The arched bridge over the Cam offers a sylvan retrospective view of the Backs. A right turn will eventually lead to Clare College, which was founded in 1326. The original buildings were ruined by fire and deterioration, and the college was rebuilt in the early seventeenth century in the style of an elegant Jacobean manor. The Clare's Fellows' Garden is considered by some Cambridge residents the finest of the college gardens and is usually open briefly to visitors on weekday afternoons. It is also open for a weekend festival in late June or July at the height of the flowering season.

North of Trinity Street is Trinity College, largest and wealthiest of the colleges at Cambridge. It was founded by King Henry VIII in 1546, and once a traveller could journey from Cambridge to the English Channel port of Dover, more than 130 miles, without leaving Trinity College property. At the great gate, completed in 1535, the majestic right hand of the statue of Henry VIII wields a weathered chairleg and not the original sceptre. A student prankster made the switch untold generations ago.

The Great Court, with its elaborate Renaissance fountain built in 1602, is the largest court of any Cambridge or Oxford college. Commissioned in 1595, it was designed by Thomas Neville, whose name has been give to the second court. The original clock tower (1432), where the race in the film *Chariots of Fire* was supposed to have taken place, is on the right, on the north side. A flight of steps on the west side leads through to the second court. Sir Christopher Wren's library here is considered one of his architectural masterpieces; its interior carvings by Grinling Gibbons are also very fine. Among the ninety thousand volumes is a first-draft manuscript of *Paradise Lost* by John Milton. The Trinity College library usually allows visitors on weekday afternoons.

If you continue through the college's New Court, you can leave by a bridge over the Cam, then follow the path north along the Backs to St. John's College. Beyond is the cloistered bridge with five unglazed windows, called the Bridge of Sighs after the bridge in Venice. In leaving St. John's through its eastern gate, you may want to cross Bridge Street to look briefly at the Holy Sepulchre Church, known as the Round Church, whose earliest parts date from the twelfth century and Crusader times.

If you still have time, continue north along Bridge Street to Magdalene College, passing a row of Elizabethan buildings restored as houses and shops. The college lies just the other side of the Cam, across a bridge where centuries ago housewives were sometimes dunked for nagging their husbands and neighbours.

Magdalene, founded in 1542 on the site of four older monasteries, has well-tended grounds and some original buildings of the sixteenth century. Samuel Pepys, a Magdalene scholar, bequeathed six volumes of his diaries to the college. Bridge Street becomes Castle Street and a huge mound can be seen, the remains of a castle built by William the Conqueror shortly after the Norman conquest of England.

As with any university town, there are other things to do in Cambridge. At the main branch of Heffer's bookshop at 20 Trinity Street, one can not only browse through the extensive stacks but also buy a list of university lectures, which are closed to outsiders. However, the tourist information office keeps track of public lectures, concerts and debates in Cambridge, which range from earnestly amateurish to impressively professional. The city library at Lion Yard shopping mall near Market Square also publishes a monthly list of local activities. Keep an eye out for posters in town advertising student events and ask about any good rugby or cricket matches scheduled.

One of Cambridge's most memorable experiences is the evensong service at King's College chapel, held weekdays at 5.30 pm. Episcopalians will be familiar with the service, but anyone who displays appropriate respect is welcome and can follow along with a special booklet of explanations available in the pews. If you get there early, you can probably sit up in the old choir stalls. The chapel has other sung services at 10.30 am and 3.30 pm on Sunday as well as an organ recital at 6.30 pm Saturday.

If you enjoy Cambridge enough to want to stay overnight, the tourist office keeps a list of approved guest houses and homes providing bed and breakfast more cheaply and charmingly than a commercial hotel. The office staff will even call and make the reservations for you, but ask as soon as you arrive during the summer tourist season.

TELEPHONE NUMBERS are all on the **Cambridge** exchange.

FOR PLOUGHMEN AND GRADUATES

TAKING A BREAK

When the sight of one medieval Cambridge courtyard starts blending into the next, stop for lunch. There are dozens of pubs. **The Old Spring** (phone 357228) between Ferry Path and Chesterton Road reopened not long ago after a renovation and includes a cheerful barman who will advise you on the nuances of British beers. **The Fort St. George** (phone 354327) on the River Cam is quainter but gets terribly crowded. Both serve hot meals as well as the traditional ploughman's lunch of cheese, bread and salad. **The Spade and Becket** (phone 311701), at the western edge of Jesus Green, another grassy common, has undistinguished food but a pleasant patio overlooking the river. In summer one can leave every hour from there on a punt ride down through the Backs. **The Anchor** (phone 353553) on Silver street and **The Granta** (which does not list its phone number) on Queen's Road also have enviable riverside locations but are more vulnerable to tour groups. Downtown, the most interesting pub is **The Eagle** (phone 353782), an old coaching inn on Bene't Street. **The Pickerel** (phone 355068) on Magdalene Street offers a particularly good quiche with salad among its lunches. If your tastes run to health food, try **Hobb's Pavilion** (phone 67480), run by a cheerful young staff, just off Park Terrace, overlooking impromptu soccer and cricket matches on grassy Parker's Piece. The pubs in particular fill up by 1 pm so unless you arrive early you may have to stand.

If you prefer a picnic, get a packed lunch for about $4.50 from **Fitzbillie's** (phone 352500), a bakery on Trumpington Street near Pembroke Street, and some wine from a shop on King's Parade. Then float down the river on a punt while you eat. Punting is popular with

Cambridge students during the short spring and summer period. A flat-bottomed punt for six persons with a pole and precautionary paddle costs about $4.60 an hour plus refundable deposit at **Scudamore's Boatyard** (phone 59750) off Mill Lane.

RESTAURANTS

Unlike Oxford, Cambridge is not noted for good dining. **The Blue Boar** (phone 63121) and **Garden House** (phone 63421) hotels cater to tourists but are thought overpriced by many local residents. The most highly recommended restaurant in town happens to be Chinese – **The Peking** (phone 354755) on Burleigh Street. **Xanadu** (phone 311678) on Fitzroy Street serves imaginative fare. **Shade's** (phone 59506) on King's Parade has a pleasant cellar wine bar with light food in addition to a more expensive upstairs restaurant looking out on King's College. Another busy undergraduate hangout is **Sweeney Todd's** pizza parlour (phone 67507) on Newnham Road.

MAKING THE OXBRIDGE CONNECTION: OXFORD

Jaqueline Wren

Oxford is not only a renowned university but also a bustling industrial city, as you will discover when you see the traffic on 'the High' as the main street is nicknamed. William Morris founded his Morris Motors here and, as Lord Nuffield, later endowed a college that bears his titled name. It is said that his wife continued to grow potatoes and raise chickens in case they lost their wealth.

Convenient express trains leave London's Paddington Station frequently and take an hour to arrive in Oxford. To conserve time, walk down the hill from the station and catch a red bus to Carfax, a downtown intersection possibly named from the French 'quatre voies,' because the roads go in the four directions of the compass. At the corner stands Carfax Tower, built in the fourteenth century. It has a clock with figures called 'quarter boys' that strike the bells every quarter hour.

From here, turn south, though it means seeing Oxford's most spectacular college first. Just a block down St. Aldate's Street from Carfax is the college of Christ Church. On the way, Oxford's tourist centre can provide inexpensive guidebooks and brochures.

The west side of St. Aldate's offers the best view of Tom Tower, the uniquely proportioned cupola over the main gate that was started by Cardinal Wolsey, who founded the college in 1525, and finished in the next century by Sir Christopher Wren. Its seven-ton bell, Great Tom, tolls 101 times at 9.05 pm every evening for the original number of students, whose curfew in those earliest days was 9 pm. (The five-minute discrepancy resulted because Oxford lies a fraction of a degree west of Greenwich, where the world's mean time is kept.)

Christ Church is one of the largest of the Oxford colleges. (There is a small entrance fee Monday to Friday, and Saturday morning. On Saturday afternoon and Sunday the buildings are closed.) It was refounded by Henry VIII, who made its small college chapel the cathedral of his new see, the diocese of Oxford. One professor, who later became college dean, was known for raising his bedroom window overlooking Tom Quad and cursing noisy undergraduates at night in

Biblical Hebrew. The breathtaking vista of Tom Quad is really an unfinished cloister, with the arcade missing. In summer its green lawn with fountain has been the scene of many a famous garden party. But don't walk on the grass. This privilege is reserved for the teaching staff.

The cathedral can be entered from a rather inconspicuous doorway in the southeast corner. Parts of the cathedral date to the twelfth century. Inside, St. Firdeswide's shrine and a Saxon archway remain from an eighth century priory.

In the quadrangle to the right outside the cathedral, a large archway with a stairway leads up to the Hall, with its rows of portraits of prominent men.

At the bottom of the stairway to the rear is the entrance to a small unfinished cloister and early English chapter house. From here one can glimpse the college gardens and, beyond, the Christ Church meadows, where the appearance of the first snowdrop flowers in late January provides a pretext for picnics. This large expanse of grass stretches to the Thames, called the Isis in Oxford, where the annual boat races take place in May.

Walk back along the eastern side of Tom Quad and turn right into Peckwater Quad, named for an inn that originally occupied the site. The library is on the second storey of the classical building on the right. The smallest quadrangle, Canterbury, lies ahead, and here one may emerge through the college's back gates into one of the oldest sections of Oxford.

Up the small hill to the left is Oriel College, whose alumini include Sir Walter Raleigh and Cecil Rhodes. It was founded in 1326 on the site of a tenement called L'Oriole. Ahead lies Merton Street and to the right is Corpus Christi College, which Bishop George Fox founded in 1517. In its main quadrangle stands a pillar with a celebrated sundial and perpetual calendar. The pelican pecking its breast atop the pillar was a common medieval symbol for the sacrifice of Christ because it was thought that the pelican fed its young with its own droplets of blood.

Farther on to the right is the gate into Merton College, which, along with University College and Balliol College, claims to be the oldest in Oxford. Merton's Mob Quad, reached by passing under the Muniment Tower, is Oxford's oldest surviving quadrangle. Its simplicity contrasts strikingly with the architecture of the relatively newer, wealthier colleges.

Merton's chapel, built between 1290 and 1450, has a splendid old tower and interior with some of the oldest stained glass in England. The original cruciform plan took on a T-shape when the chapel nave went uncompleted. Several other colleges subsequently copied this design for their chapels.

The two oldest buildings are the library and the Muniment Room. The library still has some of the original books chained on its shelves. The Muniment Tower may have been standing when the college site was originally purchased. The hall, which is reached by a flight of steps, was largely rebuilt in 1872 but retains its six-hundred-year old oak door. After leaving the college, walk to the end of Merton Street, which leads left up to High Street. If you turn right, you will pass the University Botanical Gardens, first founded in 1621. Opposite across the High is Magdalen College, one of Oxford's finest colleges. (Magdalene College, in Cambridge, is spelled slightly differently, but both are pronounced 'maudlin.') Its bell tower, which houses a ten-peal chime, was reconstructed with substantial financial help from Americans.

Magdalen, which was founded in 1458 on the previous foundation of St. John's hospital, has four quadrangles covering twelve acres and more than one hundred additional acres of grounds. These encompass a deer park where deer still graze and many lovely walks through the meadows and along the River Cherwell, which runs alongside.

Every year on May 1 at 6 am the chapel choristers sing a Latin hymn from atop the tower to greet the arrival of spring, an occasion that students and townsfolk also celebrate with picnic breakfasts, punting and morris dancing, which is costumed folk dancing complete with ribbons and bells.

Just past the college is Magdalen Bridge, where the High crosses the Cherwell, a tributary of the Thames and the river where punting, that leisurely Oxbridge boating pastime, enjoys popularity in Oxford.

Start back down the High toward the town centre. This may be as good a time as any to think about lunch or just tea. When you return to the High, you will be ready to visit New College, which despite its name was founded in 1379. It is the only one in Oxford referred to informally with *college* appended to its name. Take Queen's Lane off the High, which becomes New College Lane and winds around a great deal until it reaches the gates.

On the way, you will pass St. Edmund Hall, founded about 1270, which is colloquially called Teddy Hall. It is Oxford's smallest college. If it is open, walk at least briefly into the front quadrangle to see whether the geraniums in the window boxes are in bloom. Should you have time, walk left through the archway into the courtyard, which has the oldest cemetery in Oxford and the ancient church of St. Peter's-in-the-East, since converted into a student library.

New College is one of the colleges at Oxford that charges a small admission fee in the summer months for an adult who is not a college member or an Oxford M.A. A sister college of King's College at Cambridge (such pairings are common between colleges of each university and 'the other place,' as Oxford and Cambridge call each other), New College was built between 1379 and 1382 by William of Wykeham, the Bishop of Winchester, who also endowed it magnificently.

A serene cloistered courtyard was created for its scholars. The college was also allowed to build against the city wall as long as it maintained the wall in good order. As a result, only here can Oxford's thirteenth century fortifications still be seen in their original splendour. Every three years the Lord Mayor of Oxford arrives with his city councillors in a solemn-gowned procession to check whether the pledge is being fulfilled. The chapel at New College is particularly interesting, with a stained-glass window in its west end designed by Sir Joshua Reynolds, the eighteenth century portraitist. An elaborately carved reredos was carefully restored in the nineteenth century following the damage done to it during the Reformation. An El Greco painting of St. James is also on view, as is the bishop's gold crozier of William of Wykeham.

As you come back out of the main gate of New College, you can head straight for Broad Street, which runs parallel to the High. The Bodleian Library, centre of the old university, appears almost immediately on the left. Within can be seen the old school's quadrangle, with the ancient names still above the doors. The splendid divinity school is now a museum. Its vaulted stone ceiling dates from the early fifteenth century.

The Sheldonian Theatre, designed by Sir Christopher Wren, lies just past the Bodleian. Its cupola, which is open to tourists, offers a panoramic view of Oxford. The Sheldonian today is used for university ceremonies, which were once held in the university church of St. Mary the Virgin. This very old church, the tower of which dates from the thirteenth century, can be viewed by walking straight through the Bodleian, past the domed Radcliffe Camera toward High Street. St. Mary's spire rises 180 feet and is one of the most richly decorated in England.

As you head toward the church you will pass Brasenose College on your right. Its garden offers an unusual view of spires and towers from various periods.

To the left of the Radcliffe Camera, which now contains two library reading rooms, is All Souls College, dating from 1437. All Souls elects its members, only fifty-four in number plus a warden, from scholars and writers and provides them opportunity for research.

Back on Broad Street is Blackwell's bookstore, which is reckoned to have 170,000 books in its inventory and fills orders for customers in almost every country. A visit to Oxford would not be complete without some browsing here.

Beyond Blackwell's, after a section of gardens belonging to Trinity College, is Balliol College. Though it lays claim to being one of the oldest colleges in Oxford, its present buildings are predominantly Victorian. An exception is the fifteenth century dining hall, now the library. The pavement of Broad Street in front of Balliol contains a stone with a cross on it, marking the spot where Bishops Ridley and Latimer and later Archbishop Cranmer were burned at the stake as Protestant heretics in 1555 and 1556.

Martyr's Memorial, designed by Sir Giles Gilbert Scott in the nineteenth century to commemorate the three bishops, is around the corner, where Cornmarket Street becomes St. Giles. On the right is the entrance to St. John's College. The first quadrangle of St. John's, which dates from the fifteenth century, has gardens that are used as a setting for outdoor plays in the summer.

If you are only spending the day in Oxford, you are probably ready to return to the train station. If there's time to walk, take Beaumont Street west off Cornmarket. On the right will be the Ashmolean Museum, which contains a valuable and varied collection of archaeological treasures found or dug up by Oxford men.

Try to catch a glimpse of Worcester College, at the end of the street where Beaumont Palace once stood and Richard the Lionheart was born. The college has its own canal-fed lake and the playing fields are adjacent. Most interesting is the row of old cottages on the south side of the quadrangle, which were built for monk-scholars from various Benedictine abbeys.

The original thirteenth century Gloucester Hall on the site was dissolved in the sixteenth century, and there was not enough money for all new buildings when Worcester College was founded in 1710. These 'camerae,' with their central staircases, became an architectural model for other colleges at Oxford and Cambridge.

From Worcester College it is but a short walk to the station to catch the train back to London. If you want to stay, plan ahead. There is a variety of accommodations in Oxford, ranging from the **Randolph Hotel** on Beaumont Street (phone 247481) at about $72 a night for a double room with bath, excluding breakfast and service, to guest houses, inns and bed-and-breakfast establishments at about $25 to $75 for two, including breakfast and service but not always a private bath.

TELEPHONE NUMBERS, unless indicated, are on the **Oxford** exchange.

PUBS AND SUCH

For a provincial English town, Oxford has an impressive selection of eating spots, including pubs that serve bar snacks or simple lunches with their pints of beer. **The Turf Tavern** (phone 243235), which dates back to the seventeenth century, features a cold buffet table as well as a daily hot dish. It is in Bath Place off Holywell Street. Lunch at The Turf can run from about $3.50 to $9 a person. The Turf Tavern also offers bed and breakfast for $33 for a double room. **The King's Arms** (phone 242369) on Holywell Street and **The Nag's Head** (phone 249153) on Hythe Bridge are among the pubs frequented by Oxford students. But the most popular lunching spot is probably **The Trout** (phone 54485), a venerable pub on the River Thames, a ten-minute taxi ride from town, though many students walk to it along the towpath. Pubs in general, including The Trout, run about $3.50 to $5.25 for lunch entrees. Oxford also has an ambitious health food restaurant, **The Nosebag** (phone 721038), upstairs at 6-8 St. Michael Street, which offers a daily hot or cold dish with salad for less than $3.50. It also fills up at teatime. **Maxwell's** (phone 242192), at 36 Queen Street, is a trendy student spot serving hamburgers and salads. Snacks and tea are enjoyed at **The Wykeham** (phone 246916), an old house on Holywell Street.

RESTAURANTS

For a more elegant meal, try **The Elizabeth** (phone 242230) at 84 St. Aldate's, with entrees running up to $14 and an extensive wine list; open for lunch and dinner. **Brown's Restaurant and Wine Bar** (phone 511995) at 7-9 Woodstock Road is frequented by students for its good, uncomplicated English food. If you stay in Oxford long enough to have dinner, the best atmosphere and value are found at **The Cherwell Boathouse** (phone 52746) off Bardwell Road, where the punting begins. Reservations are essential for the fixed dinner menu, two set three-course meals that vary according to season – for example, leek and tomato soup, port with apricot sauce or roast chicken with herbs and chocolate cream pie – at about $32 for two. Students fond of Chinese food go to **The Opium Den** (phone 248680) at 79 George Street. Indian restaurants are an inexpensive staple for British students, and **The Anglo-Indian Tandoori** (phone 243390) restaurant at 84 Cowley Road is one of the best in Oxford. The finest restaurant in the vicinity is generally considered to be **Manoir aux Quat' Saisons** (phone Great Milton 230) in nearby Great Milton, which offers classic French cuisine in a country setting. The menu can include duck-liver mousse, fish soup, medallions of veal with truffles, seasonal fresh vegetables and fresh strawberries at around $45 a person.

CORNWALL: A LAND OF LEGENDS

D. M. Thomas

I go back to Cornwall at least once every year, to touch the granite, to smell the sea and generally to reaffirm that I am Cornish. I keep telling myself that I'll return for good, next year. Though nominally in England, Cornwall is a separate, Celtic land, the small sister of Wales, Scotland, Ireland. That means it exercises a magnetic pull on its children; they may go away forever, but in a sense they never leave home.

All the same, I return looking little different from the three million tourists – 'emmets,' or insects, the Cornish call them – who swarm over the western peninsula every summer. Fortunately a lot of them rush to the popular seaside resorts, such as Newquay, and so leave room, still, in the quieter, lovelier places, even in high summer.

But I recommend spring or autumn. In spring, especially, the mild Gulf Stream brings the flowers early. To savour Cornwall, go to a quiet village, leave your car, and wander down one of the lanes. The hedges, as tall as your head or taller, are a mass of sweet wildflowers. Unless you're very lucky, or fairly unlucky, the sky has Shakespeare's 'uncertain glory of an April day' (even if it's May or later): enough black cloud to worry you, enough blue sky to make you hopeful, and the sky is restive, the clouds in motion, because in Cornwall you're never more than a few miles from the sea. It's almost an island. The River Tamar, dividing Cornwall from Devon and England, starts its trickle only a Celtic giant's stone-throw from the north coast, and broadens out to flow into the English Channel at Plymouth.

You can cross the fledgling Tamar at Launceston, the ancient capital, with its Norman castle on a hilltop; or south by way of Plymouth, where a new toll bridge crosses the wide river close to Brunel's splendid old railway bridge. The northern route takes you down through Bodmin Moor, brooding and slightly sinister; but you can cheer yourself up with a drink at Jamaica Inn, which gave Daphne du Maurier the title and setting for a smuggling romance. Better still, you can turn off right, to the coast, and enjoy the bleak splendour of Boscastle and Tintagel. The former offers you a chilling Museum of

Witchcraft and, for more exalted spirits, the vision of Thomas Hardy, novelist and poet, riding with his sweetheart and – later, alas – wife, Emma Gifford, on the wild cliff heights. Tintagel offers you pseudo-Arthuriana in the spoiled village, but an authentic vision of him when you leave the car and strike down to the cliffs. I'm a great believer in the truth of stubborn legends; and I'd be surprised if the real King Arthur didn't have a castle at Tintagel. Whether he did or not – you should stand on those mighty cliffs, gaze out to sea, and dream.

If, on the other hand, you take the south route, you drive for some time through countryside that still looks greenly, charmingly English. Once upon a time you could find true Cornwall in the fishing villages of Looe and Polperro, but nowadays the locals mainly fish for tourists. But a little farther down, you should make a detour to visit Fowey. The sea dazzles; the village clings to the wooded hillside in a descending maze of narrow streets. Spare the village: leave your car at the top, and walk down. As you thread the maze, and draw closer to the white-sailed boats on the bright, enchanted water, you will begin to feel the timelessness of Cornwall.

The Arthurian past is undeniably present in and around Fowey. Almost certainly, this was the royal abode of Mark, King of Cornwall. The earthworks of his palace can still be seen at Castle Dor; by the roadside you will see a tall stone which is very likely the gravestone of Tristan. The names of hamlets and farms echo names in the earliest versions of the great love story. Tristan brought Isolde to Fowey – I know it. Drive through the lanes where they walked – and lose your way, as they did. I got lost there, once; and after an hour in which I kept coming back to the same turning, my head was spinning like Tristan's.

And you can't trust the Cornish to set you right. They hate to disappoint strangers, so they'll tell you the place you're aiming for is 'just down the road a bit of way, my lover!' (They end almost every sentence with an endearment – 'my lover,' 'my handsome,' 'my sweetheart' – regardless of your sex.) A Huguenot priest, appointed to a living at Lanteglos, on the north coast, lost his way and couldn't make himself understood. The Cornish kept pointing him down the road, and he ended up at Land's End, reining in his horse and gazing out to sea in extreme confusion.

That's the direction we have to go – west. So we find our way at last back on to the main road. The granite spine of Cornwall, running down from Bodmin Moor (itself a smaller version of Dartmoor) to smaller moors and cairns, often disappoints the stranger. It is bleak; the wind howls; the villages are poor, unpicturesque – hunched to ward off the gales. One of the bleakest is made beautiful only by its name: Indian Queens. You catch sight of ghostly pyramids, the waste

from the china-clay pits of St. Austell. Increasingly you glimpse
strange ruins by the roadside or on the hills: the enginehouses or stacks
of used-up tin and copper mines. For this is mining country. If a
Cornishman wasn't a fisherman or a farmer he was a miner. The ore
ran out – though there are a few mines still working – and he had to go
abroad. They say that wherever there is a mine in the world, you will
find a Cornishman, a 'Cousin Jack,' at the bottom of it. At least, if it's a
hard-rock mine: tin, copper, lead, iron, gold, silver, quicksilver. We
leave the soft stuff, like coal, to the Welsh.

So these poor villages on the spine of Cornwall are the signatures of
hardworking men and women; and so, for me, they have their own
beauty. My heart tightens as my car runs down toward Cornwall's
heart: past the small, attractive cathedral city of Truro, to the stony
landscape of Redruth and Camborne, dominated by the granite cairn
under which I was born: Cairn Brea. You won't want to pause in this
landscape; but, as the land narrows, the sea is even closer on either
side.

If you veer left, you will strike a different Cornwall: the lush, almost
sub-tropical, river valleys of the Fal and the Helford. There are few
trees on the cliffs and moors – they all rushed to form settlements by
the lovely rivers.

Find, if you can, Restronguet or Mylor on the Fal, Mawnan Smith
or Manaccan on the Helford; you won't need to get drunk at the
splendid riverside inns: Your senses will swim from the scent of flowers
by a path, the glint of water through trees, the constantly changing
sky.

At the mouth of the converging Fal and Helford rivers is the town of
Falmouth. It is a great harbour. Many a round-the-world voyage has
ended here; many an eccentric American has paddled to land here,
after crossing the Atlantic in a bathtub. Falmouth is a sprawling,
likeable town; so is Helston, a few miles away. Every eighth of May its
people dance in and out of houses and shops, to blow away the winter.
A week earlier, to the north, the fishing village of Padstow brings in the
summer with the help of a fearsome Hobby Horse: the seasons get
mixed in Cornwall.

South of Helston, you face the windwept, flat Lizard, ending at a
lighthouse, and the southernmost point of Britain. The flatness is so
boring (varied only by surreal tumuli which are satellite stations) that,
if you're not careful, you could shoot over the high cliffs of dazzling
serpentine to the white sand far below. The coast of the Lizard is
beautiful but merciless; the whole Cornish coast is a graveyard for
ships, but none more so than the Lizard. The Cornish got a reputation
for being wreckers: luring ships on to the rocks. It may have happened
in a few cases; but many more Cornish have given their lives in rescue

attempts than taken lives. Still, the people were poor; small wonder one priest prayed, not that a wreck should occur, but that if it did, the Lord would drive the ship onto their rocks.

We keep getting sidetracked. Well, one should get sidetracked in this land; don't stick to the main roads, or the main resorts. But we must move farther west, so back – for a while – to the atrocious modern motorway. At least it gets us quickly to Penzance. Penzance is where the railway ends, and the wildest, most Cornish, part of Cornwall begins. The ancient Celtic language of Cornwall lingered here longest: until a couple of centuries ago. That language can be seen, now, only in place-names, and the names of people. 'By Tre-, Pol-, and Pen-, You can tell the Cornishmen,' says the rhyme. There must be many good Americans, reading this, with names beginning with those Cornish prefixes, or others. Professor A. L. Rowse's book, *The Cornish in America*, gives a long list of prefixes that indicate the Americans of Cornish descent. In return, many homecoming Cornishmen have given American names to their homes. I grew up at Beverly; I bathed at Mexico.

The last of Cornwall, then: take the coast road out of Penzance, and follow it all around the peninsula. Mousehole, most charming and unspoiled of villages, still mourns the death, a few Christmases ago, of seven lifeboatmen. Here, Dorothy Pentreath was the last native speaker of Cornish. She cursed the curious visiting English with swear-words in that sad Land's End of a language. Visit the open-air Minnack Theatre at Porthcurno, its backcloth the sea. The setting is more beautiful than that of Epidaurus, though its climate is less kind. The land becomes ancient. You pass Bronze Age stones: phallic standing-stones, called Pipers, who piped to maidens turned into a stone circle for dancing on a Sunday. You pass cromlechs, guarding the dead. You crawl (if you are sick: and, as Freud said we all are) through a holed stone, a men an tol. Its meaning is lost in the moor mist; but in recent times people crawled through it to cure their ills. You should, strictly, strip naked, and crawl through it nine times against the sun. You pass roadside crosses, left by the gentle Celtic saints: as much roses as crosses.

If you must go to Land's End itself, go early or late, to avoid the other tourists. But my advice, again, is to sidetrack a little to left or right. And, when you've had your fill of gazing out to where you imagine America to be, continue the coastal crawl, starting to turn up along the north coast. Sennen Cove is fine for bathing; thereafter, just past the workaday mining town of St. Just, don't miss the discreet sign pointing to Botallack. Gaze at the mine-ruins on the cliff edge, and imagine the old miners walking out under the seabed. The most cat-footed of all the miners was a blind man: In the country of the blind, that man was king. After gazing your fill at the spectacular coast, you can eat splendidly at the Botallack Count-House, perhaps the best restaurant in Cornwall. I usually prefer to slum it cheerfully at the Trewellard Meadery, a 'converted' Methodist Chapel, just 'down the road a mile or two, my lovers.'

The Cornish, being poor and hard working, have gone for plain, substantial food which 'sticks to your ribs.' Flatter a local housewife into baking a real Cornish pasty for you, and saffron cake, but avoid the pub and shop imitations. If you're looking for a very cheap, but satisfying, meal – the Cornish equivalent of a hamburger – try the traditional fish-and-chip shops. They appeal greatly to my plebeian taste. I've also eaten well and expensively at the Lobster Pot in Mousehole; well and less expensively at the Tarot in Penzance: and even in the crowded summer I've enjoyed a pleasant, restful lunch at the Green Bank Hotel in Falmouth, with a view of the Fal estuary included in the modest prices. Good for a lunchtime rest also are the Pandora Inn at Restronguet, and the Tinners' Arms at Zennor.

Zennor is a few miles up the coast from Botallack. This is D. H. Lawrence country: he spent the First World War here, with his german wife, till the locals drove them out as suspected spies. Lawrence observed the laconic power of the Cornish, their elusiveness, their enigmatic pagan depths. This wild stretch of coast, between brooding moor and sapphire, mermaid-haunted sea, can make the skin creep on a blustery day. It seems fitting that one of the villages is called Crows an Wra, the Witch's Cross. For film-lovers, it's *Straw Dogs* country. But if you read Lawrence's short story 'Samson and Delilah' in the Tinner's Arms at Zennor, where he set it, remember that the proprietors (as of almost everything lucrative in Cornwall) are unmystical English people, now. You will gradually learn to distinguish the well-bred tones of the English from the rhythmical singsong of the native Cornish – whom you should try to get to know, for a landscape is its people.

At Zennor, in fact, you can get an insight into the unity of the Cornish landscape and people by visiting the privately, and lovingly, created Folk Museum. Then, having strolled for a while along the cliff path, and found a mermaid combing her hair in the church, drive on – through even more breathtaking scenery – to St. Ives. St. Ives is one of the brightest jewels of Cornwall, and consequently too popular; but even high summer can't rob it of its enchantment. On a fine day it is like a Cornish fishing-town miraculously transported to the Mediterranean.

Because you've made a half circle round the coast, you're still only six miles from Penzance. You can drive across the moor, and as you crest it you have the unforgettable sight of Mount's Bay, with its monastic isle, St. Michael's Mount. Seeing it amid the glittering water, you may appreciate for the first time Milton's reference to it in his poem 'Lycidas':

> *Where the great vision of the guarded Mount*
> *Looks toward Namancos and Bayona's hold;*
> *Look homeward Angel now . . .*

EXPLORING THE WEST COUNTRY

For a glimpse of Cornish folklore, start your journey at the **Jamaica Inn** on the windswept moors near Bolventor, where highwaymen and smugglers are said to have roamed. You will find Mary's and Joss's Bars filled with the tools of the villainous trades: muskets, lanterns and swords. Bar open daily, with hot and cold snacks, 11 am to 2.30 pm and 5.30 to 10.30 pm (phone Pipers Pool 250).

After a brisk walk along the cliffs of Tintagel in northern Cornwall, you might want to stop for lunch at the **Mill House Inn**, less than two miles southwest of the town. In this seventeenth century converted cornmill, you can have a bar lunch from noon to 2 pm, or stay overnight, at $43 for a double room (phone Camelford 770200).

On the opposite side of Tintagel, you find **Boscastle's Museum of Witchcraft**. Open daily from April 1, 10 am to dusk, 80 cents admission (phone Buckfastleigh 3452).

For a base from which to explore the south coast, the comfortable **Fowey Hotel** in the town of the same name offers a pleasant dining room and views of the magnificent estuary. Or try the **Riverside Hotel**, also in Fowey. Double rooms in each cost $64. Dinner for two at the Fowey (phone Fowey 2551) is about $25, or $20 for residents, or $28 at the Riverside (Fowey 2275). As you continue your journey west, try the **Pandora Inn** at the edge of Restronguet Creek, near Falmouth. This thatched, medieval building, named after a lost ship, provides a buffet (quiches, Cornish pasties, etc.) daily noon to 2 pm (bars close at 2.30 pm), and fine meals, particularly seafood, from 7.30 to 9.30 pm at $30 for two (phone Falmouth 72678).

In Falmouth, another good base, the renovated eighteenth century **Greenbank Hotel** and restaurant overlooks the historic harbour. A double room with a harbour view costs $60, with set meals at about $12 each. Restaurant open 7 to 10 pm (phone Falmouth 312440).

Farther along the coast at Penzance, try either the **Berkeley** (phone Penzance 2541) or **Harris's** (Penzance 4408) for fine homemade meals. Berkeley, with its thirties-style décor, is open only for dinner 7.30 to 10.30 pm, at about $35 for two. Harris's is also open lunchtime noon to 2 pm, and again from 7 to 10 pm. Evening meal for two: $46. Both close Sundays.

If you visit Mousehole (pronounced like touzle) between early March and late December, don't miss the family-run **Lobster Pot Hotel**, converted from a row of fishermen's cottages that overlook the sea. Here dinner (7.30 to 9.45 pm) for two will cost about $40, lunch up to $16. Double rooms cost about $60, including breakfast (phone Penzance 731251).

For cliff-top views, try the **Botallack Count-House**, where dishes include crabmeat with raw mushroom and ballotine of duck cooked in honey. Open for dinner at about $38 for two, Wednesday through Saturday, 7.30 to 9.45 pm. Sunday lunch (12.30 to 1.45 pm) runs to $7.20 (Penzance 788588).

Farther on in the picturesque port of St. Ives, you can stay at the ivy-draped **Tregenna Castle Hotel**, with spacious double bedrooms at $51. Meal for two $25, restaurant open 7.30 to 9 pm (Penzance 795254). Reservations recommended; wine excluded from prices; all rooms with bath and breakfast; prices vary with exchange rate.

FAREWELL TO
BROWN WINDSOR SOUP

R. W. Apple, Jr.

Unless you have an uncontrollable passion for kippers or steak-and-kidney pie, you probably won't go to Britain to eat, but if you go for other reasons you will find that you can eat very well indeed. Slowly, ever so slowly, over the last twenty-five years, good restaurants have come into being in almost all parts of the kingdom. Brown Windsor soup, thank heavens, is an endangered species. But you must choose where you eat carefully, and you must be prepared to pay for quality, because Britain remains a country where there is something slightly suspect about a fine meal.

The English have the strangest approach to the pleasures of the table of any European people. Only in Britain is a politican likely to be pilloried in the press for liking good wine and good food, as Roy Jenkins was, and only in Britain is good wine and good food so much the province of the more privileged elements. Go to Spain, a much poorer country, and you will find in the simplest of bars a delicious assortment of *tapas*, the little nibbles that accompany so well a glass or two of *vino*. But go to an English pub and you are in danger of finding nothing more appetizing than a Scotch egg, which consists of a hard-cooked egg rolled in sausage meat, usually served stale, to go with your pint of beer.

Bernard Levin, the London writer and critic, says in his new book, *Enthusiasms*, that his pieces about architecture or music or the theatre never arouse quite the same scorn from those who disagree with him as his pieces about food. 'To take pleasure in good food and wine, and to express that pleasure,' he writes, 'is by some considered altogether impermissible, and even arouses the most unbridled hostility.' He finds incomprehensible the view that 'because eating is something we all have to do, it is somehow wrong to enjoy a universal necessity.'

Eating in Britain, like most things, has a good deal to do with class. French families of modest means save for months to eat a superb meal on a birthday or a holiday; I remember chatting in the three-star establishment of Paul Bocuse outside of Lyons one night with the local postmaster and his wife, there to celebrate their wedding anniversary.

Neither they nor the waiters saw anything surprising about their presence in a dining room full of richer and more cosmopolitan people from a half-dozen countries. They were accustomed, they told me, to eating in restaurants about once a week, and they went to the best bistros they could afford, except for their twice- or thrice-yearly splurges. When they ate at home, I am sure, they also ate well, if simply. There are just not very many people like that in Britain, and without people like that, there is no way that good restaurants will ever be the norm, as they are in France and Italy and Belgium and to a lesser extent in Germany and Austria.

It follows that, with honourable exceptions, the British make poor waiters who know little about what they are serving and are therefore utterly incapable of guiding a client. It follows, likewise, that chefs have no status. The proprietor of the best trattoria in an Italian town is a man of some renown and not a little standing, and a cook who wins the title *meilleur ouvrier de France* is automatically Somebody. But the British rank a gifted cook just marginally above a good garage mechanic. It follows that it is still considered somewhat bad form to praise a Mayfair hostess too enthusiastically for her food. And it follows, finally, that the British in general are bad restaurant clients, lacking a sense of adventure, afraid that they will commit a social gaffe, reluctant to return a bad dish to the kitchen or to express dissatisfaction with the service when paying the bill.

There are few gastronomic magazines of general circulation in Britain, and the general level of food criticism is poor. The three excellent guidebooks (which, if one is to find the gems among the clutter, are more important in Britain than anywhere else in Europe) are the products of a French tyre company (Michelin), of an inexhaustible Hungarian émigré with deep roots in the restaurant trade (Egon Ronay) and of a band of dedicated amateurs who report without compensation (*The Good Food Guide*).

And yet, mirabile dictu, one can eat extremely well in Britain; in fact, Britain has restaurants that are the equal of the best and the next-to-best of every country I know except France and Italy.

I would far rather eat at Tante Claire in London or at Manoir aux Quat' Saisons near Oxford than in any grand restaurant in Germany, Austria, Spain or Scandinavia, and there are only a very few in the United States in their class. The chefs of both places are French, it is true, but there is an increasing supply of home-grown talent, too, including men and women like Kenneth Bell of Thornbury Castle near Bristol, Richard Shepherd of Langan's Brasserie in London, Joyce Molyneux of the Carved Angel in Dartmouth, Marion Jones of the Croque-en-Bouche in the Welsh borders and Francis Coulson of Sharrow Bay in the Lake District. They could all hold their own in any country. Michel and Albert Roux, the French brothers who own Le Gavroche in London (three Michelin stars) and the Waterside Inn along the Thames in Bray, west of Heathrow (two Michelin stars, and three from Ronay), are full of praise for their young English apprentices.

Several things have conspired to bring this about, the most important of which is the radical socio-economic change that has taken place since World War II. After the war, all but the richest members of the aristocracy found it impossible to maintain large staffs and large houses, and many began eating regularly in restaurants for the first time, creating a new clientele. Members of the new meritocracy that was encouraged by the gradual lowering of class barriers also became regular clients. The availability of cheap travel to the Continent, opened up by the jet aeroplane and all the apparatus of mass tourism, taught people whose culinary horizons had been confined to Blackpool and Brighton to appreciate the delights of Málaga and Taormina. To this was added the contribution of two seminal figures – Elizabeth David, whose sprightly cookbooks have taught two generations of British chefs as well as household cooks how to recreate the flavours and aromas of the Mediterranean in Northern Europe; and Raymond Postgate, the historian and bon vivant who founded *The Good Food Guide* in 1951 with the tart comment that 'it is quite arguable that even worse meals are today served in hotels and restaurants than in Edwardian days.'

As in the United States, the best restaurants in Britain are a heterogeneous lot. A few, a very few, are survivors from the old days. I think especially of the Gay Hussar, the last of the great Soho establishments, which serves in a warmheartedly Central European ambience the best Hungarian food in the world, especially if one takes the advice of the rotund and avuncular proprietor, Victor Sassie. Or of the Riverside, a tiny place tucked into a romantic cove in remotest Cornwall that seems to have leaped from the pages of Daphne du Maurier, where George Perry-Smith still turns out the classics – lamb boulangère, salmon in pastry with ginger and currants, St. Emilion au chocolat – that helped make his Hole-in-the-Wall in Bath the best British restaurant outside London in the 1950's and early 1960's.

Many are the products, direct or indirect, of the remarkable Roux brothers, who were private cooks in France and Britain before founding their gastronomic dynasty. They own not only Le Gavroche and the Waterside, which in my opinion competes with the Auberge de I'Ill in Alsace and Ama-Lur in Barcelona and the Four Seasons in New York for the title of prettiest restaurant in the world, but also Le Poulbot, probably the best restaurant in the City, and Gavvers, which this year's *Good Food Guide* described as 'the best value set meal in

London' (dinner there costs $25 a person, including service and wine). In addition, they have helped to finance restaurants set up by a number of their alumni, including Pierre Koffmann's quite wonderful Tante Claire, of which a further word or two in a moment, and Jean-Louis Taillebaud's very good Interlude de Tabaillau in Covent Garden (so-called because that is the way Albert Roux mangled the name).

Still others are the creations of amateurs. Paul Henderson, who runs the magnificent Gidleigh Park at Chagford in Devon (with his wife, Kay, and John Webber in the kitchen) used to be a management consultant; Tim Hart of Hambleton Hall in Leicestershire fled from the City; John Tovey of Miller How in the Lake District was an actor; and David Brown of the minuscule La Potinière in Gullane, near Edinburgh, surely the best restaurant in Scotland, was an art student. One advantage of this pattern is the eclecticism that it can produce, of which a particularly happy example is Pomegranates in Pimlico, where Patrick Gwynne-Jones offers Turkish, Scandinavian, French, Chinese, Mexican, Argentinian and Indonesian dishes that he came to love during his wanderings as a seaman and almost anything else you can think of.

Then there is the extraordinary Nico Ladenis of Chez Nico in Battersea, on the 'wrong' side of the Thames but only five minutes by cab from Chelsea. Self-taught, he is a perfectionist proud of the fact that he made it without help from the Roux brothers or anyone else. Nico's individualism and the simplicity of both the décor and the service at his place, make it all the more remarkable that he has just won a second Michelin star. His cooking is French, a careful personal version of nouvelle cuisine stripped of empty flourishes and character-ized by great depth of flavour; his blood, however, is Greek, and his temperament passionate. Natural allies, he and Ronay feuded for years before coming to terms, and the restaurant is not a place for those who treasure calm, because Ladenis is as likely to charge into the dining room to debate a gastronomic point with a client as he is to explode at a *sous-chef* who has created a microscopically thin skin on a sauce by leaving it under the salamander two seconds too long. But it is most definitely a place for those who like to eat well, because the cooking, improving every month, may soon equal the best in the country. For those on a budget, his set lunch at $16.50, including service, is a godsend.

Sadly, many of the best small places are finding it hard to survive in times of economic stringency, staff shortages and increasingly tight government regulations controlling wages and benefits. A last-minute cancellation by a party of six can wipe out Nico's profit margin for the day. Sadly, too, unknowing clients (including, in these days of the strong dollar, a fair number of Americans) who are more interested in telling their friends that they have visited an 'in' place than in eating, can frustrate chefs and cut into profit margins by ordering meagrely. Tante Claire is suffering from this at the moment.

But, saddest of all, there is no sign that the current dearth of good, simple restaurants – the equivalent of France's bistros, Italy's trattorias, Spain's and Greece's fish places – will be ending soon. It is not that Britain lacks good ingredients suitable to straightforward methods of preparation. But fishermen find no market for John Dory, the same delicate fish that Venetians and Bretons devour. Few restaurants get the most out of Scottish beef or Welsh lamb, which are among the best in the world. Fewer still take the trouble to collect the wild mushrooms that abound in the woods or the crayfish that swarm in the streams. The excellence of English cheese – not just Cheddar and Stilton but Wensleydale and Single Gloucester and Blue Cheshire – is a well-kept secret. You will find more tired tournedos Rossini and paella on menus than Lancashire hotpot and blackberry pie. A pity, especially for visitors, because no one on holiday wants to eat grandly every day (even if he or she could afford it), and foreigners would like to sample the local fare.

In a sense, the need is met by the Asian restaurants that have flourished in the last two decades, especially in London. Most are relatively inexpensive, and if you pretend that the Empire lives on, as some Brits do, you could imagine that you are eating 'local'. Try the Indian cooking at the zippy Bombay Brasserie or the cheerful, cooperatively owned Last Days of the Raj in Covent Garden; the dim sum at Chuen Cheng Ku near Leicester Square; the whole range of Chinese dishes at the Diamond in Soho (cheap, cheerful and Cantonese), the Hunan in Pimlico (Hunanese and Szechuan) or, at a rather higher price, the impressive new Zen near Sloane Square.

Somerset Maugham, who did most of his adult eating elsewhere, once said that to eat well in Britain you had to eat breakfast three times a day. Not anymore, but don't count on finding any undiscovered out-of-the-way places – good food, cheap, so very English. They don't exist.

Prices quoted indicate approximate cost of dinner for two including wine, coffee, tax and service.

LONDON

Bombay Brasserie Courtfield Close, Gloucester Road, London SW7. Telephone: 370 4040. Dinner for two: $45. Specialities: Parsee chicken dhansak with brown rice; mutton with apricots and straw potatoes; fresh tropical fruit sorbets; cobra coffee (flambéed coffee). Never closed. Lunch 12.30 pm to 2.30 pm; dinner 7.30 pm to 11.30 pm.

Chez Nico 129 Queenstown Road, London SW8. Telephone: 720 6960. Dinner for two: $75. Specialities: Coquilles St. Jacques à la crème; légère de poireaux or canette de Challons; homemade sorbets. Closed: Lunch Saturday, all Sunday, Monday, four days Easter, two and a half weeks July-August and ten days at Christmas. Lunch 12.15 pm to 2 pm; dinner 7.15 pm to 10.45 pm.

Chuen Cheng Ku 17 Wardour Street or 20 Rupert Street, London W1. Telephone: 437 1398 and 734 3281. Dinner for two: $30. Specialities: Lobster in chili and black bean sauce; quick fried prawns; stuffed bamboo shoots with pork and prawns; belly of pork and yam in a hot pot. Closed: Christmas Day. Meals served from 11 am to 11.30 pm.

Diamond 23 Lisle Street, London WC2. Telephone: 437 2517. Dinner for two: $35. Recommended: Crab with ginger and spring onions, garlicky spare ribs cooked in a paper bag. Closed: Christmas Day and Boxing Day. Meals served from noon to 4 am.

Gavvers 61 Lower Sloane Street, London SW1. Telephone: 730 5983. Dinner for two: $45. Specialities: Menu changes daily so the following dishes are just an example of the kind of food served. Feuilleté de moules au saffron; assiette de la mer au cerfeuil; confit de canard au citron vert; truffe au chocolat. Closed: Sunday, public holidays, four days Easter and Dec. 24 – Jan. 1. Lunch 12.30 pm to 2.30 pm; dinner 5.30 pm to 11 pm.

Gay Hussar 2 Greek Street, London W1. Telephone: 437 0973. Dinner for two: $50. No credit cards or foreign currency accepted. Specialities: Hot spicy clear red fish soup (szegedi); half a chicken cooked in mild paprika sauce served with noodles and cucumber salad (chicken paprikashgaluska); cheese pancakes or raspberry and chocolate torte (eszterha'zy). Closed: Sunday and public holidays. Lunch 12.30 pm to 2.30 pm; dinner 5.30 pm to 11 pm.

Hunan 51 Pimlico Road, London SW1. Telephone: 730 5712. Dinner for two: $45. Specialities: Hunan food (southwest China), which is hot and spicy; crispy pork; lettuce with dumplings; frogs legs; prawn with chili sauce; sea bass with hot bean sauce. Closed: four days at Christmas. Lunch 12 noon to 2.30 pm; dinner 6 pm to 11.15 pm; Sunday 7 pm to 11 pm.

Interlude de Tabaillau 7 Bow Street, London WC2. Telephone: 379 6473. Dinner for two: $60. Specialities: Flan of oysters with beurre blanc sauce; fillet of sea bass with spinach cream sauce or saddle of hare with green lime sauce; passion fruit tart or hot caramelized pear tart. Closed: Lunch Saturday, all day Sunday, ten days Easter, three weeks August-September and ten days at Christmas. Lunch noon to 2 pm; dinner 7 pm to 11.30 pm.

Langan's Brasserie Stratton Street, London W1. Telephone: 493 6437. Dinner for two: $55. Specialities: Artichaut farcies paloise; suprême de faisan au porto; crème brulée. Closed: Lunch Saturday, all day Sunday and public holidays. Lunch 12.30 pm to 2.45 pm; dinner 7 pm to 11.45 pm, Saturday 8 pm to 12.45 am.

Last Days of the Raj 22 Drury Lane, London WC2. Telephone: 836 1628. Dinner for two: $35. Specialities: Thali – a well-balanced assortment of meat and vegetables, vegetarian dishes; almond-flavoured ice cream. Closed: Lunch Sunday and Dec. 24-26. Lunch 12.15 pm to 2.30 pm; dinner 6.15 pm to 11.15 pm.

La Tante Claire 68 Royal Hospital Road, London SW3. Telephone: 352 6045. Dinner for two: $110. Specialities: Galette de foie gras served warm with Sauternes sauce and roast shallots; hare fillet with red wine sauce flavoured with raspberry vinegar with a drop of chocolate added; Queen's strudel served warm. Closed: Saturday, Sunday, public holidays, ten days at Easter, three weeks in August and ten days at Christmas-New Year. Lunch 12.30 pm to 2 pm; dinner 7 pm to 11 pm. It is necessary to reserve a table weeks in advance.

La Gavroche 43 Upper Brook Street, London W1. Telephone: 408 0881. Dinner for two: $125. Specialities: Mousseline de homard aux champagnes; l'assiette du boucher; soufflé aux framboises. Closed: Saturday, Sunday, public holidays, Dec. 23 – Jan. 2. Lunch noon to 2 pm; dinner 7 pm to 11 pm.

Le Poulbot 45 Cheapside, London EC2. Telephone: 236 4379. Meal for two: $60. Specialities: Boudin blanc sauce périgourdine, filets de sole Léonora, grenadines de veau Vallée d'Auge. Closed: Saturday, Sunday, public holidays and ten days at Christmas. Lunch only, noon to 3 pm.

Pomegranates 94 Grosvenor Road, London SW1. Telephone: 828 6560. Dinner for two: $65. Specialities: Gravad lax, Canard sauvage à la Normande, Mexican baked crab, homemade honey and cognac ice cream. Closed: Lunch Saturday, all Sunday and public holidays. Lunch 12.30 pm to 2.15 pm; dinner 7.30 pm to 11.15 pm.

Zen Chelsea Cloisters, Sloane Avenue, London SW3. Telephone: 589 1781. Dinner for two: $50. Wide choice of Chinese food from dim sum and dragon prawns to braised abalone with oyster sauce, sweet and sour pork fillets and baked rice with assorted meats in lotus leaves. Also sizzling dishes and vegetarian specials. Closed: Dec. 25, 26 and 27. Lunch noon to 3 pm; dinner 6 pm to 11.30 pm; Saturday and Sunday open all day, noon – 11.30 pm.

OUTSIDE LONDON

Carved Angel 2 South Embankment, Dartmouth, Devon. Telephone: North Dartmouth 2465. Dinner for two: $60. Specialities: Fish soup; Dartmouth pie (a pie made with spiced mutton and fruit); chocolate and chestnut cake. Closed: In summer, lunch Tuesday, dinner Sunday, all Monday, and public holidays. In winter, lunch Monday to Wednesday inclusive, dinner Sunday to Wednesday inclusive. Lunch 12.30 pm to 1.45 pm; dinner 7.30 pm to 10 pm.

Croque-en-Bouche 221 Wells Road, Malvern Wells, Hereford and Worcester. Telephone: North Malvern 65612. Dinner for two: $60. Specialities: Jerusalem artichoke soup: rai au beurre; rouge au vin de Bourgeuil; grilled leg of lamb, served with a sauce first made for venison by Francatelli, Queen Victoria's cook; tarte Tatin. Closed: Sunday to Tuesday. Dinner only 7.15 pm to 9.15 pm.

Gidleigh Park Hotel Chagford, Devon. Telephone: Chagford 2367. Dinner for two: $90. Specialities: Salad of mixed lettuce with braised quail served with a warm walnut oil dressing; Scotch sirloin steak with bone marrow and shallots with red wine sauce; individual baked apple tarts. Never closed. Lunch 12.30 pm to 2 pm; dinner 7 pm to 9 pm.

Hambleton Hall Hambleton, Leicestershire. Telephone: Oakham 56991. Dinner for two: $70. Specialities: Warm pigeon breast salad with pine kernels; roast wild duck with black currants or roast saddle of lamb with onion marmalade; homemade honey ice cream with hot pistachio sauce or hot chocolate and praline pudding with marbled chocolate sauce. Never closed. Lunch noon to 2 pm; dinner 7.30 pm to 9.15 pm.

Hole-in-the-Wall George Street, Bath, Avon. Telephone: Bath 25242. Dinner for two: $55. Specialities: Fettucine with cream, ham and mushroom sauce; goose braised with brandy and tomatoes served with sugared onions and chestnuts; crêpe Normande. Closed: Sunday and public holidays to non-residents and two weeks at Christmas. Lunch noon to 1.30 pm; dinner 7 pm to 10 pm.

Horn of Plenty Tamar View House, Near Tavistock, Gulworthy, Devon. Telephone: Tavistock 83 2528. Dinner for two: $70. Specialities: Roast Cornish sea bass with mustard sauce; veal medallions with saffron and sage sauce; chocolate meringue cake. Closed: Lunch Friday, all Thursday and Christmas Day. Lunch 12.30 pm to 2 pm; dinner 7 pm to 9.15 pm.

La Potinière Gullane, Lothian, Scotland. Telephone: Gullane 843214. Dinner for two: $47. The set menu is always changing, but the accent is invariably French. The chef specializes in soups, mousselines, soufflés, marinated dishes and interesting desserts. Closed: Lunch Saturday, all Wednesday, Jan. 1 and 2, Dec. 25 and 26, one week June and October. Lunch at 1 pm; dinner Saturday only at 8 pm.

Manoir aux Quat' Saisons Great Milton (near Oxford). Telephone: Great Milton 230. Dinner for two: $95. Specialities: Pâté of oyster and scallops; layered dish of fillet of turbot, soufflé, flaked crab flavoured with ginger and grapefruit, au gratin; biscuits glacé aux framboises de Maman Blanc (recipe inspired by Raymond Blanc's mother). Closed: Sunday,

Monday, public holidays, four days at Easter, two weeks in July, two weeks at Christmas. Lunch 12.15 pm to 2 pm; dinner 7.15 pm to 10 pm.

Miller Howe Hotel Restaurant Rayrigg Road, Windermere, Cumbria. Telephone: Windermere 2536. Dinner for two: $60. No specialities as such because a set five-course meal is served (no choice until dessert). Menu changes daily. An extensive range of vegetables is one of the hallmarks of the restaurant. Closed Dec. 5 to mid-March. Dinner only at 8.30 pm, Saturday 7 pm and 9.30 pm.

Riverside Helford (near Helston), Cornwall. Telephone: Manaccan 43. Dinner for two: $65. Specialities: Salmon baked in pastry with ginger and currants, bourride with aioli and rouille, brandade of smoked mackerel in pastry with dill cream, St. Emilion au chocolat. Closed: End of October to beginning of March. Dinner only 7.30 pm to 9.30 pm.

Thornbury Castle Thornbury (near Bristol), Avon. Telephone: Thornbury 412647. Dinner for two: $70. Specialities: Wye salmon marinated in white wine, orange and lemon juice; breast of chicken flamed in Pernod and cream; Thornbury treacle tart. Closed: two weeks at Christmas. Lunch 12.30 pm to 2 pm; dinner 7 pm to 9.30 pm.

Waterside Inn Ferry road, Bray-on-Thames, Maidenhead. Telephone: Maidenhead 20691. Dinner for two: $125. Specialities: Warm oyster feuilletés with raspberries: grilled rabbit fillets with marrons glacés; warm peach soufflés. Closed: Lunch Tuesday, all Monday, also dinner Sunday in winter, public holidays, Dec. 26–Jan. 25. Lunch 12.30 pm to 2 pm; dinner 7.30 pm to 10 pm.

Book in good time for all these restaurants except Chuen Cheng Ku and Diamond, the two Chinese restaurants that serve meals without closing in between lunch and dinner.

PARIS
AND BEYOND

MY PARIS

Saul Bellow

Changes in Paris? Like all European capitals, the city has of course undergone certain changes, the most conspicuous being the appearance of herds of tall buildings beyond the ancient gates. Old districts like Passy, peculiarly gripping in their dinginess, are almost unrecognizable today with their new apartment houses and office buildings, most of which would suit a Mediterranean port better than Paris. It's no easy thing to impose colour on the dogged northern grey, the native Parisian grisaille, flinty, foggy, dripping and for most of the year devoid of any brightness. The gloom will have its way with these new *immeubles*, too, you may be sure of that. When Verlaine wrote that the rain fell into his heart as it did upon the city (referring to almost any city in the region) he wasn't exaggerating a bit. As a onetime resident of Paris (I arrived in 1948), I can testify to that. New urban architecture will find itself ultimately powerless against the grisaille. Parisian gloom is not simply climatic, it is a spiritual force that acts not only on building materials, on walls and rooftops but also on your character, your opinions and judgements. It is a powerful astringent.

But the changes – I wandered about Paris not very long ago to see how thirty-odd years had altered the place. The new skyscraper on the Boulevard du Montparnasse is almost an accident, something that had strayed away from Chicago and come to rest on a Parisian street corner. In my old haunts between the Boulevard de Montparnasse and the Seine, what is most immediately noticeable is the disappearance of certain cheap conveniences. High rents have done for the family bistros that once served delicious, inexpensive lunches. A certain decrepit loveliness is giving way to unattractive, overpriced, overdecorated newness. Dense traffic – the small streets make you think of Yeats's 'mackerel-crowded seas' – requires an alertness incompatible with absent-minded rambling. Dusty old shops in which you might lose yourself for a few hours are scrubbed up now and sell pocket computers and high-fidelity equipment. Stationers who once carried notebooks with excellent paper now offer a flimsy product that lets the ink through. Very disappointing. Cabinetmakers and other small artisans once common are hard to find.

My neighbour the *emballeur* on the Rue de Verneuil disappeared long ago. This cheerful specialist wore a smock and beret, and as he worked in an unheated shop, his big face was stung raw. He kept a cold butt-end in the corner of his mouth – one seldom sees the *mégots* in this new era of prosperity. A pet three-legged hare, slender in profile, fat in the hindquarters, stirred lopsidedly among the crates. But there is no more demand for handhammered crates. Progress has eliminated all such simple trades. It has replaced them with boutiques that sell costume jewellery, embroidered linens or goose-down bedding. In each block there are three or four *antiquaires*. Who would have thought that Europe contained so much old junk? Or that, the servant class having disappeared, hearts nostalgic for the bourgeois epoch would hunt so eagerly for Empire breakfronts, Récamier sofas and curule chairs. Inspecting the Boulevards I find curious survivors. On the Boulevard St. Germain, the dealer in books of military history and memorabilia who was there thirty-five years ago is still going strong. Evidently there is a permanent market for leather sets that chronicle the ancient wars. (If you haven't seen the crowds at the Invalides and the huge, gleaming tomb of Napoleon; if you underestimate the power of glory, you don't know what France is.) Near the Rue des Saints Pères, the pastry shop of Camille Hallu, Ainé, is gone, together with numerous small bookshops, but the dealer in esoteric literature on the next block has kept up with the military history man down the street, as has the umbrella merchant nearby. Her stock is richer than ever, sheaves of umbrellas and canes with parakeet heads and barking dogs in silver. Thanks to tourists, the small hotels thrive – as do the electric Parisian cockroaches who live in them, a swifter and darker breed than their American cousins. There are more winos than in austere postwar days, when you seldom saw *clochards* drinking in doorways.

The ancient grey and yellow walls of Paris have the strength needed to ride out the shock waves of the present century. Invisible electronic forces pierce them but the substantial gloom of courtyards and kitchens is preserved. Boulevard shop windows, however, show that life is different and that Parisians feel needs they never felt before. In 1949 I struck a deal with my landlady on the Rue Vaneau: I installed a gas hot-water heater in the kitchen in exchange for two months' rent. It gave her great joy to play with the tap and set off bursts of gorgeous flame. Neighbours came in to congratulate her. Paris was then in what Mumford called the Paleotechnic age. It has caught up now with advancing technology, and French shops display the latest in beautiful kitchens – counters and tables of glowing synthetic alabaster, artistic in form, the last word in technics.

Once every week during the nasty winter of 1950 I used to meet my friend, the painter Jesse Reichek, in a café on the Rue du Bac. As we drank cocoa and played casino, regressing shamelessly to childhood, he would lecture me on Giedion's *Mechanization Takes Command* and on the Bauhaus. Shuffling the cards I felt that I was simultaneously going backward and forward. We little thought in 1950 that by 1983 so many modern kitchen shops would be open for business in Paris, that the curmudgeonly French would fall in love so passionately with sinks, refrigerators and microwave ovens. I suppose that the disappearance of the *bonne à tout faire* is behind this transformation. The post-bourgeois era began when the maid of all work found better work to do. Hence all these *son et lumière* kitchens and the velvety pulsations of invisible ventilators.

I suppose that this is what 'Modern' means in Paris now. It meant something different at the beginning of the century. It was this other something that so many of us came looking for in 1947. Until 1939 Paris was the centre of a great international culture, open to Spaniards, Russians, Italians, Rumanians, Americans, to the Picassos, Diaghilevs, Modiglianis, Brancusis and Pounds at the glowing core of the modernist art movement. It remained to be seen whether the fall of Paris in 1940 had only interrupted this creativity. Would it resume when the defeated Nazis had gone back to Germany? There were those who suspected that the thriving international centre had been declining during the thirties, and some believed that it was gone for good.

I was among those who came to investigate, part of the first wave. The blasts of war had no sooner ended than thousands of Americans packed their bags to go abroad. Among these eager travellers, poets, painters and philosophers were vastly outnumbered by the restless young, students of art history, cathedral lovers, refugees from the South and the Midwest, ex-soldiers on the G.I. Bill, sentimental pilgrims, as well as by people, no less imaginative, with schemes for getting rich. A young man I had known in Minnesota came over to open a caramel-corn factory in Florence. Adventurers, black marketeers, smugglers, would-be *bon vivants*, bargain hunters, bubble-heads – tens of thousands crossed on old troopships seeking business opportunities, or sexual opportunities, or just for the hell of it. Damaged London was severely depressed, full of bomb holes and fire weed, whereas Paris was unhurt and about to resume its glorious artistic and intellectual life.

The Guggenheim Foundation had given me a fellowship and I was prepared to take part in the great revival when and if it began. Like the rest of the American contingent I had brought my illusions with me, but I like to think that I was also sceptical (perhaps the most tenacious of my illusions). I was not going to sit at the feet of Gertrude Stein. I had no notions about the Ritz Bar. I would not be boxing with Ezra Pound, as Hemingway had done, nor writing in bistros while waiters brought oysters and wine. Hemingway the writer I admired without limits, Hemingway the *figure* was to my mind the quintessential tourist, the one who believed that he alone was the American whom Europeans took to their hearts as one of their own. In simple truth, the Jazz

Age Paris of American legend had no charms for me, and I had my reservations also about the Paris of Henry James – bear in mind the unnatural squawking of East Side Jews as James described it in *The American Scene*. You wouldn't expect a relative of those barbarous East Siders to be drawn to the world of Mme. de Vionnet, which had in any case vanished long ago.

Life, said Samuel Butler, is like giving a concert on the violin while learning to play the instrument. That, friends, is real wisdom. I was concertizing and practising scales at the same time. I *thought* I understood why I had come to Paris. Writers like Sherwood Anderson and, oddly enough, John Cowper Powys had made clear to me what was lacking in American life. 'American men are tragic without knowing why they are tragic,' wrote Powys in his autobiography. 'They are tragic by reason of the desolate thinness and forlorn narrowness of their sensual mystical contacts. Mysticism and Sensuality are the things that most of all redeem life.' Powys, mind you, was an admirer of American democracy. I would have had no use for him otherwise. I believed that only the English-speaking democracies had real politics. In politics continental Europe was infantile and horrifying. What America lacked, for all its political stability, was the capacity to enjoy intellectual pleasures as though they were sensual pleasures. This was what Europe offered, or was said to offer.

There was, however, another part of me that remained unconvinced by this formulation, denied that Europe-as-advertised still existed and was still capable of gratifying the American longing for the rich and the rare. True writers from St. Paul, St. Louis and Oak Park, Illinois, had gone to Europe to write their American books, the best work of the 1920's. Corporate, industrial America could not give them what they needed. In Paris they were free to be fully American. It was from abroad that they sent imaginative rays homeward. But was it the European imaginative reason that had released and stirred them? Was it Modern Paris itself or a new universal Modernity working in all countries, an international culture, of which Paris was, or had been, the centre? I knew what Powys meant by his imaginative redemption from desolate thinness and forlorn narrowness experienced by Americans, whether or not they were conscious of it. At least I thought I did. But I was aware also of a seldom-mentioned force visible in Europe itself to anyone who had eyes – the force of a nihilism that had destroyed most of its cities and millions of lives in a war of six long years. I could not easily accept the plausible sets: America, thinning of the life-impulses; Europe, the cultivation of the subtler senses still valued, still going on. Indeed a great European prewar literature had told us what nihilism was, had warned us what to expect. Céline had spelled it out quite plainly in his *Journey to the End of the Night*. His Paris was still there, more there than the Sainte Chapelle or the Louvre. Proletarian Paris, middle-class Paris, not to mention intellectual Paris, which was trying to fill nihilistic emptiness with Marxist doctrine – all transmitted the same message.

Still, I had perfectly legitimate reasons for being here. Arthur Koestler ribbed me one day when he met me in the street with my five-year-old son. He said: 'Ah? You're married? You have a kid? And you've come to *Paris*?' To be Modern, you see, meant to be detached from tradition, traditional sentiments, from national politics and, of course, from the family. But it was not in order to be Modern that I was living on the Rue de Verneuil. My aim was to be free from measures devised and applied by others. I could not agree to begin with any definition. I would be ready for definition when I was ready for an obituary. I had already decided not to let American business society make my life for me, and it was easy for me to shrug off Mr. Koestler's joke. Besides, Paris was not my dwelling place, it was only a stopover. There was no dwelling place.

One of my American friends, a confirmed Francophile, made speeches to me about the City of Man, the City of Light. I took his rhetoric at a considerable discount. I was not, however, devoid of sentiment. To say it in French, I was '*aux anges*' in Paris, wandering about, sitting in cafés, walking beside the green, medicinal-smelling Seine. I can think of visitors who were not greatly impressed by the City of Man. Horace Walpole complained of the stink of its little streets in the eighteenth century. For Rousseau it was the centre of amour propre, the most warping of civilized vices. Dostoyevsky loathed it because it was the capital of Western bourgeois vainglory. Americans, however, loved the place. I, too, with characteristic reservations, fell for it. True, I spent lots of time in Paris thinking about Chicago, but I discovered, and the discovery was a very odd one, that in Chicago I had for many years been absorbed in thoughts of Paris. I was a longtime reader of Balzac and of Zola, and knew the city of Père Goriot, the Paris at which Rastignac had shaken his fist, swearing to fight it to the finish, the Paris of Zola's drunkards and prostitutes, of Baudelaire's beggars and the children of the poor whose pets were sewer rats. The Parisian pages of Rilke's *Malte Laurids Brigge* had taken hold of my imagination in the thirties, as had the Paris of Proust, especially those dense, gorgeous and painful passages of *Time Regained* describing the city as it was in 1915 – the German night bombardments, Mme. Verdurin reading of battlefields in the morning paper as she sips her coffee. Curious how the place had moved in on me. I was not at all a Francophile, not at all the unfinished American prepared to submit myself to the great city in the hope that it would round me out or complete me.

In my generation the children of immigrants *became* Americans. An effort was required. One made oneself, freestyle. To become a Frenchman on top of that would have required a second effort. Was I being invited to turn myself into a Frenchman? Well, no, but it seemed to me that I would not be fully accepted in France unless I had done everything possible to become French. And that was not for me. I was already an American, and I was also a Jew. I had an American outlook, superadded to a Jewish consciousness. France would have to take me as I was.

From Parisian Jews I learned what life had been like under the Nazis, about the roundups and deportations in which French officials had cooperated. I read Céline's *Les Beaux Draps*, a collection of crazy, murderous harangues, seething with Jew-hatred.

A sullen, grumbling, drizzling city still remembered the humiliations of occupation. Dark bread, *pain de seigle*, was rationed. Coal was scarce. None of this inspired American-in-Paris fantasies of gaiety and good times in the Ritz Bar or the Closerie des Lilas. More appropriate now was Baudelaire's Parisian sky weighing the city down like a heavy pot lid, or the Paris of the Communard *pétroleurs* who had set the Tuileries afire and blown out the fortress walls. I saw a barricade going up across the Champs-Elysées one morning, but there was no fighting. The violence of the embittered French was for the most part internal.

No, I wasn't devoid of sentiments but the sentiments were sober. But why did Paris affect me so deeply? Why did this imperial, ceremonious, ornamental mass of structures weaken my American refusal to be impressed, my Jewish scepticism and reticence; why was I such a sucker for its tones of grey, the patchy bark of its sycamores and its bitter-medicine river under the ancient bridges? The place was, naturally, indifferent to me, a peculiar alien from Chicago. Why did it take hold of my emotions?

For the soul of a civilized, or even partly civilized, man Paris was one of the permanent settings – a theatre, if you like – where the greatest problems of existence might be represented. What future, if any, was there for this theatre? It could not tell you what to represent. Could anyone in the twentieth century make use of these unusual opportunities? Americans of my generation crossed the Atlantic to size up the challenge, to look upon this human, warm, noble, beautiful and also proud, morbid, cynical and treacherous setting.

Paris inspires young Americans with no such longings and challenges now. The present generation of students if it reads Diderot, Stendhal, Balzac, Baudelaire, Rimbaud, Proust does not bring to its reading the desires born of a conviction the American life impulses are thin. We do not look beyond America. It absorbs us completely. No one is stirred to the bowels by Europe of the ancient parapets. A huge force has lost its power over the imagination. This force began to weaken in the fifties and by the sixties it was entirely gone.

Young M.B.A.'s, management-school graduates, gene-splicers or computerists, their careers well started, will fly to Paris with their wives to shop on the Rue de Rivoli and dine at the Tour d'Argent. Not greatly different are the behavioural scientists and members of the learned professions who are well satisfied with what they learned of the Old World while they were getting their B.A.'s. A bit of Marx, of Freud, of Max Weber, an incorrect recollection of André Gide and his Gratuitous Act, and they had had as much of Europe as any educated American needed.

And I suppose that we can do without the drama of Old Europe. Europeans themselves, in considerable numbers, got tired of it some decades ago and turned from art to politics or abstract intellectual games. Foreigners no longer came to Paris to recover their humanity in modern forms of the marvellous. There was nothing marvellous about the Marxism of Sartre and his followers. Postwar French philosophy, adapted from the German, was less than enchanting. Paris, which had been a centre, still *looked* like a centre and could not bring itself to concede that it was a centre no longer. Stubborn de Gaulle, assisted by Malraux, issued his fiats to a world that badly wanted to agree with him, but when the old man died there was nothing left – nothing but old monuments, old graces. Marxism, Eurocommunism, Existentialism, Structuralism, Deconstructionism could not restore the potency of French civilization. Sorry about that. A great change, a great loss of ground. The Giacomettis and the Stravinskys, the Brancusis no longer come. No international art centre draws the young to Paris. Arriving instead are terrorists. For them, French revolutionary traditions degenerated into confused leftism and a government that courts the Third World make Paris a first-class place to plant bombs and to hold press conferences.

The world's disorders are bound to leave their mark on Paris. Cynosures bruise easily. And why has Paris for centuries now attracted so much notice? Quite simply, because it is the heavenly city of secularists. *Wie Gott in Frankreich* was the expression used by the Jews of Eastern Europe to describe perfect happiness. I puzzled over this simile for many years, and I think I can interpret it now. God would be perfectly happy in France because he would not be troubled by prayers, observances, blessings and demands for the interpretation of difficult dietary questions. Surrounded by unbelievers, He, too, could relax toward evening, just as thousands of Parisians do at their favourite cafés. There are few things more pleasant, more civilized than a tranquil *terrasse* at dusk.

DISCOVERING THE HIDDEN PARIS

John Vinocur

One man's exoticism is another man's Hoboken. My theory is that Paris is a marvellous, extraordinary place for a visitor, on the condition that the city be treated like Cleveland or Bujumbura, Burundi. That means embracing its alienness, its exoticism and its vitality by running after what is both common and hidden.

It is not just a question of avoiding places where you will be seated next to two junior high school classmates or, for the second night out of five, across from a couple from Tenafly who are surely nice, gracious and intelligent people. She may be a brain surgeon, and he an expert in Darius Milhaud, but their presence should serve as a sign that Paris is slipping past.

It happens very easily. The world is such that every ambitious restaurant or good boutique in Paris literally has a counterpart in Munich, London or New York. At more than seven francs to the dollar, at this writing, Paris is certainly more manageable now for a visitor than a resident, buying food and getting his shirts washed, but the emergence of a kind of unwritten international franchising system really means that the good, expensive Paris restaurant is the mirror image of another restaurant in another place, the reflection including the same diners wearing the same clothes. A Saint Laurent boutique, moreover, is a Saint Laurent boutique is a Saint Laurent boutique.

There's absolutely nothing wrong with these places: Go, please. But there's not a trace of the vaguely original about them, either; they are deserts of predictability, and spending much time in them usually results in feeling like a mirage, a person who doesn't exist beyond paying the bill. I don't propose touting people off anything standard in Paris, neither the Tuileries Gardens nor the Eiffel Tower, Hermès or the Galeries Lafayette. Instead, I'm offering some mild sociology, a little looking at things that don't look quite like yourself. They may be as basic as Cleveland, but they also require a kind of Bujumbura approach, a sense of wilful immersion in the foreign, a deliberate but not overwhelming disorientation. The French have a very great understanding for this point of view and they have a word, missing from English, that explains the phenomenon: *dépaysement*. It's the feeling of not being assaulted by the familiarity of things, a change in surroundings where there is no immediate point of reference. The French have always been big on the exotic, as long as it creates no inconveniences and can be followed by a proper meal with respectable wines.

This is exactly the approach that I want to recommend. James de Coquet, a French journalist who covers big criminal trials and then writes about food between verdicts, maintains that 'Americans don't travel to be *dépaysés*, but to find a home away from home.' I wouldn't dispute this, but I could add that those who do look for a little *dépaysement* in France generally like the place a lot. Individually, and in corners where they are not expected, Americans can pass for exotics themselves. This means interest, or at least curiosity, and very often kindness on the part of the locals. It's a lot better circumstance for having a good time than being the eight hundred and eleventh tourist of the day to ask for a Perrier with lots of ice at Le Café Flore.

Here is an unsystematic list of things to augment the glorious and the obvious. They are places to walk, places to eat, things to do. They don't substitute for anything famous, extraordinarily beautiful or culturally uplifting. They are things to do in between, and I think they suggest a little bit of what Paris is like if you're not visiting for just a week or a few days. The city's magnificence is never really common-place, but some of its ordinariness is unique, fascinating and, in the best sense, exotic.

THINGS TO DO

The brain surgeon and her husband, if I know anything of their habits, will have bought copper pots for their kitchen, eaten chez Michel Rostang and, running into you again, will propose you accompany them to the big Marché aux Puces (flea market) at St. Ouen, a scabrous industrial suburb just northeast of the city line. You answer yes, of course, if it's Sunday, spend fifteen minutes looking around the mostly miserable antiques and assorted junk, and then slip away, saying there is something else to do in the neighbourhood. Which is true.

There is Le Red Star. Red Star is a second-division soccer team that plays at the Stade St. Ouen. Its link to Paris life is roughly that once held by the Jersey City Giants of the International League in relation to New York City. But Le Red Star is as marvellous in its permanent ineptness as its stadium is in its decrepitude. There are rarely more than three or four thousand people at a game, and they are worth the trip. The mix is classic: straight proletariat in hats with pompons and, on the edges, a few paler types in tweed jackets with the collars turned up, students there for a spiritual soak in the baths of the nether world. Since Red Star never wins, the essence of an afternoon at St. Ouen is the hectoring and bemoaning, with a kind of *gouaille*, or Paris lip, that Jean Gabin turned into a fortune and a horse-racing stable. No translations are needed and everybody talks to everybody else. If you're there, the assumption is you're okay. If anybody asks how you washed up in St. Ouen, my suggestion is telling them you're scouting for the Cosmos. The best flea markets – nowhere near St. Ouen, by the way – are those at Kremlim-Bicetre at the Porte d'Italie, and the one at the Porte de Montreuil. Go as early as 8 am.

There are nightime corollaries to the Red Star experience, the best being boulevard theatre. It always goes like this: Arlette, Jacques's wife, goes off to visit her sick aunt in Nantes. While she's away, Jacques picks up a Danish au pair at St. Germain-des Prés and installs her for the weekend in the family apartment. But Aunt Edith dies earlier than expected and Arlette returns unannounced. Jacques is surprised, there are people running in and out of doors, and Arlette shouts that she's leaving with Edith's enormous inheritance.

By the end of things, Arlette and Jacques are back together, the money held in escrow by a notary with a Marseilles accent, and the Danish girl is marrying the couple's nephew. The titles change, but the plays never really vary, as immutable as Kabuki. The actors are always called Maurice Baquet or Bunny Godillot, and they look very much like everybody in the audience. The mood is very lower middle class, joyously vulgar, rough and grainy, and far less ambitious than Broadway. The odds are very small you'll meet anybody you know. Tickets costs the equivalent of from $5 to $17. The weekly entertainment guides like *Pariscope* carry complete listings for what's available.

I have slightly mixed feelings about another suggestion that, depending on the mood of the people involved, can brush very close to the campy and self-conscious. It's going to be a *bal populaire*, where you run the risk of turning into a phoney participant, a disguised gawker. There are a couple of dance halls, like the Balajo and La Boule Rouge on Rue de Lappe, that run along the thin edge between naturalness and self-pastiche. There are tangos and polkas, café waiters in blue suits on their night off and women holding grenadine and mint drinks, the same shade of red and electric green as the little spotlights in the ceiling. The best time to go is probably on a Sunday night. There is probably less latent hoke, though, at the dance hall downstairs at La Coupole, on Boulevard Montparnasse, where most of the activity is late in the afternoon, with accompaniment by a band that sometimes wears Cossack outfits. The old Joe E. Lewis line about liking a family audience fits well there: in the dim light, most of the dancers look like aunts and their nephews.

EATING

Any fool can eat well in Paris. It is not always certain, though, that he'll eat what he wants to eat. It's a waste of time to go somewhere that's trying very hard to be original, and then eat a steak, but it's also silly to be there in the first place if a steak is what you really want. This terrible confession, this shameful state of affairs, this resistance to the urge for a steak, is an American malady in Paris, one absolutely not shared by the French. The result is that if you go to a French steak restaurant, you're moving close to authenticity and about as far away from the guidebook and nouvelle-cuisine circuit as you can get.

There is a steak-house row on Avenue Jean Jaurés near where the old slaughterhouses once stood at La Villette. Most of the licence plates on the cars (big Peugeots, Mercedeses) parked in the area come from the provinces. This means that the guy with the biggest truck dealership in Auxerre, who is in town for a couple of nights with his wife, has headed for La Villette. You can trust his judgement. The decoration in most of the places is furniture-store still-life, but the meat is terrific, and the pretentiousness nonexistent. There are five steak houses bunched together, and one of them, **Au Cochon d'Or**, gets a Michelin star, and very few foreign visitors. Count on spending from $20 to $30 a person with wine.

I recommend another place, too, because it is so deep-France, so much the antithesis of anything modish that is seems extraordinary. It is **Chez E. Marty**, 20 Avenue des Gobelins, which really should be marked down for Sunday lunch. Most everyone there seems as if they've come straight from mass – couples, whole families, and some old people by themselves, spruce and dignified and sipping port. The people tend to look like retired general officers, their widows or their grandchildren. For reasons unexplained, there is also a nasty-looking stuffed boar, a pheasant with very long feathers, and a brown animal with a lot of little pointy teeth that could put you off walking in the woods for a while. But the service, particularly from the waitresses in black uniforms with lace aprons, is time-warp stuff: decorous, kind, patient. If you steer clear of the lobster, which is expensive, the bill should be between $15 and $20 per person. A friend, Françoise Labro, says she knows a place on the Rue de Babylone, **Au Pied de Fouet**, that is so beyond time that the regulars are given personal napkins, napkin rings, and drawers to stow them in between meals. For my notions of the intemporal, Marty is as close as you get.

MUSEUMS

The problem with Paris museums is again the problem of the glorious and the obvious. There's really no right time to go. People with strong concentration last hours, other crack in twenty minutes; the crowds can be that bad. They exhibit paintings in the Brussels metro, but in Paris the metro sometimes seems to have entered the **Louvre**. There is a quiet corner, though. If you go in the **Pavillon de Flore** entrance, you can do French sculpture from the Renaissance to the nineteenth century almost by yourself. There are a lot of other good, less-trampled museums where you may even get the notion of having seen something out of the ordinary and in relative calm: **Nissim de Camondo**, 63 Rue Monceau, is remarkable for the French eighteenth century. You may have to wake up the concierge to get in, but the **Musée Gustave Moreau**, 14 Rue de la Rochefoucauld, is a unique place with the remarkable work of the early symbolists. Nobody goes much either to the **Musée de la Chasse et de la Nature**, 60 Rue des Archives, which has interesting things from the seventeenth and eighteenth centuries, and weapons from the Louis XV period. One of the very best visits is to the **Musée National des Antiquités**, which is far away enough, in St. Germain-en-Laye, to discourage many. Actually it's an easy ride on the R.E.R. express metro, and the Gallo-Roman collection is terrific.

WALKING
After Le Red Star and Balajo, someplace bourgeois may be required. As far as up-market sociology goes, the Champs-Elysées these days is car showrooms and Burger King and McDonald's boxes. With the certainty of the moon and the tides, Rue du Faubourg St. Honoré means bumping into the brain surgeon again. Aim instead for the Place St. Augustin, where there are two stores, Berteil and Tunmer, that have the same relationship that Brooks Brothers and Abercrombie and Fitch used to have on Madison Avenue. Nobody goes to one without going to the other. Berteil is French preppy, Shetland-and-tassle loaferland, while Tunmer is a very big sporting-goods store.

French preppiedom is essentially an Anglophile graft, rather studied, and carries a genuine class feel. If you listen to the accents in Berteil, there's a good chance you'll hear some pure sixteenth *arrondissement* mumbling and diphthonging, an arch but rough equivalent of Locust Valley lockjaw.

Tunmer gets itself involved only in upwardly mobile exercise – skiing, tennis, hunting – and then provides the very right instruments for all the planned exertion. A visit to the shops has a political sense, too, since anyone who wanted to fit in among the young men around Valéry Giscard d'Estaing was advised to have at least one Oxford grey V-neck sweater for wearing in aeroplanes that would pass muster at Berteil. Both stores carry men's and women's lines. A word of caution: Men who do not eat quiche may find it hard to get fitted at Berteil. The sizes seem to me to run small.

On Saturday or Sunday morning, I say go round to the entrance to the Jardin du Luxembourg in Rue Auguste Comte. Inside, just beyond the tall iron gates, are lawns and sandy walks, peopled mostly by daddies assigned to offering a morning's fatherliness to their small children, invariably dressed in Oshkosh overalls and a certain kind of English boarding-school sandals.

The fathers are usually a pretty good slice of what's young and upcoming in France in publishing, in the universities, in government. They are aides to cabinet ministers, and television producers, and they try hard not to read the paper too much and to play with their kids. When they give up on the lawn, they move toward the marionette theatre, the carousel and the playground inside the garden. The playground has its own fence, and benches, inside and out. Inside, the daddies, and some mummies, can sit and talk together and not feel too guilty about it since the kids are busy on the slides and swings. Outside, at a proper anthropological distance, you can sit and watch them all, the French ruling class to come. Native rites for next to nothing! But the chair ladies still make you pay for your seat if they catch you.

– THE LOUVRE –
PALACE OF MASTERWORKS

Michael Brenson

The Louvre may be the most intimidating of the world's great museums. Not only is it enormous – the largest museum in the West and the largest building in Paris – but it was built as a palace, not as a museum, and has the formality and weight of a neglected urban Versailles. Furthermore, the Louvre was constructed and pieced together over eight centuries, and there is no single unifying architectural concept, just as there is no overriding logic to the installation.

Not knowing which way to proceed or how to cope with what may seem to be a morass of masterpieces, the first-timer's visit to the Louvre may turn out to be a rainbow-coloured nightmare. I remember how much I looked forward to my first visit and how relieved I was, like a kid at school breaktime, when I stepped into the fresh air afterwards.

There is something that might be called the Louvre first-visit blues, and everyone who has spent time in the museum recognizes it. It begins with dragging feet, continues with ever more dutiful glances at famous works and ends with a heaving crash into one of the overused cushions along the great hall.

Such a fate is not, however, inevitable. Although it may be impossible not to feel overwhelmed during the first visit, it is also possible to feel exhilarated. Even if the formality of the building and the size of the collection seem excessive, if not irrational, the French do know something about measure, and it is with a sense of measure that one should prowl the Louvre's corridors and halls.

This cannot be done without finding a way to shed that sense of duty or obligation that does more to diminish the enjoyment of palaces and monuments than anything else. If you like a painting or sculpture and don't want to move on, don't.

What follows is less a guide than a three-visit approach to a museum whose resources could not be exhausted in a lifetime of visits. Two of the itineraries are orientated by specific paintings and sculptures, the third more by an attitude to the relatively unfamiliar periods in question.

Ideally one would put aside at least two and a half hours for each visit. There are places to sit in many of the painting and European sculpture galleries and a cafeteria on the second floor (for the French, the first floor) that is conveniently located for the first two itineraries.

Since most people know the Louvre for its paintings, the painting collection is a good place to begin. Painting's main rival for attention, the ground-floor Greco-Roman section, has been restored and was reopened again in 1984. Some of the Roman collections are on display in the restored rooms known as **Anne of Austria's apartments** (on the ground floor to the right of the **Daru Staircase**.) The remainder of the Greco-Roman section, including the *Venus de Milo* and the restrained and elegant *Hera of Samos*, is temporarily on view in the **Salle des Cariatides** (ground floor, left after the Daru Staircase).

The paintings are largely confined to the second floor. Assuming one enters by the **Porte Denon,** the main entrance, and climbs the Daru Staircase, one will arrive at the *Nike of Samothrace,* who propels herself toward the main body of the museum as she once reached out toward the open sea. If one turns right and walks to the end, one will end up in the **Salon Carré,** where the Louvre's history of French painting begins.

The first major work is the *Avignon Piéta,* a fragile fifteenth century panel painting attributed to Enguerrand Quarton that is justifiably one of the landmarks of the museum. As with many of the best late Gothic paintings and sculptures, the work can be understood through the details, through the hands and drapery alone.

After the room of fifteenth and sixteenth century French painting, one is in the **Grande Galerie,** the corridor, two football fields long, of French and Italian paintings – hung alongside, never on top of, each other, and whenever possible at eye level – that must surely be the largest space of its kind in any museum. Most of the seventeenth century paintings, not just those by Poussin, Claude Lorrain and Georges de La Tour, are worth looking at because of the demanding classical approach to composition.

With Poussin, try looking at the colours. There is a Poussin blue that is unlike any other. If one experiences it finally not as a colour but as another element, like earth and water, something important about the roots of the Abstract Expressionist approach to colour and paint may become clear.

Nobody should be put off by the apparent modesty of Louis le Nain's 1642 *Peasant Meal* and 1648 *Peasant Family*. They are works that can be looked at a long time. Le Nain had a first-rate compositional mind, and the geometrical thinking with which he composed these paintings is unusually accessible. One may find there a key both to Cézanne and the photographer Paul Strand.

In the **Salle des Etats,** a large room about one-third of the way down the Grande Galerie to the right, one is suddenly in sixteenth century Italy. It is in this room that one finds the painting that launched a thousand tourist agencies and camera shops. The *Mona Lisa* was bought by Francis I, the French king who patronized Leonardo, founded the royal art collection and transformed the Louvre from a thirteenth century fortress-castle into a palace.

If the *Mona Lisa* cannot be reached because of the crush of people, keep in mind that among those deserted works on the same wall there are five other Leonardos. And with all the Raphaels and Titians, do not overlook the most conspicuous painting in the room, Veronese's 1563 *Marriage at Cana.* It is in every way an immense work, as much a world as a painting can be.

Meanwhile, back in the Grand Galerie, the journey through French painting continues with the rococo work of the early and mid-eighteenth century. The last time I was in the Louvre, there was no one in front of Watteau's *Embarkation for Cythera* and *Gilles.* If there is any inclination to enter Watteau's quiet, wistful, precarious world, it is worth the effort. The restrained lyricism, melancholy and content of his works are more suggestive of eighteenth and nineteenth century poetry than painting.

At the other end of the **Mollien Wing** – perpendicular to the Grande Galerie – with its Bouchers and Chardins and Fragonards, one enters the **Salle Mollien** and late eighteenth century French painting. If one turns right again and walks east, one will reach perhaps the most awesome room in the museum. The nineteenth century **Daru Room** contains, among other things, Géricault's *Raft of the Medusa*, Delacroix's *Death of Sardanopolis* and Courbet's *Burial at Ornans*.

A word of advice here. Many people wait for a rainy day to go to a museum. Because the Daru Room, like many other rooms, including the Salle des Etats, is dark, the Louvre should be visited when there is maximum natural light.

(There is another area of nineteenth century French painting, which provides a more intimate view of Géricault, Delacroix and Courbet, as well as an important selection of work by Corot and Daumier. The area can be reached most easily by a small staircase almost at the end of the second-floor **Egyptian section**.)

A second visit to the museum would take in the rest of the paintings and most of the museum's collection of European sculpture. It would begin back where French painting ended in the Grande Galerie and Italian painting really begins.

There is little in the Italian section, from Cimabue's thirteenth century altarpiece to Carpaccio's sixteenth century *Preaching of St.*

Stephen, that is not worthy of attention. In the context of the contemporary art desire to accept and work with banality, look at Fra Angelico's fifteenth century *Coronation of the Virgin*. It is a saccharine, wedding-cake vision that is serious and totally convincing. There is a dramatic juxtaposition between the Fra Angelico and Uccello's *Battle of San Romano*, on the opposite wall, with its dark colours and hammerlike rhythm that beats out the sense of a cold, irresistible fatality.

Italian painting and the Grande Galerie ends with the **Van Dyck Room** of seventeenth century Flemish painting. One painting, Rubens's *Kermesse*, dominates everything else in the room. It presents a peasant festival after dance and drink have torn off the bonds of rules and reason. The painting has a diabolical energy that seems to pour out of the canvas and invade everything around it.

The **Galerie de Médicis** contains the twenty-one paintings Rubens did for Marie de Médicis's Luxembourg palace. These works remind me of all those Romanesque tympani that depict a struggle between good and evil, which always present good as victorious, and which always leave the modern viewer finding the evil side more interesting and somehow indomitable.

Continuing on the east-west axis, I would pick and choose very carefully. In the **Dutch, Flemish and German galleries** of the **Petits Cabinets,** which one reaches by staircases just beyond the Galerie de Médicis, look for Dürer's self-portrait and two Vermeers: *The Lace Maker* and *le Philosophe*.

With the exception of Caravaggio's *Fortune Teller*, one could skip the corridor of seventeenth and eighteenth century Italian painting and move on to the **Beistugui Collection** with its first-rate eighteenth century portraits. Just up the stairs is the **Pavillon de Flore** and Spanish painting. There are fine works by Goya and Velázquez and Ribera, but, with the possible exception of Zubaran, the section does not give a satisfying sense either of the artists represented or Spanish painting in general.

In the **Basement of the Flore Wing** are Michelangelo's *Slaves*. One flight down is the corridor of European – mostly French – sculpture, from the Middle Ages through the nineteenth century. The medieval and Gothic French collection is of real interest. The strongest seventeenth to nineteenth century room is devoted to Pierre Puget. There are three major works of his, including the intensely three-dimensional *Milo of Cortona*.

The one other room that should not be missed in the west side of the museum is the **Picasso Donation**. The works by other artists that Picasso owned and left to the French state. The room can be reached by a staircase along the corridor of seventeenth and eighteenth century Italian painting. There are some surprises here, works by Le Nain, Matisse and Balthus one may not easily identify with one of the giants of modernism. What Picasso surrounded himself with provides a larger perspective not only on him but on those influenced by him.

A third trip to the museum would concentrate on the Louvre's fabulous collection of ancient art, most of which is located in the **Cour Carrée**, in the eastern part or back of the Louvre. The first major ancient section one encounters on the second floor, behind the *Nike of Samothrace*, is Egyptian. Instead of discussing individual works, perhaps I can suggest why it may be worthwhile going through the dense display of Egyptian works very carefully.

An argument could be made that Egypt, as much as Greece, is the cradle of Western art. There is an Egyptian combination of geometry and imaginative freedom that shows up in the Egyptian menagerie: birds, snakes, strange hybrid creatures like the Sphinx, that has become part of an artistic archetype. So has the Egyptian sculpture's tendency to contain and sometimes embed figures in blocks of stone; the relation between figure and stone in Michelangelo's *Slaves* can be traced back to this.

Furthermore, Egyptian artists were extremely sophisticated. Because they knew how to create volume and space, they could be monumental in small works as well as large. Also, even though Egyptian heads may seem abstract, there is in many of them a strong element of empirical truth. If one catches on to what is happening in those crowned or uncrowned heads that seem to swell or expand in the back, one may never see 'realistic' heads – like those by Houdon – the same way again.

The small Egyptian works are on the second floor, the large works on the ground floor, which one reaches by the stairs at the southeast corner of the Cour Carrée. At the end of the ground-floor Egyptian display, down another flight of stairs, is the beginning of the **Assyrian section**. Anyone who has seen the Assyrian reliefs in the British Museum does not need to be convinced of what the Assyrians could do.

Many of the qualities of Egyptian art are also present in the art of Mesopotamia, which can be reached by turning left at the northeast corner of the Cour Carrée, at the end of the Assyrian section. One of the rooms one must pass through to get there contains Persian brick reliefs, and they should not be missed either.

If there is any curiosity and energy left, go back to the section of medieval objects that begins at the end of the second-floor Egyptian galleries, to the left. The quality of the craftsmanship is predictable; the formal and contemporary interest of some of these works may not be. In the small thirteenth century ivory *Joseph Carrying the Body of*

Christ Dead, in the fourth room, there is in the composition an original and expressive approach to form. In the same room there is a northern Italian ivory altarpiece made up of rows of narrative boxes that suggest not only Louise Nevelson but conceptual art. Particularly during this third visit to the museum, one may gain a strange and unexpected perspective on contemporary art.

COPING WITH THE MUSEUM

Most of the Louvre is open every day except Tuesday from 10 am to 6.30 pm. However, some sections, such as the Petits Cabinets and the Assyrian, Mesopotamian and Persian collections, are only open on Mondays and Wednesdays, 10 am to 5 pm. Some parts of the museum close between twelve noon and 2 pm. Admission is free for those under eighteen years, about 75 cents for those eighteen to twenty-five and over sixty-five years, and about $1.50 for everyone else. Admission is free on Sundays.

The cafeteria, or *salon de thé*, where one can stop for coffee or tea and a snack, is situated between the Mollien Wing and the Salle Mollien, at the point where eighteenth century French painting ends and nineteenth century French painting begins.

Rest rooms are scattered throughout the museum. Even when they are conveniently situated, however, as they are in the painting sections, they are almost never conspicuous. One pretty much has to ask a guard in order to find them.

The museum shop, near the main entrance at the Porte Denon, is often crowded and not particularly attractive, but the people at the information desk speak English and the shop is unusually complete. There are books of all kinds, on almost all subjects touched upon in the collections. There is a broad selection of guides, and a vast number of postcards. The gift shop has some quality reproductions, particularly of jewellery and sculptures. (There is a more limited selection of cards and books at the head of the Daru Staircase, near the *Nike of Samothrace*.)

If one is looking for a good restaurant within easy walking distance of the museum, one almost has to cross the river to the Left Bank. **Le Voltaire**, on the Quai Voltaire, is a good restaurant frequented by professionals in the art and entertainment worlds. A meal for one with wine will cost about $15.

PASSPORT TO
PARIS FASHION

Bernadine Morris

Along with the food, art and architecture, fashion is certainly one of the chief attractions of Paris. It can be contemplated passively by sitting in a café and watching people pass by, or pursued more actively by dropping into any of the multitudinous boutiques, either those with world-renowned names such as Hermès or Vuitton or the small, little-known ones where the venturesome shopper can make her own discoveries.

There is a third way: total immersion in the rarefied world of haute couture, or made-to-order clothes. This alternative is not restricted to moguls and pashas, though many are certainly aficionados. Nor is it a closed society, into which you have to be born – or arrive with impeccable credentials. Anyone can attend a Paris couture fashion show. The atmosphere is no more posh than that of any expensive dress salon, though the prices can be considerably higher.

Many visitors to Paris who head immediately for the Louvre or have no qualms about making reservations at a three-star eating establishment such as Taillevent or L'Archestrate are diffident about turning up at a couture house, except perhaps to buy a scarf or some perfume at its street-floor boutique. They do not realize that the couture itself is considered by the French to be one of their national monuments and, as such, worth showing off to foreigners.

In fact, the Chambre Syndicale de la Couture Parisienne, the trade association of high-fashion houses that establishes the rules and regulations of the couture industry, dictates that each member put on regular showings of its collection for at least two months a season. There is no charge for people who are not involved with the fashion industry, though if a woman decides to buy any of the styles she is shown it can turn out to be an expensive visit.

Prestige aside, it is the purpose of the showings to attract customers, and on a not-too-busy day visitors are likely to be assigned a *vendeuse*, or salesperson, to guide them through the finer points of the collection.

To build goodwill, some couture houses even schedule special shows for tour groups; these must be arranged in advance. The viewer may not necessarily be a candidate for a couture dress, which normally costs from $2,000 to $3,000 at some of the smaller houses for a relatively simple style (the more elaborate beaded evening designs can go as high as $15,000). But she is a potential customer for the couturier's perfume, cosmetics or ready-to-wear items, which may also be available in the visitor's neighbourhood store back home.

'The couture is expensive, but not extravagant,' says Emanuel Ungaro, whose prices start at about $4,000. This is considerably more than the $1,200 to $2,500 one would have to spend for a jacket, skirt and blouse from his ready-to-wear collection.

From the middle of the nineteenth century until about twenty years ago, the haute couture in Paris was the undisputed arbiter of fashion throughout the world. Ready-to-wear clothes may have flourished in the United States and elsewhere, but all over the world women aspired to go to France to have their clothes made to order – at least their important dresses.

In the social upheaval of the 1960's a new form of dressing evolved, based on such simple items as T-shirts, sweater dresses and trousers. Ready-to-wear houses, never significant in France, developed to supply them. It was no longer necessary to travel to Paris to acquire a French label.

Haute couture, seeing which way the wind was blowing, began organizing its own ready-to-wear collections; several years ago Alix Grès, whose couture house dates to the 1930's, was the last couturier to succumb to the ready-to-wear boom. Meanwhile, houses such as Christian Dior and Yves Saint Laurent had built thriving manufacturing operations that overshadowed their couture businesses.

Still, designers consider the couture operation essential. 'It gives you a chance to be in touch with what women want,' observed Marc Boham, the Dior designer who leaves his workrooms to preside over fittings of such clients as Queen Noor of Jordan and Jacqueline de Ribes of Paris.

The clothes are still made largely by hand, out of the most luxurious fabrics in the world. To display them, dressmakers around the turn of the century devised the fashion-show formula so that their customers would not have to muss their hair or remove their clothes. They employed mannequins to slip on the clothes and parade them informally before potential clients.

If a dress appealed to her, the customer could pick her own colours, change a fabric or a neckline and have it made to fit her body. She came back regularly for fittings until the style was satisfactory. This system still prevails, although the fashion show itself has been standardized.

Twice a year, new collections are developed and presented in mammoth shows to the press, some important clients and manufacturers, who pay for the privilege of reproducing the styles. (Until a decade ago many of the manufacturers were from the United States; today they tend to be from West Germany, Switzerland and Japan.) The autumn and winter styles are introduced at showings the last week in July; the spring and summer shows are traditionally presented the last week in January.

The week after the openings, the regular showings begin. They are held from two to five times a week, depending on the house; they usually begin at 3 pm and last about an hour. It is advisable to arrive fifteen minutes early. The salons hold from 20 to 150 people and it may be necessary to reserve a few days in advance; the shows are usually more crowded earlier in their run. Showings continue for two to five months.

Some of the smaller houses, such as Carven, are aware that women may enter a couture salon with a good deal of trepidation. A Carven spokesman said his salon makes a special effort to make new visitors feel at home. One of these was Danielle Mitterrand, whose husband was elected President of France in June 1981. Soon afterward she visited couture houses for the first time and bought clothes at two of the smaller ones, Torrente and Louis Féraud. Later she worked her way up to Yves Saint Laurent.

To visit, it is necessary to have a reservation, but this can be secured easily be telephoning the couture house and asking for the receptionist. Most receptionists speak English and will report on the next scheduled showing. It may, of course, be easier to have your hotel concierge make the call.

Some houses, such as Dior, will call back to confirm that the visitor is actually registered at the hotel. This is to keep out the copyists and it is not always successful. To prove you are not in the fashion business, it is a good idea to bring your passport with you.

While the couture fashion show as an institution has had a long run, it may not be permanent. Several houses – Lanvin, Ungaro, Saint Laurent and Hanae Mori – have switched from live models to video presentations. Others are contemplating the same move.

Emanuel Ungaro explained why: 'It costs a lot of money and you never recapture the excitement of the first show,' he said. 'The production becomes tired and there is always the problem of finding the right models. Like the theatre the show runs down when it's been going too long.'

The opening, or press show, is videotaped and later presented on a large screen while the audience sits in comfortable chairs. The clothes that potential clients want to see again are shown afterward by live mannequins.

'A live show does keep the staff alert,' Mr. Ungaro said, somewhat wistfully. 'I would like to do one occasionally, if it could be arranged.'

While the nature of the showings may change, the couture, he says, must go on. 'It is my laboratory – a chemical factory has a laboratory, where it can experiment with new ideas. I can do anything I want, without having to worry about production problems. It is the last luxury a creator can have.'

WHERE TO SIT, TO SEE, AND
TO BE SEEN

Patricia Wells

It is impossible to imagine Paris without cafés. The city has about seven thousand, varying in size, grandeur and significance, as diverse as the French themselves. Cafés are for grabbing a café au lait on the way to the office, for arguing politics or reading *Le Monde*, for people-watching or improving a tan, for sipping a late-night cognac or flirting with strangers. While most cafés serve snacks or meals, people don't really pay careful attention to the food. Rather, the café serves as an extension of the French living room, a place to start and end the day, to gossip and debate, a place for seeing and being seen.

Long ago, Parisians lifted to a high art the human penchant for doing nothing. The French have always done as they pleased, and at the famous sidewalk cafés along Boulevard du Montparnasse and Boulevard St. Germain they made an art of doing as they pleased in public.

No book on Paris literary, artistic or social life is complete without detailed descriptions of who sat where when with whom and what they ate and drank. One wonders how writers and artists accomplished all they did if they really whiled away all those hours perched on the sidewalks downing Vichy water and *ballons* of Beaujolais. Max Jacob is said to have disciplined himself to the extent that he hung a sign on his wall warning: 'Do not go down to Montparnasse.'

He did, of course, as did Ernest Hemingway and Gene Tunney, Henry James and Jean-Paul Sartre. The sidewalk cafés along Boulevard du Montparnasse – Le Dome, La Rotonde, Le Select and, later, La Coupole – were the strongholds of artists; those along Boulevard St. Germain – Les Deux Magots, Le Flore and Lipp – were the watering holes and meeting halls for the literary. When the 'lost generation' of expatriates came after World War I, they established themselves along both boulevards, often drinking and talking themselves into oblivion.

Le Flore was the home of the existentialists, while **Les Deux Magots** served as the birthplace of Surrealism. Both cafés claimed Simone de Beauvoir and Sartre as regulars. Camus came to Le Flore, but apparently not so often, because of disagreements with Sartre, while Picasso settled in at Le Flore every evening, drinking a bottle of mineral water and chatting with his Spanish friends.

Le Dome and **La Coupole** still serve as bourgeois symbols to French radicals and any time there is political trouble – as in 1968 and 1980 – the windows at the cafés along Boulevard du Montparnasse are systematically shattered.

Lipp remains the hangout for the literary élite, and on any given day you can find editors from nearby publishing houses downing hearty platters of *choucroute* and giant goblets of Alsatian beer as they plot writers' futures. François Mitterrand has always favoured Lipp.

The café billed as the oldest in Paris is **Le Procope**, opened in 1685 by a Sicilian, Francesco Procopio dei Coltelli, the man credited with turning France into a coffee-drinking society. Le Procope served such greats as Voltaire and Rousseau. It still exists at the original address, 13 Rue de l'Ancienne Comédie near Odéon, but today, it is a rather insignificant restaurant, not a café.

Many cafés, such as **La Closerie des Lilas**, actually began as *guinguettes*, open-air taverns where one could drink, dance, eat and play at various games. At one time billiards were featured, but the game was banned in 1895 because of excessive gambling.

Not all of the notable cafés have survived. At the now-vanished **Café Mecanique**, clients filled out their orders at the tables, which vanished into the basement, soon to reappear with the order.

The people you see today at Les Deux Magots, Le Flore and Lipp may not be the great artists of the past, but faces are worth watching just the same. Linger a bit on the sidewalk and you will see that the Paris clichés are alive and well: the surly waiters and red-eyed Frenchmen inhaling Gitanes; old men in navy berets; *clochards* hauling bright pink shopping bags holding all their earthly possessions; ultra-thin women with hair dyed bright orange: and schoolchildren decked out in blue and white seersucker, sharing an afternoon chocolate with mother and siblings.

On the sidewalks of Les Deux Magots you might even see a struggling American writer pull up on his motorcycle, lift a portable typewriter from his saddlebags and sit down to continue his novel. Cafés are still there for discreet – or not so discreet – rendezvous. When a French magazine recently published a café picture of a young woman gazing rather longingly at a middle-aged man, the gentleman in question threatened to sue.

At one time, cafés supplied writing paper, newspapers and magazines for their customers, but today a request for writing paper will get you a typical Gallic shrug. Ask for a newspaper and at most cafés the waiter will send you to the nearest kiosk.

Café food and drink have changed little since the early days. Coffee, beer and licorice-flavoured *pastis* remain the staple drinks, along with various fruit juices, sweetened with sugar. A *citron pressé* is a good shot of fresh lemon juice, served with a jug of tap water or bottled Vichy and a few packets of sugar, for sweetening to taste. *Orange*, as well as *pamplemousse*, or grapefuit *pressé* are also standbys. (You know it's a classy café if they serve the sugar in silver-topped shakers, instead of paper packets.)

At Lipp, try the Vittel Cassis, a few inches of thick black-currant syrup served with a bottle of Vittel mineral water. Popular everywhere is the *diabolo-menthe*, the drink Americans call peppermint soda. It's a splash of bright green mint syrup served with a bottle of tap or mineral water.

The *croque-monsieur* – a thick cheese-and-ham sandwich fried in egg batter – and the *sandwich mixte* – a thickly buttered baguette filled with Gruyère cheese and thin slices of *jambon de Paris* – are still the favourite café snacks. For larger meals, there are always giant platters of fresh Belon oysters, plates of Baltic herring, chunks of pistachio-studded sausage served with mounds of potato salad.

While Parisians willingly share space with tourists at the famous spots, it is the neighbourhood cafés that really typify everyday Paris. You can't walk two steps without tripping over a café or *café tabac* with maybe a table or two extending onto the sidewalk. There is little real physical difference between a café and tabac, unless you're buying cigarettes. At the former, cigarettes can be sold only to clients who are eating or drinking there, while at the latter, cigarettes can be sold to clients walking in off the street.

It's also worth knowing where you can eat and where you can drink. If the tables are covered with cloths, even little paper ones, the table is reserved for dining. If it is bare, you are welcome to sit down for just a drink.

Many a young Frenchman feels his day has not begun until he's downed a quick *café calva*, or thick espresso with a shot of calvados, with his friends. Historically, most of the city's café owners come from the Auvergne, the southern central region of France known as the Massif Central. Years ago the Auvergnats came to Paris in droves, working as dealers in wood and coal and, incidentally, opening cafés. Café owners still have their own chatty newspaper, fittingly called *L'Auvergnat de Paris*. This is why you still see firewood stacked in front of little neighbourhood cafés all over town and why the hearty dishes of the region, including country hams and Cantal cheese, appear regularly on the brief menus.

Most cafés are distinguished by a décor more practical than aesthetic, but a few are worth visiting simply on architectural merit. A personal favourite is **Au Petit Fer à Cheval** in the Marais. The tiny, popular neighbourhood café dates back to 1903, when the Combes family opened it as the Café de Bresil. It still boasts a marble-topped horseshoe bar, mirrored walls and the original patchwork tile floor. The patron, André Collin, has embellished the room a bit but retained the feel of authenticity when he added another mirror, a giant chandelier and shelves of glass and brass.

Unlike many café owners, eager for every extra centime, Mr. Collin has seen fit to omit the most unpleasant and unfortunate additon to the contemporary café scene, the noisy flipper, or pinball machine. Instead, there's classical music and a solid, local crowd. Au Petit Fer à Cheval may well be the only Paris café with a Manhattan telephone directory stashed behind the bar, should customers have need of one. The book is a souvenir of Mr. Collin's single visit to New York, to run in the city's marathon.

Equally appealing is **Le Cochon à l'Oreille**, a tiny café lost in the jumble of Les Halles. The walls here are covered with ceramic murals depicting life in the old Les Halles market and, hidden in the corner, there is a wonderful mural in the style of the famous French poster artist Eugene Grasset. The bar is of zinc, the floor is covered with peanuts and you will have to stand five deep to share a *pastis* with the locals.

If you're in the Les Halles neighbourhood and feeling sort of peckish, it's worth stopping at **Aux Deux Saules** on the pedestrian-filled Rue Saint-Denis, where they serve a rather decent bowl of onion soup. Most of the action here goes on outdoors, where a trendy young crowd hangs out at the large, communal picnic tables on the patio. There's also a busy carryout *frites* stand and a noteworthy interior, featuring the same sort of murals as Le Cochon à l'Oreille.

Le Clown Bar is not in any of the guidebooks because it's not the kind of place that appeals to tourists – unless, of course, you have a passion for clowns or circuses or more Belle Epoque ceramic murals. The good part is that the place probably hasn't changed during the last fifty years. The bad part is that it probably hasn't been cleaned in as long. But along with the dirt-encrusted windows and walls papered with photographs of stars of the Cirque d'Hiver down the street, there's a lot of history and a rather grubby sort of charm, with red and yellow murals of circus clowns, acrobats and other circus figures.

TWENTY SIDEWALK FAVOURITES

Patricia Wells

If you know how to nurse a beer or coffee for hours, café-sitting can be one of the city's best buys. No matter how crowded a café may be, waiters will respect your graceful loafing and won't insist that you order another round just to hold the table.

A *café simple*, or tiny cup of thick black espresso coffee, will cost about $1 if taken on one of the famous terrace cafés along the boulevards, and about fifty cents if you stand at the bar of a neighbourhood café. A *demi-pression*, or glass of draught beer, will cost about $1.25, a simple *sandwich mixte*, $2, a little glass of Muscadet or Beaujolais $1 to $1.25.

But if you intend to spend an afternoon café-hopping, the adventure can be an expensive one, particularly if your tastes tend toward anything stronger than wine or beer. A shot of calvados will cost $4 on the terrace of Le Dome and a taste of Lipp's eau-de-vie will cost the same.

The price of a full meal at any of the café-restaurants, such as Lipp, La Closerie des Lilas or La Coupole, will cost about $35 a person for a first course, main dish, dessert and half-bottle of moderately priced wine. A light lunch or snack – including perhaps a salad, a bowl of onion soup and a half-bottle of wine – will cost about $10.

Following is a listing of many of the more popular and lively Paris cafés. Some are included because of their historical significance, others for architectural reasons and still others because they are nice little places to sit on a sunny afternoon. Athough most are open through much of the day and into the night, note days and months of closing.

Café de la Paix, 12 Boulevard des Capucines (260-33-50). Metro: Opéra. Open daily, 10 am to 2 am. This open, expansive café near the Opéra represents a sort of gaiety of days past. You can still sit and sip your 'limonade' under the crisp green-and-white umbrellas lining the sidewalk and watch the spectacle of the passing crowd, but you'll also see a large share of tourists.

La Closerie des Lilas, 171 Boulevard du Montparnasse (326-70-50). Metro: Port-Royal. Open daily, noon to 1 am. The lilacs are long gone, but the romance of days when men like Henry James and Ernest

Hemingway gathered here is still very much alive at this popular café-restaurant. Beneath the colourful green-and-white awnings amid a garden of greenery, you can sit outdoors sipping coffee, move to the enclosed terrace for an authentic salade Niçoise or dine in the open-air covered garden. Try the restaurant's still-famous *loup de mer flambé au fenouil* (whole grilled sea bass that arrives in a flame of dried fennel branches). A comfortable place for Sunday lunch in August, when much of Paris is closed. This is still a hangout for French movie stars and chic young Frenchmen and one spot where you can linger reading the copies of *L'Express* and *Paris Match* provided for clients.

Le Clown Bar, 114 Rue Amelot (700-51-18). Metro: Filles-du-Calvaire. Open 7.30 am to 7.30 pm. Closed Saturday. A dive, to be sure, but an honest *café de quartier,* worth visiting for its colourful turn-of-the-century ceramic murals depicting circus scenes.

Au Petit Café Cluny, 20 Boulevard Saint-Michel (354-23-64). Metro: Saint-Michel. Open daily, 7 am to 2 am and all night Saturday. This is one of those large and rambling cafés of the great boulevards, where people don't go for the décor or food, but simply to watch other people and to relax. It is a few steps from the Cluny Museum and at one of the city's busiest crossroads, the corner of Boulevard St. Michel and Boulevard St. Germain.

La Coupole, 102 Boulevard du Montparnasse (320-14-20). Metro: Vavin. Open daily, 8 am to 2 am. Closed in August. Still Montparnasse's favourite meeting places for artists, models and tourists and the haunt of young Americans since its opening in 1927. For years Jean-Paul Sartre and Simone de Beauvoir came every afternoon. But they made a point never to come in the evening hours, reserved for the bourgeoisie. Though few artists can still afford to live in this popular district, where artists' studios rent for $400 to $500 a month, little seems to have changed here over the last fifty years. Artists still come and sit at the left, under posters of current exhibitions, while the chic set dines on the right. Sunday is for family lunches, when reservations are at a premium. During off hours, the old-timers fill the tables, sitting at the same table they've occupied for decades, reading the papers that hang from bamboo frames. The food is above average for such a popular, cavernous place. Try the briny Belon oysters, the grilled lamb chops, the moist pistachio-studded sausage or the Baltic herring served with mounds of *crème fraiche* and chunks of fresh apples. This is one place you can always go for a snack or a full meal and never have a sense of being rushed.

Les Deux Magots, 170 Boulevard St. Germain (548-55-25). Metro: St. Germain-des-Prés. Open daily, 8 am to 2 am. Closed in August. The ultimate Paris café, great for observing the current fashion scene and for restoring yourself with a steaming cup of good hot chocolate on cool afternoons. Deux Magots still offers more than twenty-five different whiskies, and coffee is still served in thick bistro-style cups. Sidewalk entertainment varies from fire-eaters to organ grinders, from talented mime groups to junior Bob Dylans. The interior is calm and appealing, with its mahogany red banquettes and brass-edged tables, walls of mirrors and waiters decked out in crisp, floor-length aprons and neat black vests. You can sit under the famous wooden statues of the two Chinese dignitaries, or *deux magots,* which gave their name to the café. The owner recalls watching Sartre indoors, from 10 to 12.30 every morning, writing while smoking cigarette after cigarette. Right after World War I, Hemingway came 'for serious talk' and to read aloud the poetry he'd written.

Aux Deux Saules, 91 Rue St. Denis (236-46-57). Metro: Les Halles. Open daily, noon to 1 am. This historic café is a breath of fresh air amid a sea of sex shops and fast-food hangouts. Sit outdoors on the unvarnished picnic tables set along this pedestrian passage and enjoy a good $1.50 bowl of onion soup *gratinée* and a glass of cheap red wine. Next, go inside and down a quick coffee at the bar, facing the fabulous ceramic murals depicting life in old Les Halles. This is a popular spot for the young, chic crowd of the district.

Le Dome, 108 Boulevard du Montparnasse (354-53-61). Metro: Vavin. Open 10 am to 2 am. Closed Monday. When Le Dome first opened at the turn of the century, it was just a drinking shack and Montparnasse a suburb of the Latin Quarter. Today, the neighbourhood is a mix of old-timers and tourists, and the restored interior of Le Dome has an unappealing plastic-coated sheen. But the assortment of live ferns on the open-air terrace adds a touch of warmth and Le Dome is still a fine place for lingering over a coffee, a *ballon* of rosé, a *croque-monsieur* or *sandwich mixte.*

Café Le Flore, 172 Boulevard St. Germain (548-55-26). Metro: St. Germain-des-Prés. Open daily, 8 am to 2 am. Closed in July. The rival of Les Deux Magots next door, this was always more of a literary hangout, popular with Sartre, Simone de Beauvoir and Camus. Although most artists gathered in Montparnasse, Picasso used to come here every night during the late 1940's sitting at the second table in front of the main door, sipping a bottle of mineral water and chatting with his Spanish friends. Little is changed here, with its simple and classic Art Deco interior: red banquettes, walls of mahogany and mirrors, and a large sign suggesting that, while pipe smoking is not forbidden, *'l'odeur de certaines tabacs de pipe parfumes incommode le plupart de nos clients.'* In other words, courteous clients don't smoke pipes here. The large sidewalk café is neither as pleasant nor as accessible as that at Les Deux Magots, yet equally popular.

Le Flore en L'Ile, 42 Quai d'Orléans (329-88-27). Metro: Pont-

Marie. Open daily, 11 am to 1.45 am. The décor in this combination café-restaurant-tea salon on Ile St. Louis is nothing special, but if you can get a seat at the open-air windows along the sidewalk, the view of Notre Dame is breathtaking. Settle in to read one of the French or English publications that hang from bamboo racks and enjoy one of the famous and fabulous Berthillon *sorbets* or ice creams sold here. Tea does not come from a tea bag but is freshly brewed and steaming hot, and the classical music in the background helps one enjoy a moment of peace and a nice breeze on a warm summer's day.

Fouquet's, 99 Avenue de Champs-Elysées (723-70-60). Metro: George V. Open daily, 9 am to 2 am. Fouquet's is always making society news, as starlets and journalists talk about and write about their rendezvous here. Paul Bocuse loves the food and company at Fouquet's, but most don't come to dine but to grab a snack before or after viewing one of the dozens of first-run films playing at cinemas along the avenue. Sexism lives at Fouquet's, where a sign warns, 'Les Dames seules ne sont pas admises au bar.' Mr. Casanova insists that the sign, which has been up at the seven-stool bar since the restaurant opened more than eighty years ago, is there to protect women, not insult them. Most women see it otherwise. (Fouquet's is pronounced to rhyme with *bets,* not *bay,* incidentally, in a survival of a fashionable fascination with *l'anglaise* early in the century.)

L'Innocent, 12-14 Rue Berger (236-55-31). Metro: Les Halles. Open daily, noon to 1 am. There is no lack of sun-kissed sidewalk cafés in the Les Halles area, but of those on the tree-lined plaza, L'Innocent offers the most charm. Indoors, the décor is total Deco, with walls of bevelled white metro tile covered with posters for current art exhibitions. There are *Le Monde* and *Le Matin* for leisure-time reading, and a choice spot under the sun facing the giant Renaissance Fountain of the Holy Innocents. Or you can retreat to the shade of umbrellas, away from the pedestrian hordes.

Brasserie Lipp, 151 Boulevard St. Germain (548-53-91). Metro: St. Germain-des-Prés. Open 8 am to 12.45 am. Closed Monday and the month of July. Perhaps the city's most famous café-restaurant, still a late-night spot for politicians such as François Mitterrand, publishers from Grosset, Gallimard and Hachette, and scores of beautiful people. During the day, the rather cramped and airless terrace is filled with American, German and English tourists, drinking the delicious Alsatian beers and sharing platters of *jambon* and *cornichons* or *pâté en croute.* The interior is classically dark and dingy, but in a felicitous way. Colourful ceramic tiles painted with parrots and cranes give the main-floor dining room a lighter feel, and the bright lights of the old-fashioned chandeliers turn night into day. Despite the fact that the food is barely edible – the famous *choucroute* is third-rate, the popular *gigot* is tasteless and the pastries tired and soggy – Lipp packs them in night after night. They don't take reservations by telephone and a good deal of fuss is made of securing a table on the main floor. People who eat upstairs don't talk about it.

Lutetia, 23 Rue de Sèvres (544-38-10). Metro: Sèvres-Babylone. Open daily, noon to midnight. Although one is welcome to sit outdoors at the tiny espresso bar for a tea or coffee, I love the brilliant Art Deco interior, all mirrors and silver, with a horseshoe zinc bar dominating the room. Lutetia caters to an older, well-heeled crowd, which comes here for onion soup and little salads of mixed greens and smoked goose breast. This is a busy area, with the Bon Marché department store, Poilâne bakery and numerous boutiques, as well as a lovely little park nearby, at the foot of the pedestrian street, Rue Récamier.

Ma Bourgogne, 19 Places des Vosges (278-44-64). Metro: St. Paul. Open 8 am to 1 am. Closed Monday. A classic little café under the arcades of Paris's oldest square. Sit outdoors on the traditional red-and-beige rattan chairs, absorbing the beauty of the architecture, which dates back to 1407.

Au Petit Fer à Cheval, 30 Rue Vieille-du-Temple (272-47-47). Metro: Hôtel de Ville. Open 7.30 am to 8.30 pm. Closed Sunday. The name of this perfectly rare café comes from the horseshoe-shaped bar that absorbs the space of this tiny local meeting place. There are plants and classical music, an elegant chandelier and André Collin, certainly one of the friendliest patrons in Paris. The locals rave about the pastries.

Brasserie du Pont Louis Philippe, 66 Quai de l'Hôtel de Ville (272-29-42). Metro: Pont-Marie. Open noon to 3 pm, 7.30 pm to 11.30 pm. Closed Monday. This little café across from Pont Louis Philippe gets the simplicity award for décor: plain white walls, giant white vases filled with lilacs, oval bevelled mirrors and wide windows that open to the streets. On nice days sit on the white folding chairs in the sun, reading whatever it is you've found at the booksellers along the *quai*.

La Rotonde, 105 Boulevard du Montparnasse (326-68-84). Metro: Vavin. Open daily, 8 am to 2 am. Lenin and Trotsky sipped their *café crèmes* here in 1915, along with others of the international intelligentsia who made the café famous. It has all been remodelled and lost its charm, but in the afternoon La Rotonde and Le Select (next door at No. 99) get the sun, so the Montpartnasse crowd camps out here, sipping *diabolo-menthe* and smoking Gitanes.

Le Cochon à l'Oreille, 15 Rue Montmartre (236-07-56). Metro: Les Halles. Open 4.45 am to 4.30 pm. Closed Sunday. I passed this café for years, never noticing the incredible interior, with its priceless ceramic murals depicting scenes of life in old Les Halles. It's still a place where local meat-market wholesalers and other area merchants gather. You may have to stand five deep at the zinc bar for your *pastis* or coffee, but it will be well worth it.

La Palette, 43 Rue de Seine (326-68-15). Metro: Mabillon. Open daily from 8 am to 2 am. Closed in August. This Left Bank café is perfect on a sunny afternoon, when the sidewalk tables expand as far as law and reason will allow. Everyone is in a light mood, and seems to know everyone else, so La Palette has a particularly intimate, Parisian air. The patron wanders about, shaking hands and chatting with the brightly dressed clientele – almost all artists – who come for a solid cup of coffee and to snack on open-faced sandwiches made with fresh Poilâne bread.

THE REFINED GLITTER OF THE PLACE VENDÔME

Susan Heller Anderson

The Place Vendôme resembles an old-fashioned Cartier watch – a slightly elongated square with bevelled corners and an air of well-bred understatement. Roughly equidistant from the traffic-clogged Places de l'Opéra, de la Madeleine and de la Concorde, the Place Vendôme is a serene pocket of harmonious architecture and seventeenth century sumptuousness in the hectic heart of Paris. Its shop windows, filled with jewellery and luxury goods, reflect the opulence of France's costliest products. Originally conceived as an ornament for the Paris of Louis XIV, whose equestrian statue was to be its chief monument, the Place Vendôme was designed in 1686 by Jules Hardouin-Mansart. It was built as a beautiful façade, behind which academic and cultural institutions were to be housed. The lots behind this façade remained vacant, to be gradually sold off to individual builders in Paris's first real-estate development.

Now classified as a historical monument, Mansart's façade has remained intact. All the buildings are identical, with street-level arcades topped by a rhythmic series of pilasters that rise two stories to a steeply pitched roof with Mansart windows. Not a single tree disrupts the harmony of this elegant, honey-coloured testimony to early city planning.

Towering above the Place Vendôme is a bronze column with a statue of Napoleon dressed as Caesar perched on top. The material for the column came from 1,200 cannons captured at the Battle of Austerlitz in 1805. The statue is a replica of the original; the Place Vendôme has had several statues, beginning with the one of Louis XIV, which was destroyed in the Revolution.

Chopin died at No. 12 Place Vendôme. Dr. Mesmer, the father of hypnotism, lived at No. 16. The Ritz sits at No. 15. The Ministry of Justice, at No. 13, was once the Royal Chancellery, and the official measure for the metre is still embedded in its façade. There are several banks, Rothschild and Morgan Guaranty among them.

The streets leading into the Place Vendôme on the northeast and southwest are, in the French fashion, also called the Place Vendôme, though they are not inside the square. Here, and in their extensions on the Rue de la Paix and the Rue de Castiglione and the nearby streets, are some of Paris's finest shops.

South of the Place Vendôme, the Rue St. Honoré, between the Rue Royale and Place du Theâtre Française, where the Comédie Française is situated, is bordered with luxury boutiques:

Cassegrain, at No. 422 Rue St. Honoré, sells thick, creamy stationery and wonderful gifts, among them a cellar book (*livre de cave*) in black or red leather with columns for records and wine-tasting notes. **Le Nain Bleu,** No. 406, is filled with unusual and very expensive toys from all over Europe.

At No. 392, **Dana** specializes in co-ordinated suits, blouses and beautifully tailored clothes for women. Made-to-measure clothing is available at about a third higher than ready-made items and takes two weeks for delivery.

Selleries de France, No. 265, has ostrich handbags, briefcases and change purses. **Louis Féraud,** No. 265, specializes in wearable ensembles in unusual prints, with styles that are classic. Another classic couturier, **Pierre Balmain,** has a boutique at No. 237, with slightly démodé styles.

Soft, fluffy mohair and cashmere sweaters for men and women are the speciality of **Richard Grand,** No. 229.

Heavy, dramatic jewellery that evokes ancient Greece is the signature of **Zolotas,** No. 370. His competitor, **Ilias Lalaounis,** at No. 364, has recently designed a glittering collection in carved rock crystal. Extravagant necklaces in leather, metal or even yarn are a theme at **Ancolie,** No. 233. More conservative animal pins and necklaces can be found at **Brecy,** No. 392. **Jean Vendôme,** No. 352, designs geometric pieces that approach sculpture.

Punctuating the luxury are the earthy aromas wafting from **Gargantua,** No. 284, one of the area's better charcuteries, where one can fuel a shopping trip with delicious, bite-size pastries and tiny sandwiches. More substantial fare can be found around the corner in the Place du Marché St. Honoré, which is solid with bistros.

L'Absinthe, No. 24, has a Belle Epoque décor, lots of pretty people and serves late, a disappearing tradition. The menu offers such specialities as duck with turnips. Across the square at No. 23, **La Sardegna** has acceptable Italian fare at modest prices.

Michelin gives a star to **Le Bistro d'Hubert,** at No. 36, which has a bistro on the ground floor and more serious food at serious prices upstairs; either way, it's nouvelle cuisine, sometimes good, sometimes overreaching. (It must also be mentioned that a group of American women recently received notably rude service here.)

Back on the Rue St. Honoré, **Goyard,** at No. 233, specializes in luxury luggage and leather goods. Reasonably priced made-to-measure shoes, in every colour imaginable, and boots for ladies are the attraction at **Le Savetier d'Aya,** No. 207.

To the west of Place Vendôme on Rue Cambon, **Chanel,** at No. 31, is still queen of the walk and guardian of the little suit. To go with your suit from the ready-to-wear collection, at somewhere around $1,000, you will of course need a matching silk blouse, several Chanel fake jewelled chains, beige sling-back shoes with black toes and perhaps a coat, if you can afford it.

Lanvin, at No. 2 Rue Cambon, has luxurious men's clothing and dashing hats. At **Andrea Pfister,** No. 4, you will find high-styled shoes that can be half the price they are in the United States. **Le Clan,** No. 20 has kilts, cashmeres and hand-knit sweaters for men and women. **Laura Biagiotti,** at No. 29, has Italian clothes such as cashmere dresses with lots of flair at high prices. Lacy lingerie is the speciality at **Cordelia,** No. 21, and **Cadolle,** No. 14, which also features figure-flattering beachwear and will do made-to-measure corsetry.

For eating in the neighbourhood, **Prunier Madeleine,** at 9 Rue Duphot, has lost its stars and its allure, but not its wonderful oysters and Art Deco architecture; shun the upstairs dining room. **La Table de Jeannette,** at No. 12, dishes up vaguely Gascon cooking. One block west, at 7 Rue Richepanse, the slightly less expensive **Chez Bosc** is a cosy, modern room (crowded with regulars at lunch) with excellent food and well chosen wines.

Leading into the Place Vendôme from the south is Rue de Castiglione. At No. 2, **Sulka** is trying to change its classic image with expensive, sharply tailored Italian menswear. **Willoughby,** No. 7, has created a fold-up hat for men and women. **Godiva,** on the corner of Castiglione and St. Honoré, has good factory-made Belgian chocolates. (Handmade is really far superior, though – try **Fauchon,** in the nearby Place de la Madeleine.)

The Rue du Mont Thabor, which intersects the Rue de Castiglione, is a good restaurant street. **André Faure,** No. 40, has a large hors-d'oeuvre selection and low prices. **Le Soufflé,** No. 36, serves light meals, as the name implies. To the north of the Place Vendôme on Rue de la Paix, one can find gorgeous fabrics for men's clothing at **Zegna,** No. 10, along with jackets in cashmere and suits in superfine wool. **Michel Swiss,** No. 16, on the second floor, is among the top perfume and cosmetic shops with generous discounts. **Tecla,** No. 2, specializes in pearls, marrying them with lapis lazuli, coral and jade.

For refreshment, **Harry's Bar,** just off the Rue de la Paix at 'Sank Roo Doe Noo' (5 Rue Daunou), is as popular with Parisians as with visitors, stocks 160 types of whisky and harks back to the 'Lost

Generation.' Diagonally across the street is a café serving beers from all over the world and plump mussels and *frites*, in the Belgian style.

Returning to the Place Vendôme itself, there is **Charvet,** at No. 8. Although the establishment's renowned made-to-measure shirts pale in comparison to the British products, there are nevertheless such worthy luxury items for men as silk shantung dressing gowns in deep, sensuous colours. **Guerlain,** at No. 2, sells its perfumes only from its own boutiques in Paris.

Finally, there are the grand jewellers. In jewellery as in fashion, Paris has both haute couture – or *haute joaillerie* – and ready-to-wear. The *haute joaillerie* shops cluster in and around the Place Vendôme. These are **Boucheron,** No.26; **Cartier,** 13 Rue de la Paix and Nos. 7 and 23 Place Vendôme; **Chaumet,** No. 12; **Mauboussin,** No. 20; **Mellerio,** 9 Rue de la Paix; **Poiray,** 8 Rue de la Paix, and **Van Cleef et Arpels,** No. 22 Place Vendôme. Prices are as high as anywhere in the world.

The juxtaposition of opposites is much of the delight of many quarters of Paris. Just to the east of the luxury shopping around the Place Vendôme, for example, are some of the best bargains in town. **Gigi's Soldes,** at No. 30 Place du Marché St. Honoré, off Rue St. Honoré, has shoes and boots for men and women at low prices. The shop also has a small selection of high-quality French and Italian handbags.

One block further east, at 31 Rue de la Sourdiere, is the **American Parfumery,** with a wide range of perfumes and cosmetics at 20 per cent off the retail price. And yet another block east, **A Vos Souhaits,** 49 Rue St. Roch, discounts such trendy designers' clothes as Castelbajac, Per Spook and Thierry Mugler.

Secondhand jewellery from the Place Vendôme's most famous names, but at considerably lower prices, is sold in several shops on the Rue St. Honoré between Rue Royale and the Place Vendôme. Try **Halphen Meyer,** No. 241; **Jansey,** No. 267; **Arthur Helft,** No. 366; **Oxeda,** No. 390; and **Gustave,** No. 416. The wares are still not cheap, however.

A reminder: non-French visitors should always ask for a refund of the value-added tax built into retail prices. Two conditions prevail: You must spend a minimum – recently about $100, but the exact figure varies from time to time – in one store and carry the goods and the refund document issued by the store through customs for inspection upon leaving the country. 'Discount' perfumeries often make an exception to the first rule. If purchases are made with a credit card, you can arrange to have the tax refund credited directly to your account.

THE RITZ THEN AND NOW

A. E. Hotchner

Ernest Hemingway, who introduced me to the glories of the Ritz Hotel, used to say: 'When in Paris, the only reason not to stay at the Ritz is if you can't afford it.' For Ernest, Paris was the Ritz Hotel, and vice versa.

'When I dream of afterlife in heaven,' he once said, 'the action always takes place in the Paris Ritz. It's a fine summer night. I knock back a couple of martinis in the bar, Cambon side. Then there's a wonderful dinner under a flowering chestnut tree in what's called 'Le Petit Jardin.' That's the little garden that faces the Grill. After a few brandies I wander up to my room and slip into one of those huge Ritz beds. They are all made of brass. There's a bolster for my head the size of the Graf Zeppelin and four square pillows filled with real goose feathers – two for me, and two for my quite heavenly companion.'

Not too long ago I spent the better part of a week at the Ritz, without heavenly companion, alas, but I can assure you that it is still worthy of Ernest's afterlife. It has changed little from what it was when the likes of Marcel Proust, Coco Chanel and F. Scott Fitzgerald stayed there; in fact, a complete $50 million face-lift has, among other things, provided new Persian and Chinese carpets in the entryways and stairs, a refurbishing of all the rooms and a restructuring of the dining facilities (with Chef Guy Legay, lured away from the two-star Ledoyen, now in charge). Hemingway's haunt, the Little Bar on the Cambon side, has been reconstructed; there are also plans in the works for a swimming pool and health centre.

I have stayed in a few hotels in the world more opulent than the Ritz, but what makes the Ritz unique for me is its aura of being not so much a hotel as a grand country house where I have been invited for a festive weekend. There is no lobby, as such, just an entry dominated by a noble staircase that rises beyond view. I did indeed sleep in a large brass bed festooned with down pillows; on awakening, I pushed a button on my night table and within minutes a porter appeared to light the wood fire in the fireplace that faced my bed.

There was virtually no wait for breakfast, nor for the *femme de chambre* who cheerfully took my shirts and returned then to me perfectly-laundered at 5 o'clock that afternoon. Although the ratio of employees to guests has been somewhat reduced from the two-to-one formerly maintained, there are nevertheless almost 440 employees to pamper the occupants of the hotel's 210 rooms. A third or more of these employees have been there for more than twenty-five years. André, who is on duty in the Vendôme entrance, told me he is in his forty-second year, and I knew Claude, in his fifties now and in charge of the Vendôme bar, when he was a seventeen-year-old groom running errands for clients of the Little Bar.

One day I lunched in the high-ceilinged, mirrored dining room with a friend who was disappointed when informed by the maître d'hôtel that *fraises de bois* were out of season and not on the menu. But my friend was subsequently heartened by the Belon oysters, caviar omelette, fresh asparagus with hollandaise and Montrachet wine that he was served. And then, precisely in time, a groom appeared carrying a square object covered with a wrapper of white cloth. He brought it to our table and handed it to the captain, who, in turn, peeled back the cloth to reveal a ruby-coloured collection of *fraises de bois*. To my friend's astonishment, the maître d'hôtel had risen to the occasion by dispatching the groom to Fauchon, the renowned delicacy shop where nothing is ever out of season.

The Ritz menu is extensive and varied, the unobtrusive service anticipates every need and the seventy tables are discreetly spaced. Unless you get carried away by the *carte des vins* (there are 120,000 bottles in the Ritz cellars), the bill is around $70 a person. About half the hotel's clientele is American, with only an occasional small tour group. Since no two rooms are alike, it is difficult to generalize about prices, but singles begin at about $150, doubles at $220 and small suites at $400 – with gradations all the way up to the Imperial Suite, which goes for $5,000 a day.

During the German occupation in World War II, the Ritz was the only hotel in the city where the Nazi brass shared occupancy with French civilians. The Ritz was divided down the middle, the Nazi bigwigs occupying the Vendôme side (Hermann Goering, for instance, had the Imperial Suite) while civilians were permitted to stay in the Cambon section, where people like Coco Chanel lived; the dining rooms and other areas were common to all the residents.

No side arms were permitted in the hotel – officers were obliged to check their weapons in a special gun repository situated just inside the Vendôme entrance. Goering's excuse for his extended stays at the Ritz was that it put him closer to the Blitz he was conducting against England. It also put him closer to all the art that had been confiscated from the Rothschilds and other Paris Jews, the cream of which Goering acquired for his great mansion near Berlin.

The unique quality that permeates the Ritz is, needless to say, directly attributable to the genius of its founder, César Ritz, who first opened its doors to the public in 1898. It is hard to believe that this man whose name has become synonymous with luxury the world over, this man who really invented the modern luxury hotel, was the thirteenth child in a poor peasant family that lived in the little Swiss village of Niederwald. He had scant education, and at sixteen he went to work as a busboy in a hotel dining room in the little town of Brig, which was close by. He only lasted a couple of months. When his employer discharged young César, he told him: 'In the hotel business you need an aptitude, a flair – you haven't a trace of it.'

There then followed a succession of jobs in restaurants from which Ritz was invariably fired after a brief tryout. But finally he caught on as a waiter in a Paris restaurant, and afterward worked in fashionable resort restaurants in Germany and Switzerland. By the time he was offered the managership of the troubled Hotel Savoy in London, he had evolved his own philosophy about running a hotel: See all without looking, hear all without listening, be attentive without being servile, anticipate without being presumptuous. He coined a phrase that has now become a cliché: 'The customer is always right,' he told his staff at the outset of his tenure at the Savoy. He put the kitchen in charge of an assistant chef he had met during one of his stints as a waiter in Paris, a chef by the name of Escoffier.

After turning the Savoy into one of London's grandest hotels, Ritz went back to Paris, with Escoffier, to try to realize his life's dream – to create a hotel that was uniquely in his image. And fundamental to this image was the concept that the hotel would be like a country house rather than the grand, ornate establishments favoured at the time. On the elegant, historic Place Vendôme he found just the place he had been dreaming of, a town house that had once been the residence of the Duc de Lauzun, who had commanded the French troops at Yorktown. The house provided the atmosphere Ritz wanted, that of a house in the country that might have been inhabited by French aristocracy. To that end he provided a lobby with no sitting room, elegant restaurants, garden areas for tea and drinks, a profusion of flowers raised in greenhouses that he ran himself and rooms of rather simple elegance, each with a wood-burning fireplace and furnishings that were costly reproductions of Louis XVI pieces to be found at Versailles. To extend the original house, Ritz acquired a building that backed up against it on the Rue Cambon.

From the day it opened its doors, the Hotel Ritz was the talk of Europe. The Vendôme and Cambon buildings were linked by a long corridor lined with display cases that contained some of the most luxurious and unusual items that Paris had to offer. It was, and is, aptly called 'Temptation Walk'.

The Ritz bathrooms had, and still have, a dimension and a marbled elegance all their own. One of their features is the king-size bathtub that was invented by César Ritz after the corpulent King Edward VII, who delighted in bathing with young lovelies, got stuck in an ordinary bath. Ritz also invented the king-size bed, indirect lighting and closets that are illuminated on opening the door. And he established the basic, now universal, raiment for the dining room: white tie for the waiter, black tie for the maître d'hôtel. He put brass buttons on the bellhop.

The bar on the Cambon side, presided over by the legendary Georges, became a focal point of Paris visitors, especially the fabled figures of the 1920's. President Teddy Roosevelt – laughing, big-voiced, robust – back from an African hunting expedition, surrounded by listening friends. The Prince of Wales, thin and dapper, constantly in the news because of his tumbles off his horse – and later, more importantly, when he abdicated the throne for the woman he loved. Garbo at the height of her career, often at an obscure table in the corner. Noel Coward at his special table; Scott Fitzgerald and Hemingway, sometimes arguing; Douglas Fairbanks, Sr., and Mary Pickford, holding hands; Winston Churchill and Duff Cooper, drinking Scotch; Rockefeller and F. W. Woolworth; J. Pierpont Morgan and his aide, Major Hodge; Andrew Carnegie; Tommy Manville and his wife of the moment; Wallace Beery, with his booming frog-voice and his infinite capacity for companionship and drinks. Dietrich, but never in pants.

Hemingway once told me about the evening he was having drinks in the bar with Scott Fitzgerald, when a rather decadent-looking Englishman came in with a young lady whose dazzling beauty excited Scott. Scott asked Georges to send out a groom to fetch a box of orchids, which he promptly sent to the beauty's table with a note suggesting that they meet at a later time. The young lady just as promptly rejected the box and sent it back to Fitzgerald, who opened it up and, in his misery, ate the orchids, petal by petal.

'The amazing part of it,' Ernest said, 'was that it worked and Scott got his way with that beauty. Afterwards, I always referred to such ruses and manoeuvres as the Orchid Ploy.'

Proust once explained his preference for the Ritz by saying, 'I prefer to be where there is no jostling.' There is still no jostling, and Proust would be as pleased with the dining room today as he was back then, when petite marmite at lunch and chocolate soufflé at dinner were his favourite dishes.

When César Ritz first opened his hotel he remarked, 'It is a little house to which I am very proud to see my name attached.' If he were alive today, he would be just as proud.

THREE-STAR GALAXY

Patricia Wells

What's the best restaurant in Paris? The search for perfection in Paris dining would certainly begin with the grand restaurants, the four that the Michelin guide has awarded its top three-star rating, meaning the dining rooms are not only worth a detour but a special journey as well.

But like many lists, the three-star designation tells you little. The four – L'Archestrate, Jamin, Taillevent and Tour d'Argent – are as different from one another as the seasons of the year. Each has qualities to recommend, each has its own shortcomings. Each appeals to different clientele and each has its staunch defenders and vigorous detractors.

In the end, each restaurant takes on the personality of the man responsible for its day-to-day operation. If you like what he projects, you'll like the restaurant. If not, you will not return.

L'Archestrate is proud and self-important, while Jamin is elegant and sophisticated, but in a forthright, cosy sort of way. Taillevent is discreet, attentive and well bred, while Tour d'Argent is theatrical and unabashedly bourgeois. And none can be understood in a single visit.

Taillevent and Tour d'Argent are restaurants of tradition. Diners go there to do business or socialize, to see and be seen. In some cases, paying more attention to the décor, service and amenities than the food. L'Archestrate is a veritable temple of nouvelle cuisine and people go for the food, to be surprised, to see what chef Alain Senderens is up to now, while Jamin, the newest of the three-stars, attracts the most serious gourmands, including the finest chefs of France, who come to taste Joël Robuchon's remarkable creations.

For some, dining in a three-star is a daily affair, for others it is a once-in-a-lifetime experience. Ideally, it should be a special event, like going to the opera or the theatre, one reserved for celebration or marking a special occasion. Since the bill is likely to average $50 to $75 per person, it ought to be very special indeed. If there's one mistake many out-of-towners make, it is to try to squeeze in all four in a single week's visit. Some visitors even turn suicidal, devouring two three-star meals in a single day. The overall effect is diluted, the meals begin to run together, and one hasn't the time to savour each experience.

People go to three-stars for different reasons. For some Parisians, places such as Taillevent and Tour d'Argent serve as private clubs where businessmen dine several times each week, conducting business well into the afternoon, finishing with a fine cognac and cigar. Travellers go to have a good time, to say they've been, to spar with Michelin, to collect three-star experiences. People who love to cook go to discover new dishes to try at home, while wine-lovers go to discover a new wine or sample an old, familiar one.

How, then, does one choose and how does one judge? I judge a restaurant by how I feel when I leave. Was the total experience pleasant? Did I feel as though my money was well spent? Did the lack of service obliterate any good feelings about the quality of the food on the plate? It's no secret and no surprise that the kind of experience you have often depends upon who you are, your age, your nationality, your sex, your mood at the moment and that of the chef. Here, then, are some observations on the Paris four.

TAILLEVENT

The Paris restaurant that comes closest to perfection. This clublike *hôtel particulier* embodies the qualities one looks for and comes to expect in a great restaurant: excellent food, comfortable surroundings, impeccable service and reasonable prices. The wine list is complete and most fairly priced, and whether you're a client who dines here daily or once in a lifetime, service is likely to be exquisite and democratic.

With its high ceilings, oak-panelled walls, antique cane chairs and crystal chandeliers, Taillevent's setting is much like a grand old salon, a bit dark, heavy and yet cosy and welcoming. One rarely leaves Taillevent disappointed.

It's no surprise that three-quarters of those who dine here come regularly, several times each week. Jean-Claude Vrinat, the owner and ideas man in the kitchen, oversees the dining room like a stern inspector, albeit a well-bred one, with nary a hair out of place. Over the years he has lightened and updated the cuisine, yet the food here is still quite classic, and far from trendy. At Taillevent, diners are graciously encouraged to share portions, a practice one rarely finds in grand restaurants. And if you display a bit of indecision – you can't decide between *foie gras d'oie* and *foie gras de canard* – the waiter will quickly offer you a small sampling of each.

With a staff of forty-eight to serve eighty diners at each meal, it's still Mr. Vrinat who pays attention to the most minute details, remembering diners who've come perhaps just once before, years ago, and sending out Christmas cards to those who have visited throughout the year. Here, each bottle of wine is personally sampled by Mr. Vrinat or one of the staff before being offered to diners. And mineral water is dispensed freely, and without charge, throughout the meal. Ask the sommelier for the wine lable, so that delicious Bordeaux can be remembered, and a few moments after the bottle is emptied he'll deliver a plain white envelope on a silver platter. Inside will be the wine label, neatly dried and flattened.

'I realize that, for many people, dining here may be a once-in-a-lifetime experience, and I don't want them to go away disappointed,' explains the director.

Mr. Vrinat echoes the words of the chefs and owners of other grand Paris restaurants when he explains that the average age of his clientele has dropped markedly during the last decade. While three-star restaurants were once reserved for well-heeled Frenchmen and foreign diplomats well on in years, the average diner is now in his thirties and may be American, Swiss, German or Japanese as well as French.

Taillevent offers many signature dishes you won't find elsewhere. While Mr. Vrinat conceives each new dish, it is his able chef, Claude Deligne, who carries out the instructions. The two dine together regularly, after the lunch hour is over, sampling, changing, updating dishes that will be added to the menu. Mr. Vrinat also uses regular diners as 'samplers' from time to time, offering them between-course tastings of new creations. Dishes that have become classics here include the *cervelas de fruits de mer*, a feathery light sausage of lobster, langoustine and pike, studded with bright green pistachios and black truffles, and the *pintade en pot au feu*, a fresh, farm-raised guinea fowl surrounded by crisp vegetables, including potatoes, carrots and turnips in an elegant sauce.

The wine list is extensive, and Mr. Vrinat attends to it with care, often spending the weekend visiting vineyards in search of worthy additions. The price range is equally varied. As the director says, 'When people look at a wine list, they shouldn't feel abused.'

Taillevent is also one of the few grand Paris restaurants without a 'table royale' or single, most coveted table. When one corner banquette did attract attention some years ago, the dining room was rearranged to make room for democracy.

L'ARCHESTRATE

Few Paris restaurants are as controversial as L'Archestrate. I have never been able to leave Alain Senderens' temple to nouvelle cuisine without my stomach churning in anger, even when I've dined better than I might almost anywhere else in France. Other critics, among them the food writers Henri Gault and Christian Millau, rate

L'Archestrate along with Taillevent as the top restaurants in Paris.

The problem most diners face at L'Archestrate is not the food, but the attitude: querulous and pretentious. If you pay more attention to your dinner conversation than to what is on your plate, the waiter pouts. If the sommelier does not approve of your wine selection, he'll wear you down with contentiousness until you cave in and let him have his way. Ask for a simple salad, and the waiter informs you that 'One does not come to L'Archestrate for a simple salad.' In short, the excellence of the kitchen is generally undermined by the attitude that the restaurant exists as a showcase for the chef and his staff, not for the pleasure of those dining here.

Alain Senderens goes to great pains to make the food perfect. He bakes his own bread with specially selected flour, twice a day. He makes his own chocolates and yet says, frankly, he doesn't think that most diners notice and, what's more, don't really care.

Annually he visits the Michelin offices to dicuss any shortcomings that have come to their attention during the year. He considers his restaurant the haute couture of food, yet says he could make more money if he opened a simple bistro.

L'Archestrate is the smallest of the Paris three-stars. There is a single tiny, elegant dining room decorated in shades of chocolate brown and terracotta, with contemporary cane wallpaper. With a kitchen staff of fourteen and a total staff of thirty, Mr. Senderens serves about thirty diners for lunch, fifty for dinner. Eighty per cent of those who dine at L'Archestrate order the *menu dégustation* priced at about $55, not including wine and service.

Mr. Senderens is scholarly, perhaps even brilliant, and his food is personal, and utterly nouvelle. Some diners complain that it is 'too Chinese,' with lots of unfamiliar, heavy spices, and that portions are too small. Whatever one's opinion, dining at L'Archestrate is always a culinary surprise.

The menu changes often and follows the seasons. Excellent dishes including the *salade de ris et de veau*, a colourful sweetbread salad that combines artichoke hearts, leeks and red peppers with a shower of fresh coriander and parsley; the *morue fraîche roti*, or fresh cod combined with aubergine purée and tiny, deep-fried julienne of courgettes; and a classic, bittersweet chocolate cake.

TOUR D'ARGENT

If you stopped a stranger on the streets of Paris and asked him to name the city's most famous restaurant, chances are he'd say Tour d'Argent. He might also know that the speciality of the house is duck, and that the view from the penthouse dining room overlooking Notre Dame is among the most coveted in Paris.

The restaurant's owner, reed-thin, nattily dressed Claude Terrail, is as much a bon vivant, raconteur, actor and politician as he is restaurateur. He sees dining at Tour d'Argent as theatre, as a festival, as history, as one of the utterly seductive experiences of Paris. Mr. Terrail compares Tour d'Argent to the Seine, Notre Dame and the Louvre, and views them all as public monuments. He says little about the food, and neither do those who dine here.

La Tour d'Argent is extremely popular with Americans, and on a given night you can hear more English than French spoken in the spacious, traditionally decorated blue and gold dining room.

'Some people write six to eight months in advance of a visit and say that they never come to Paris without dining here, and that their first or their last meal in France is always taken at Tour d'Argent,' explains Mr. Terrail. The restaurant, in fact, has one full-time employee who does nothing but handle correspondence for reservations.

The make-up of the 150 people who dine here each day is indeed remarkable. Presidents and ambassadors, company presidents and politicians come to 'La Tour' to get away from boardrooms and meetings, to gaze out across the Seine and share a great old bottle from the restaurant's famous cave.

The question of the 'best table' – the one with the clearest, most direct view of Notre Dame – is probably the only one that makes Mr. Terrail a bit nervous.

'I've solved it by never coming down for lunch or dinner until everyone has been seated. This way even my friends can't blame me when they don't get what they think is the best table,' he says with a laugh.

Many changes have been made during the last few years. The chef of some fifteen years was let go and replaced by the young, ambitious Dominique Bouchet, who brought with him his own staff of twenty. Slowly he's streamlined and updated the menu. Yet duck – of which they serve 450 each week – is still the dish to order.

JAMIN

Jamin's young chef and owner, Joël Robuchon, has risen to stardom quicker than any French chef in recent years. For many, the quietly ambitious and highly regarded chef appeared to come out of nowhere. Although Mr. Robuchon had quickly won two Michelin stars at the Les Célébrités restaurant in the Hotel Nikko in Paris, barely anyone, save a few critics (among them, of course, Michelin), knew of him.

Quietly, with little fanfare, he took over the long-established Jamin, which already had a strong reputation, in December 1981. Since that time Mr. Robuchon has astonished the culinary world with his solid and very personal style of cooking. He has taken several nouvelle cuisine concepts and conceits – smaller portions, new combinations and constantly changing seasonal menus – and created a stylishly beautiful yet hearty and full-flavoured sort of cuisine. His most popular dishes include a simple, thyme-flavoured lamb roast in a salt crust; salads showered with fresh, fragrant truffles; giant raviolis filled with langoustines; and some of the finest breads and rolls in town; all served in an atmosphere that is generally unpretentious and welcoming.

The dining room is small, serving just forty-five diners at each meal, decorated with chintz, floral-print tableclothes and bright, fresh flowers that create a light and discreet atmosphere for dining. The staff is young and dedicated, and one has the sense that they worked together as a team to get to the top, and are now humbly proud to be there.

Jamin, which is near the Trocadero, offers one of the city's best food bargains. It has a menu, available at both lunch and dinner, that is priced at about $20, not including wine or service. Although the menu is limited, and usually offers only a few choices, it does allow those on a budget to sample some of the finest, most creative food now available in France.

In any field, part of the game is keeping an eye on who is coming up from the minors. In Paris, chef-watching is indeed a popular sport.

Who will be the next Paris three-star chef, and when? Who are the rising stars? And why are some popular and famous restaurants left out of the guide altogether?

Michelin, the most powerful of France's hotel and restaurant guides, is cautious and conservative in its restaurant ratings. Even when the Michelin jury determines that a restaurant merits a change in rating, it usually waits a year or more before conveying its opinions via the guide. Ratings change slowly, and once stars are awarded, they're seldom taken away casually.

However, when the 1983 guide appeared, many were surprised to find the first change in the three-star lineup since 1980. Two three-star restaurants, **Grand Vefour** and **Vivarois**, were downgraded to two stars. Michelin explained that the restaurants were demoted because the chef-owners were not attentive enough, were too often absent and not in charge of their kitchens. Grand Vefour, 17 Rue Beaujolais (296-56-27), had held its third star since 1953, Vivarois, 192 Avenue Victor Hugo (504-04-31), since 1973.

It is unusual for a restaurant to gain a Michelin star during its first year of operation, but changes began occurring in 1982, when two Paris restaurants – **L'Ambroisie**, 65 Quai de la Tournelle (633-18-65), and **Quai des Ormes**, 72 Quai Hôtel de Ville (274-77-22) – were awarded stars just months after opening. L'Ambroisie was awarded two stars in 1983. Many hope such moves signal a change in what has been a rather hopelessly conservative rating system, a rigid one that does not seem to reflect France's rapidly evolving contemporary restaurant scene.

Both L'Ambroisie and Quai des Ormes are run by chefs who have worked in various three-star establishments, and both restaurants quickly attracted a steady clientele and positive notes from critics. When Parisian three-star chefs and owners were asked to name the chefs they were watching, both Bernard Pacaud of L'Ambroisie and George Masraff of Quai des Ormes were mentioned. One chef called Mr. Pacaud 'the most talented chef' he'd ever seen. Jean-Claude Vrinat, who observed Mr. Masraff's talents in the kitchens at Taillevent, declared that the Egyptian-born chef was one of the half a dozen in Paris 'worth watching.'

L'Ambroisie is a tiny, nine-table Left Bank restaurant with a simple but solid menu, refreshingly casual service and contemporary grey and burgundy décor. Quai des Ormes is larger, offering a small upstairs terrace for summer dining. The restaurant is having problems maintaining quality and service, and while Mr. Masraff is an inventive chef, many dishes are overambitious and overcomplicated.

Also on most chef-watcher's lists are the one-star **Guy Savoy**, 28 Rue Duret (500-17-67), and two-star **Michel Rostang**, 10 Rue Gustave Flaubert (763-40-77). Each chef runs a solid, welcoming establishment. Mr. Savoy's cuisine is more self-consciously nouvelle, while Mr. Rostang combines nouvelle conceptions with simpler, classic preparations.

Two newer Paris two-stars – **Le Bernardin**, 18 Rue Troyon (380-40-61), and **Au Trou Gascon**, 40 Rue Taine (344-34- 26) – are likely to maintain their ratings for several years, but both have the potential of joining the top ranks. If Le Bernardin, an elegant and popular restaurant that serves only fish and shellfish, were to receive three stars, it would signal an abrupt change for Michelin, which has up to now forced restaurants into a rather strict mould. The balance of the menu, the décor, the wine list – even the washrooms – of all the top establishments follow a rather strict formula, and up to now, no fish restaurant has been awarded three stars.

Alain Dutournier, chef-owner of Trou Gascon, has the kind of talent and ambition that may net him three stars, assuming he finds a more upscale location. Au Trou Gascon, currently located in the rather out-of-the-way twelfth *arrondissement*, in southeastern Paris, offers a blend of nouvelle cuisine and the heartier country dishes of France's southwest.

Among themselves, chefs even talk about 'buying' a third star, for they know that unless certain amenities – décor, the wine list, service and location – are attended to, Michelin will not upgrade them. A move to a new location, a greater sense of opulence or a larger menu and wine list gives the chef a serious chance at a third star, but even that only puts one in the waiting line, where there's lots and lots of competition.

And what about the wonderful restaurants that are not even listed in Michelin, such as the popular and still rather undiscovered **L'Ami Louis**, 32 Rue Vertbois (887-77-48)? Here, in a rather rumpled bistro in the forgotten third *arrondissement*, chef Antoine Magnin, well past his eightieth year, still holds forth. He serves up some of the best old-fashioned foie gras, a roast chicken that would stun your grandmother with envy, and some of the freshest sizzling fries in Paris. He's not listed in the Red Guide, and, what's more, doesn't care about a word from Michelin or anyone else. Perhaps that's the answer.

In the end, what does one do when a Michelin-rated restaurant pleases or disappoints? Write to Michelin. The 100,000 letters they receive each year are filed away with the ratings of the twelve male Michelin inspectors who travel about France throughout the year. The reaction of every single diner does, they insist, make a difference.

The following are the Michelin guide's top-rated Paris restaurants, with suggestions on when to go, and where to sit, and a few suggestions of special dishes. Note, however, that menus change frequently. Note closing days and holidays, and credit card information. The average bill is based on a first course, main course, dessert and half a bottle of wine priced at under $25. Reserve in all cases, either by mail or telephone. If reservations are made more than a month in advance, it is a good idea to reconfirm the day before.

L'Archestrate, 81 Rue de Varenne, Paris 7 (551-47- 33). The smallest and most expensive of the three-stars in Paris, featuring the very personal nouvelle cuisine of chef Alain Senderens. Received first star in 1970, second in 1974, third in 1978. Preferred for lunch, when the rather dark-toned dining room is more airy and welcoming. Menu dégustation, about $55, not including wine or service. Average bill: about $75. Closed Saturday and Sunday, first three weeks of August and Christmas week. Credit cards: American Express, Diners Club and Visa. Reserve two weeks in advance for dinner, the same day for lunch.

Jamin, 32 Rue de Longchamp, Paris 16 (727-12-27). The newest of the Paris three-stars, Jamin offers a small, bright and airy dining room featuring the solid, creative and modern cooking of chef/owner Joël Robuchon. Received first star in 1982, second in 1983, third in 1984. Equally appealing at lunch and dinner. Although there is no single preferred table, groups of six to eight will probably be happiest at one of the round centre tables, while couples may wish to be seated at the tables along the sides of the dining room, where the banquettes are very comfortable. Average bill: about $50 to $60. Menus at $17 and $43, not including wine or service. Closed Saturday, Sunday and the month of July. Reserve eight days in advance for dinner, three to four days ahead for lunch.

Taillevent, 15 Rue Lamennais, Paris 8 (561-12-90). The Paris three-star that comes closest to perfection, with pleasant, club-like dining rooms and the most careful service of just about any restaurant in France. It's also the least snobbish, and offers one of the most extensive and reasonable wine lists in France. Received first star in 1949, second in 1953, third in 1973. Best tables: all tables are good. Taillevent offers two equally appealing dining areas: a small dining room just off the entryway features well-spaced tables that provide exceptional dining privacy, while the main, oak-panelled dining room is very warming, with rectangular tables and comfortable banquettes. Good at lunch and dinner. Average bill: about $50. Closed Saturday, Sunday and holidays, Easter week, the last week in July and the first three weeks of August. No credit cards. Reserve one to two months in advance for lunch and dinner.

Restaurant de la Tour d'Argent, 15 Quai de la Tournelle, Paris 5 (354-23-31). The most famous and theatrical of the three-stars, with a spectacular view of Notre Dame cathedral. The famous wine cellar can be toured before or after the meal. First awarded three stars in 1939. When the restaurant re-opened after World War II, it was awarded two stars in 1949 and the third in 1951. Best tables: those near the window, looking out over Notre Dame and the Seine. Good at lunch and dinner, although one can dine less expensively at lunch. The daytime view, though a bit less romantic and theatrical, is equally appealing. At lunch there is a $25 menu that does not include wine or service. Average bill: about $70. Closed Monday. Credit cards: American Express and Diners Club. Reserve the same day for lunch, two weeks in advance for dinner.

THE SMALL HOTELS OF PARIS

Patricia Wells

Paris still offers some of the world's most charming little hotels. Many are narrow, four-storey affairs full of history and legend and sprays of fresh flowers, run by a fiercely proud owner who has dedicated his or her life to restoring, repainting and redecorating the establishment and to welcoming the assortment of international travellers who pass through the city.

Many travellers hoard their carefully compiled and hard-earned 'black books' of small Paris hotels and share their lists with only the closest, most deserving friends. When a friend of mine discovered that her preferred hotel would be included in this article, she quickly dispatched a letter revealing an acquaintance's guarded favourite. 'Why should others be spared total exposure?' she wrote, a bit vexed.

Some small establishments manage a loyalty usually reserved for football teams and next of kin and, like almost all Paris hotels, most of them are fully booked year round. It's no surprise. Frequent travellers fed up with hotel-modern want a touch of home when they travel, and that's what many small hotels offer, even if that touch of home translates as well-worn and threadbare.

Many small hotels lack the amenities of larger establishments – quick room service, an adjacent restaurant, a concierge to book a seat at the Opéra and an English-speaking staff – but most make up for that in other ways. Because the hotels are small and offer fewer services, the staff usually has more time to attend to a guest's personal needs, such as offering advice on restaurants, nearby shops and galleries. Even if the person at the front desk isn't the proprietor, he will have the same small-businessman's pride and will offer visitors a friendly, personal view of the city and the neighbourhood, a service one may not find in large hotels.

What follows are sketches of twenty-five small hotels, selected for a variety of reasons from the hundreds of small establishments in Paris. Each offers something special in the way of décor, location, individuality and price. Some need a touch of paint, most have unbearably small lifts, and some lack a doorman to handle baggage. Before you contemplate staying in one, also bear in mind that learning to love French décor can be much like learning to love the French. It requires patience and a lot of time, and in the end you may not succeed.

The selection of hotels, grouped by neighbourhood and all personally visited, is not meant to be exhaustive but to suggest a few spots that might make a stay in Paris more memorable. With the dollar worth approximately eight francs at this writing, even hotels that might have been out of reach a few years ago now seem like bargains. Rates for a stay of one night vary from a low of $21 for a single at the Vieux Marais to a high of $238 for a suite at L'Hôtel, an elegant establishment on the Left Bank. Unless otherwise noted, the rates given below indicate the range between a room for one person and a suite for two or more, and include tax and service. Remember that reservations are almost always necessary, in many cases far in advance.

THE RIGHT BANK

Régent's Garden, 6 Rue Pierre Demours, Paris 17 (574-07-30), forty-one rooms. This large town house on an active though relatively quiet market street not far from the Arc de Triomphe was built by Napoleon III for his personal physician. The hotel is in the process of being renovated, and the spacious, newly decorated rooms have a wonderfully homey feel, with large marble fireplaces, lots of intricate plasterwork, chandeliers and huge mirrors. Particularly pleasant in the summer, for many rooms overlook a large, flowered terrace and garden. No. 1, on the main floor facing the garden, has a certain appeal with its crisp, classic pink-and-white décor. One of the few small hotels to offer room service for such things as sandwiches and quiche and concierge service for booking theatres, restaurants and private tours. Rate: $44 to $61, plus $3 a person for breakfast. American Express, Diners Club, MasterCard, Visa. Reserve ten days to two weeks in advance.

Résidence du Bois, 16 Rue Chalgrin, Paris 16 (500-50-59), twenty rooms. Also an old Napoleon III mansion with a tiny front garden and a pleasant, park-like garden in the rear. The décor is a bit overbearing, with clashing prints and patterns, but the hotel offers calm and tranquillity just blocks from L'Etoile – now officially called Place Charles de Gaulle. Rate: $78 to $119, breakfast included. No credit cards. Reserve one to two months in advance.

Alexander, 102 Avenue Victor Hugo, Paris 16 (553-64-65), sixty-two rooms. This pleasant hotel is just a few minutes from Place Victor Hugo on one of the city's most fashionable streets, an avenue leading off from the Arc de Triomphe. The hotel's rooms and baths are larger than average and tastefully decorated. No. 122 is particularly nice, in shades of pink and brown, with a huge wardrobe and an enormous pink marble bathroom. Rate: $49 to $61, breakfast included. No credit cards. Reserve at least three weeks in advance.

Raphael, 17 Avenue Kléber, Paris 16 (502-16-00), eighty-seven rooms. A grand and elegant hotel with enormous rooms that make you feel as though you're hidden away in a very private mansion. Halls and many rooms are lined with dark, polished wood panelling. Many rooms have stone fireplaces, walk-in wardrobes and huge bathrooms. No. 7 on the main floor has Oriental rugs, a little sitting area and wood-panelled walls. Rate: from $68 to $125, breakfast included. American Express, Diners Club, MasterCard, Visa. Reserve several weeks in advance.

La Pérouse, 40 Rue la Pérouse, Paris 16 (500-83-47), eleven rooms, twenty-five suites. This is a luxury hotel, offering more services than most small establishments. There's a tiny, pleasant restaurant and bar and meeting rooms for conferences or meals. The hotel, built of stone around the turn of the century, was completely renovated in 1979. Rooms tend to have a bit of that chain-hotel look, but if it's size that you are after, this is the place. The suites are enormous, with all the big-hotel amenities, and immaculately clean. No. 63, one of the smaller rooms in the eaves, has a balcony just big enough to step out onto and a view of the Eiffel Tower. Rate: $93 to $188, plus $6 for breakfast. American Express, Diners Club, MasterCard, Visa. Reserve at least ten days in advance.

Atala, 10 Rue Chateaubriand, Paris 8 (562-01-62), fifty rooms. The huge garden at the back is superb, but the rooms lack charm and attention. For a spectacular view, ask for No. 82, with its large though tattered balcony and panorama of the city. Rate: $60 to $82, plus $3 a person for breakfast. American Express, Diners Club. Reserve at least ten days in advance.

Résidence Lord Byron, 5 Rue Chateaubriand, Paris 8 (359-89-98), twenty-six rooms. A calm, popular hotel off the Champs-Elysées, with trellised garden and tastefully decorated rooms, particularly Nos. 2 and 4. Two main-floor rooms in back look out onto the garden. Rate: $37 to $39, plus $2.50 for breakfast. No credit cards. Reserve two to three weeks in advance.

West End, 7 Rue Clément-Marot, Paris 8 (720-30-78), sixty rooms. A friendly, small, moderately priced hotel in an elegant quarter, full of great shops and little restaurants. Spotless and in the process of being redecorated. Highly recommended for single women: the front desk keeps a careful, concerned eye on who's coming and going. Rate: from $41 to $62, breakfast included. American Express, Diners Club, Visa.

La Trémoille, 14 Rue la Trémoille, Paris 8 (723-34-20), 104 rooms. A grand hotel with a lovely entry and sitting room and an intimate, luxurious feeling. Friendly staff, sparkling clean, calm, elegant décor, enormous bathrooms with live greenery. Air-conditioned. Recommended: No. 303, on the corner, with a little balcony and three large French windows overlooking the street; and No. 312, an elegant, large suite with a chandelier, Oriental rugs and coquettish, fabric-covered walls. Guests may sign for meals at the nearby Relais-Plaza, and the charges will be added to their hotel bills. Rate: $130 to $173 plus $5 for breakfast. American Express, Diners Club, Visa.

Roblin, 6 Rue Chauveau-Lagarde, Paris 8 (265-57-00), seventy rooms. The place to stay if you'll spend a lot of time at such food shops as Fauchon and Hediard or if you plan several nights at the Opéra, a five-minute walk away. Rooms are large, with an elegant French air. No. 3, facing the Madeleine, is enormous, with a large sitting area, pink faille spreads and a large marble fireplace. Rates: $44 to $56, breakfast included. Reserve two weeks in advance. American Express, Diners Club, Visa.

THE LEFT BANK

Solférino, 91 Rue de Lille, Paris 7 (705-85-54), thirty-four rooms. This is the cosy – and just slightly threadbare – sort of place that's nice to come home to after a long day's touring. Oriental rugs are scattered about; rooms are decorated with floral-patterned wallpaper; and Rue de Lille, one of the quieter Left Bank streets, lends a restful air. Rooms are tiny but reasonably priced, and there's a plant-filled breakfast and sitting room. No. 14 is especially pretty, decorated in warm shades of blue. Rate: $29 to $31, breakfast included. No credit cards. Reserve at least three weeks in advance.

Lenox, 9 Rue de l'Université, Paris 7 (296-10-95), thirty-four rooms. A calm and tasteful jewel, one of the few little hotels with crisp, contemporary décor. Completely renovated in 1976, it is popular with the fashion world and has a pretty little corner bar. Warm shades of grey and blue prevail, and there are several delightful rooms. Try No. 54, an attic duplex with tiny skylight and small balcony. Rate: $31 to $62, plus $2.50 a person for breakfast. Visa. Reserve at least ten days in advance.

Angleterre, 41 Rue Jacob, Paris 6 (260-34-72), thirty-one rooms. A classic small hotel. The rooms offer little in the way of charm, but the narrow, picturesque garden is appealing in summer, and there's a grand piano in the salon. Nearby is Le Petit St. Benoît, one of the neighbourhood's best bistros. Rate: from $33 to $44 plus $2.50 a person for breakfast. No credit cards. Reserve two weeks to a month in advance.

St. Germain-des-Prés, 36 Rue Bonaparte, Paris 6 (326-00-19), thirty rooms. This may not be the quietest hotel in Paris, but its location, just behind Café des Deux Magots, couldn't be more central. The staff is friendly, and the owner has taken great pains to restore the tiny seventeenth century building. No. 36, all in blue with antique armoires and exposed beams, is pleasant, as is No. 45. A little greenhouse garden graces the breakfast room. Rate: $43 to $46, breakfast included. No credit cards.

L'Hôtel, 13 Rue des Beaux-Arts, Paris 6 (325-27-22), twenty-five rooms. A delightful little hotel with giant sprays of fresh flowers, fabric-covered walls, antiques and marble baths. Just like home. The entrance is stunning, with a winding staircase, marble columns and stone floors. You can stay in the room where Oscar Wilde died or choose the room once occupied by Mistinguette, the Paris dance-hall star. Her room is an Art Deco dream, with the bed set on a pedestal and mirrors everywhere. Rate: from $106 for one or two to $238 for a suite for up to five guests. Breakfast is $6 a person. Reserve several months in advance.

Ferrandi, 92 Rue du Cherche Midi, Paris 6 (222-97-40), forty rooms. This sober little hotel on an active, though quiet residential street is popular with international businessmen. The blue-and-brown décor is basic but comfortable. Rooms look out at the sculptured façade of the Musée Hubert, across the street. The view from No. 43 is particularly good. The hotel has a lovely winding wood staircase and a quiet lounge for small, informal meetings. Down the street at No. 86 is Belusa, a cosy little tea shop where a collection of antiques such as teapots and cups and saucers is for sale. Rate: $39 to $60, plus $2.60 a person for breakfast. No credit cards. Reserve at least ten days in advance.

Abbaye St. Germain, 10 Rue Cassette, Paris 6 (544-38-11), forty-five rooms. This is a gem, oozing with charm, good taste, greenery and calm. The establishment, also known as Hôtel de l'Abbaye, occupies an eighteenth century convent and has a large, pleasantly decorated lobby. Ask for Nos. 2 or 3, on the main floor. They look out onto a trellised courtyard with a flower garden. Rooms are homey and elegant, with matching wallpaper and curtains, and all have marble baths. Rate: $46 to $53, breakfast included. No credit cards.

Esmeralda, 4 Rue St. Julien-le-Pauvre, Paris 5 (354-19-20), nineteen rooms. This hotel is in a class by itself and has a loyal following from the theatrical crowd. Rooms can be dim and rather dingy, but they have a particular charm and cosy clutter, and several offer a narrow view of Notre Dame and a direct view of the little park of St. Julien-le-Pauvre. The Esmeralda has a sauna, and there are three cupboard size rooms that go for an unbelievable $8 a night. Rate: $26 to $30, plus $2.50 for breakfast. No credit cards. Reserve at least two weeks in advance.

Colbert, 7 Rue Hôtel Colbert, Paris 5 (325-85-65), forty rooms. If it's a view of Notre Dame you're after, this hotel has it. Unfortunately the décor is a bit dingy and characterless, and the place is mildly musty. But No. 41 – a little studio with a sitting room and especially good view – can take your mind off the negatives. The hotel is convenient for Left Bank shopping and just a few blocks from President François Mitterrand's apartment on Rue de Bièvre, so you are well guarded. Rate: $29 to $44, plus $2.50 a person for breakfast. American Express, Visa. Reserve at least two weeks in advance.

ILE ST. LOUIS

Deux Iles, 59 Rue St. Louis-en-l'Ile, Paris 4 (326-13-35), seventeen rooms. A superb entrance hall with lots of flowers and greenery. Rooms are small, but there's a popular downstairs bar with a warming, open fire. Rate: $35 to $42, plus $3 for breakfast. No credit cards. Reserve at least a month in advance.

Lutèce, 65 Rue St. Louis-en-l'Ile, Paris 4 (326-23-52), twenty-three rooms. A gracious, well-appointed hotel, centrally located on Ile St. Louis. Small rooms, exposed beams and a friendly staff. Rate: $42 to $45, plus $3 for breakfast. No credit cards. Reserve at least a month in advance.

THE MARAIS

St. Merry, 78 Rue de la Verrerie, Paris 4 (278-14-15), fourteen rooms. This is unquestionably the most bizarre hotel in Paris. It not only backs onto the Gothic Church of St. Merri (for which it seems to be named, even though the spelling is different) but is also part of it. A flying buttress from the church edges into Room No. 9, forming a rather formidable canopy for the large, Gothic bed. Rooms are decorated with church pews (used as benches), Gothic chairs, Oriental rugs, highly varnished armoires and dark, demoniacal oil portraits. One of the hotel's wardrobes used to be a confessional, and a communion rail has been reincarnated as a banister. Certainly a curiosity for anyone who has tired of hotel-modern. Rate: $22 to $44, plus $2 a person for breakfast. No credit cards or lift. Reserve at least two weeks in advance.

Vieux Marais, 8 Rue du Platre, Paris 4 (278-47-22), thirty rooms. A friendly, unpretentious little hotel. Rooms are decorated in pink-and-blue floral prints, and there's a bright, pleasant breakfast room. Rate: $21 to $35, plus $2 for breakfast. No credit cards. Reserve at least two weeks in advance.

Bretonnerie, 22 Rue Ste. Croix-de-la-Bretonnerie, Paris 4 (887-77-

63), thirty-two rooms. A classic establishment, near Pompidou Centre. A restored seventeenth century town house with exposed beams, tasteful décor and tranquillity. No. 1 is a duplex, warmly decorated in blue and brown, with a first-floor sitting room and an upstairs bedroom. Rate: $27 to $35, plus $2 a person for breakfast. Master-Card. Reserve at least three weeks in advance.

Place des Vosges, 12 Rue de Birague, Paris 4 (272-60-46), sixteen rooms. Besides its reasonable price, the best thing about this tiny, rather characterless hotel is its location, just steps from the sixteenth century Place des Vosges, one of the most chic spots in Paris, with many boutiques carrying the latest fashions nearby. Rate: $25, plus $2 a person for breakfast. American Express, Visa. Reserve ten days to two weeks in advance.

A TOAST TO BEAUNE

Frank J. Prial

Beaune is a wine town. It is inhabited by wine shippers and wine growers, and it is invaded regularly by wine buyers and wine tourists. It stands on millions of gallons of wine in its cellars and is surrounded by thousands of acres of wine grapes. It would be possible to visit Beaune and ignore the wine, but it would not be easy. It would be like visiting Las Vegas and ignoring the casinos.

Beaune is the wine capital of Burgundy, and the embodiment of the Burgundian spirit. This is important: Burgundy is actually more a state of mind than a place. Even the French, who hunger after order as only a people who have no hope of achieving it can, have not tried to define Burgundy's borders. Burgundy as a political entity ceased to exist after the death of Charles the Bold, the last of the powerful Valois dukes of Burgundy, in 1477.

Today's Burgundy is a ruddy face under an old beret, the sound of a shotgun on a chill, autumn morning, the dark, foresty taste of the bird it killed. It is the twelfth century abbey at Pontigny, where Thomas à Becket sought refuge, now restored to pristine condition; it is the tranquil Canal de Bourgogne, defined by rows of poplars standing with military precision along its banks. It is good food in fine restaurants and it is the wines whose sonorous names are almost as delightful as the wines themselves: Montrachet, Monthelie, St.-Veran, Savigny, Santenay, Richebourg, Romanée, Pommard, Puligny. It is the tiny villages that produce the wines, most of them consisting of only a few houses, in spite of their international renown – such places as Aloxe Corton, Meursault and Nuits-St.-Georges, with their little museums, cellars for tasting, modest restaurants and cafés where feet can be rested and thirsts slaked with beer, not wine. Wine only makes you more thirsty.

At the centre of all this, about three and a half hours from Paris by the Autoroute du Sud, is Beaune. Beaune, with its narrow cobbled streets and old houses, its ancient trees and hidden gardens, its steep roofs and handsome ramparts. Beaune also with its fleets of tour buses and their sheeplike passengers, its overpriced gift shops and its endless signs: STOP HERE AND TASTE. DIRECT SALES OF WINE. VISIT OUR CELLARS.

The pace slows in autumn. The vines and the leaves on the trees turn red and yellow, and if the year promises a good harvest there is a sense of excitement in the air. Many, but not all, of the summer's tour buses are gone, and there are rooms to be had – at the **Hôtel de la Poste,** which is as much a Burgundy landmark as Beaune itself, at the attractive little **Le Cep** and at the half-dozen or so other hotels in and just outside of town.

'One must have time to live,' the French say, and there is time in Beaune in autumn. Time to visit the cool, dark cellars, to taste the wines, to stroll around the ramparts and through the little wine museum installed in one of the former residences of the dukes of Burgundy. There is time to wander through the church of Notre Dame, with its deep porch, typical of Burgundian architecture, and its superb late fifteenth century tapestries depicting the life of the Virgin. And there is time, above all, to savour the riches of the Hospice that was founded by Nicolas Rolin, Chancellor of Burgundy, in 1443.

The Hospice, which has been a working hospital since its founding, is actually two major buildings, the Hôtel-Dieu and the Hospice de la Charité. The Hôtel-Dieu is Beaune's grandest attraction, with its perfectly preserved Burgundian-Flemish architecture and priceless art collection. Its sombre stone façade is surmounted by a vast, steeply sloping roof, tiled in a lozenge pattern of red, yellow, black and white. Inside, its most striking feature is the Grand'Salle, or Paupers' Room, 160 feet long, still displaying the original fifteenth century furnishings, including the twenty-eight red-canopied and red-curtained beds used by the patients of five centuries ago. The Hôtel-Dieu is open all year long, and the modest entrance fee buys a guided tour (no individual visits permitted) of the Grand'Salle, the old pharmacy and kitchen and the museum full of art treasures.

The masterpiece of the museum — and, indeed, one of the masterpieces of the whole canon of western art – is the polyptych of the *Last Judgement* by the Flemish artist Roger van der Weyden that Chancellor Rolin commissioned to hang in the Grand'Salle. Also on display are superb tapestries, among them the covers once used on the beds in the Grand'Salle. Elsewhere in the Hôtel-Deiu can be seen some of the habits worn by the Dames Hospitalières, the nuns who ran the hospital until 1961; several collections of rare pewter and the visitors' book of the hospital, opened to the signature of Louis XIV.

But, like most places in Beaune, the Hospice is also concerned with wine. It owns pieces of vineyards all over Burgundy and, each year on the third weekend of November, sells its wine at auction. For prominent wine buyers throughout the world, attendance at the auction, at least every two years or so, is de rigueur.

The wines, which are only two months old, are available for tasting on Saturday morning in the Hospice cellars and are auctioned the next afternoon in a draughty, chilly hall in the centre of town. The prices are unconscionable because the high bidders like to get the publicity, and besides, the money goes to charity.

The Hospice auction weekend is the most exciting in Beaune's calendar but not necessarily the best time for a visit, unless you are in the wine business. All the hotel rooms and all the best restaurants are booked long in advance; waiters, clerks and guides are harried, and it is difficult not to feel left out when everyone else in town is dashing off to dinners, parties and tastings.

But a happy few will not be left out. They will have received invitations to one of the grand dinners given at the Clos de Vougeot. There are seventeen a year, eight in the autumn and eight in spring, as well as one on the feast of St. Vincent, patron of wine makers, in January. The most important are the three that coincide with the auction at the Hospice. They are called Les Trois Glorieuses – The Three Glorious Evenings.

The Trois Glorieuses and other festive dinners are the preserve of the Confrérie des Chevaliers de Tastevin, a promotional group created during the Depression to promote Burgundian wines. Its members rig themselves out in mock-medieval robes, give big dinners, drink good wines and manage to have a lot of harmless, if fattening, fun.

The Chevaliers own the **Clos de Vougeot,** a former monastery a few miles north of town in the middle of the vines. The main hall of the Clos seats 550 people, and that is how many are invited to each Confrérie dinner. The dinners are for members of the Confrérie and occasionally their friends; now and again an unconnected visitor manages to wangle an invitation through the management of his hotel. Each dinner costs about $100.

Imagine the scene: It is a cold November night. A half dozen Americans are sitting around the lobby of the Hôtel de la Poste, dressed in evening clothes, sipping champagne. They are trying to look as if they always sit around the lobby of the Poste in evening clothes, drinking champagne. Actually, they are nervous.

The Americans think that a dinner at the Clos de Vougeot is serious business. They adjust their ties too often and discuss the vintage self-consciously. At the appropriate time they climb into their rented cars and head north. They get a huge surprise. There is singing, shouting, much backslapping and laughter. Wines are rarely mentioned, and no one seems to care whether or not any of the Americans knows the difference between a Beaune Clos des Mouches 1961 and a jug of Spanish plonk bottled last week. The most profound wine comment is a sip, a frown, a big smile, a dig in the next man's ribs and a 'Hey, hey, not bad, eh, *mon vieux?*'

The truth is that, like much in and around Beaune, the dinners at the Clos de Vougeot have only one purpose – to sell wine. But the sight of the Clos, dark against a full moon, with a blaze of light spilling into the courtyard as the guests enter – this is very stylish selling.

As for buying wine in Burgundy, it is probably better not to, unless you know what you are doing. Knowledgeable buyers who have a supplier they know and trust can do well, but the casual tourist must rely on the shops around the Place Carnot in Beaune, where prices are often higher than they are in New York. Better to taste around, try different wines with meals, then search them out back home. It is likewise better not to visit Beaune without reservations. Not just hotels, but also restaurants, are apt to be booked months in advance for the best autumn weekends. The restaurants are not to be missed – Burgundian food can be as glorious as Burgundian wine. It is, traditionally, hearty fare, the food of farmers hungry after long days in the fields and vineyards. Snails cooked in their shells, coq au vin, an enormous variety of sausages and salamis, terrines of pork and veal, all kinds of game in season – these are the bases of the best Burgundian cooking. Beaune has two excellent restaurants, the new **Auberge St. Vincent** and that of the **Hôtel de la Poste** presided over by Marc Chevillot, whose brother runs two New York restaurants, La Petite Ferme on Madison Avenue and Les Tournebroches in the Citicorp Building. (Mr. Chevillot, who speaks perfect English, might as well be the mayor of Beaune as far as visitors are concerned – besides offering his own fine table, he knows where the best country restaurants are, the best drives through the vineyards, and the best places to buy gifts and wine.)

Just outside town, in an old house, **Au Petit Truc** is a country restaurant in the best tradition; Gault and Millau commend it highly and award it special marks for décor (the Michelin guide has not yet listed it). There are only twenty covers, so reservations are essential. **L'Ermitage de Corton,** in nearby Chorey, to which Michelin awards a star, is excellent, as are the one-star **Rôtisserie du Chamertin** in Gevrey-Chambertin and the moderately priced **Relais de la Diligence** at Meursault. And at Chagny, ten miles south, is the **Hôtel Lameloise,** with only twenty-five rooms, but with a restaurant that may be classified as a temple of gastronomy, one of the score to which Michelin gives its three-star rating.

These restaurants are not inexpensive, except by New York standards: a dinner of such specialties as terrine of salmon and sole, crayfish in cream sauce and roast quail at the Hôtel de la Poste can easily cost $50 a person with wine, even when the dollar is strong, while at Lameloise a meal of foie gras with red currants, steamed salmon and roast hare can be slightly more.

Yet the wine remains the thing. It is not a bad idea to write to Beaune shippers for appointments to see their cellars – some, though admittedly few, offer no tours or tastings; other are particularly hospitable to visitors who write in advance. In any event, never hesitate to take wine tours or to visit vineyards because of a fancied or real lack of knowledge of the subject. The Beaunois have been spreading the word about their wines since Pliny wrote about the Gauls drinking wine at Auxerre in the fifth century. The present-day Gauls will be happy to tell you whatever you need to know, and to sell you a couple of bottles as well.

PROVINCE OF HIDDEN TREASURES

Frederic Raphael

'Whereabouts in the South of France do you live exactly?' people sometimes ask, in a tone implying precise knowledge of the untrodden tracks between the Grand Hôtel du Cap-Ferrat and the three-star restaurants of Mougins and La Napoule, those magnets for travellers for whom heaven itself will have to be on American Express or they won't want to go. Actually we cannot claim to belong to that South of France at all, even though the mimosa flowers as frothy-yellow and as early in our sheltered valleys as it does on the slopes behind Cannes.

The department of the Dordogne, where we do live, lies in the southwest of France; our climate, though temperate, is Atlantic, not Mediterranean. The region lacks the *douceur* of Provence, but winter is seldom prolonged, or very cold – though our eaves have once or twice been fringed with alpine icicles. But March is not always warm nor July always hot; we can be bombarded by summer storms, the sky exploding in a volcano of white nimbus, the rain daggering thick gravy out of the terrace. Yet there is always hope: The most sullen day can yield to a golden-delicious evening with a Turner sunset.

Dordogne is a great shield-shaped province, with a prominent east-pointing nose to spoil its hexagonal symmetry. This nose, which appropriately includes Cyrano's hometown of Bergerac, sniffs at Bordeaux, without quite reaching it.

But to say that we live 'in the Dordogne' would, to a Frenchman, imply that we were fish: 'the Dordogne' refers always to the river, not the district. To the native, our region is the Périgord, rarely 'Dordogne'; its inhabitants Périgordins, never Dordognais.

There have been residents here since before the dawn of history. The oldest *gîtes*, or cave shelters, had tenants some thirty thousand years ago, give or take a millennium. Our first visit here was during a hot March more than twenty years ago. We were driving toward the Mediterranean and decided to make a large detour to take in the caves at Lascaux, then open to all. (The remorseless lichens, brought to life by the oxygen imported with the tourists, had not yet started to consume the bison, deer and bulls which nameless genius had pastured on the walls.) The caves have now been sealed against outside air, and Montignac, a riverside town briefly rich on the paintings' fame, has relapsed into a holiday centre *'comme les autres.'*

The now undisputed mecca for prehistorians is Les Eyzies, where excellent restaurants, particularly the **Centenaire** (Michelin gives it two stars), impeccably run by young Alain Schooly, compensate for the rather raw, charmless village. Limestone cliffs, riddled with as many holes as an Emmenthal cheese, dominate and pinch the main street. The vicinity offers a mazy and amazing variety of caves that, though they lack the astonishing dimensions of Lascaux, contain murals in both black and white and full colour. For my money, however, the most evocative site is just outside the strict Dordogne boundaries, at Cougnac, near Gourdon, where the cave paintings all but equal the vividness of Lascaux.

But the richness of the prehistoric heritage does not merely cower in the recesses of hillsides or do time in the many small museums. It is present in the fabric of the land. On our first trip, in 1956, we went to buy some wine and discovered the farmer to be an amateur archaeologist in the nicest sense. He was in love with the region's past. On a walk round his smallholding, at Sergeac, above the V-shaped banks of the trout-rich Vezere, he bent down and scratched at the red-brown earth. He came up with a tooth the size of a little finger. 'Sabre-toothed tiger,' he said. In that moment, I was converted to the Périgord.

It may be that the farmer regularly buried that tooth, the better to enchant naïve visitors, but I think not. Fossils are ubiquitous and bones no rarity; any rooting bulldozer unearths abundant hunting grounds for the part-time paleontologist. The riches of the stratified rock are even said to include gold, though luckily in insufficient quantities to provoke a Klondike.

The châteaux of the Périgord lack the flashy narcissism that turns the Loire Valley into a string of fat pearls. Here were the homes of fighting men, not pampered favourites or bewigged financiers. Although nothing now seems more peacefully reminiscent of *vieille France*, the region did not become unquestionably French until well into the fifteenth century, when the English were finally evicted, though they never fully lost their footing: Bordeaux owes its prosperity not least to the English appetite for claret. It is not, I like to think, mere wishful thinking to believe that English-speaking tourists are particularly well received in Aquitaine. On a visit to the looming castle of Sauveterre, with its honeycomb vaults for storing corn against a siege, we were greeted by the custodian with the assurance that he, too, was *'anglais'*. Neither accent nor style confirmed this, but his name, he said, was Freeman, and his family had been there since the Hundred Years' War.

The châteaux and fortified villages vary from unadorned strong-points to elegant, if rugged, aristocratic seats. The château of Biron, in the extreme south of the Périgord, combines both elements; it contains both a surly donjon and a graceful chapel within its high-shouldered enceinte. We visited it recently on a day of precociously springlike weather, with the whole landscape seemingly reserved for our private pleasure, under a sky worthy of Greece. (The poet Byron springs from a branch of the Birons who supposedly accompanied William the Conqueror to England.) We scarcely passed another car as we cut through the oak, chestnut and pine forests, home of the furtive truffle, the bulbous cèpe and the other flukish fungi that, in their season, enrich local menus. In the clearings, sudden deer bounced, dithered and sprang for cover. The sawn wood stacked along the side of the road in precise lengths was typical, in its practical and harmonious beauty, of the local style. Périgord farmers and merchants may be self-centred, but they also subscribe to a communal tradition that graces everyday tasks with respect for nature. Craft and craftiness conspire to repay the generous earth with due interest.

When we reached Biron and stood in the commanding *place d'armes* within its walls, it seemed that we were on the hinge of the world. The low hills curved toward the gleaming valley of the river Lot to the south; to the north, the earth bent to a silvery green horizon where the Dordogne shone under the last of its mist. The Renaissance chapel of Biron was built after one of the warrior counts had returned, with culture and profits, from Italy; the chapel's founder is entombed in front of the altar. His sarcophagus is decorated with panels depicting the resurrection of Lazarus, under which, as a sort of three-dimensional footnote, is a row of smiling skulls, happy to know that they too can one day expect a new coat of flesh.

We have now had a house here for almost thirteen years. Like all newcomers, we like to imagine that we arrived before the rush. It is a quiet life, but not a dull one.

Our nearby village, like most, has become increasingly depopulated since 1945. On our hilltop, before the war, there were eleven *feux*, or hearths; now there are two. Yet village life does not lack vitality: there are fairs, weddings, dances and fêtes. The young are less inclined to leave the land than they were a decade ago; the recession makes them count the blessings of self-sufficiency. The tractor has replaced the horse and the oxen, once necessary for the heavy ground, but the mixed farm, with its picturesque, noisy yard, is still the rule. The farmer and his wife are equal partners, almost, and to watch them ride out, high on their tractors, to harvest or planting is to see how essential women now are to the farm economy.

The deep freeze and convenience foods are here to stay, but our friend and neighbour, Christianne, still kills her fatted pig in January and prepares many weeks' pleasure and sustenance from its meat. The essence of Périgord cookery lies less in its luxury than in the cook's wily use of every scrap. Christianne's kitchen, during the days after the slaughter, is full of bowls and tureens in which joints are marinating, fat is being hardened, offal conserved for pâtés and *rillettes* and blood saved for *boudin*, a rich black sausage to be savoured in thin slices over a glass of homemade cassis.

The habit of generosity works alongside calculation. No favour is asked here without another being rendered; none is given without balancing the recompense. The farmer may work for himself, but he will lend 'days' to a neighbour when there is a harvest to gather or an emergency to meet. The *vendange*, or grape picking, is a party as well as a back-breaking chore. A sixth sense – and a wide cousinage – alerts the whole *coin* (the Périgordin refers thus to his own corner of this many cornered land) when something goes wrong. A death will bring comfort from all over, a stream of visitors to share and allay grief. The sense of community does not preclude rivalry and enmities of course, but it is strong and magnanimous.

There is one piece of furniture that perhaps typifies the district: very occasionally, in old farmhouses, you may still see a table with bowls scooped out of the wood in front of each diner's place. Channels run from a central point to each individual hollow. The custom was for the cook to pour the soup directly onto the table. Thus all the diners were served at once, without precedence. What happier symbol of ingenious and labour-saving equality?

The pleasures of the Périgord are legion, but they are not for sale. This is a *pays* in which to lose yourself, and find yourself, a Virgilian landscape of neat valley farms and of bony hillsides buzzing with bees, of trout streams and game, of crutched walnut trees, towering chestnuts, rooty oaks, and of figs, never olives. It is a land of sudden vistas, craggy castles and steepling hill towns (Domme is a beauty), of trooping sunflowers and unpretentious vines (yielding 'small' but refreshing wines). Do I know where you can still get a sumptuous meal of six or seven courses for less than $10 a head? Certainly I do, but – forgive me – I shan't be telling you. You must develop a nose for your own truffles.

One thing: you will find no Riviera sophistication here; you have been warned – and promised.

PREHISTORIC ART AND ARTIFACTS

The major display of locally discovered palaeontological artifacts is in the **Musée National De Prehistoire** at Les Eyzies-de-Tayac, a small town situated on the Vézère River, about twenty-five miles southeast of Périgueux. The museum, installed in a twelfth century fortress, contains objects and works of art from the many caves along the river. Exhibits are arranged chronologically, with helpful explanatory charts. The museum is open daily except Tuesday, 9.30 am to 12 am and 2 pm to 6 pm. Admission about $1.50 on Sunday.

The nearby cave at **Font-de-Gaume** is painted with horses, bison and mammoths; the one at **Combarelles** has drawings of nearly three hundred animals. There are guided tours daily except Tuesday, at 9 am, 11 am, 2 pm and 5 pm; admission: $1.

Other displays are at **Les Gisements de Laugerie,** northwest of Les Eyzies; the **Musée de Périgord** at Périgueux; the **Fernand Desmoulin Museum** at Brantome, seventeen miles north of Périgueux; and at the **Ernest Rupin Museum** at Brive-la-Gaillarde, forty-five miles east of Périgueux.

A reproduction of the Lascaux caves at Montignac, which have been closed to the public since 1963, is scheduled to be open to the public in about two years.

BRITTANY'S RUGGED NORTH COAST

Richard Eder

There are, to be sure, single-purpose holidays: to see Europe, to get a suntan, to improve your tennis. But single purposes torment us all year; and we wear out lopsidedly, like the rug beneath the dining-room table. To go to northern Brittany and sit for a month is restorative vagrancy: living at walking speed, pursuing small and easily distracted objectives, and coming away with a harvest of particularities.

None of them add up to a theme: artichoke fields in moonlight, a duck race, sheets flapping in a thunderstorm. Ernestine's recollection of drowned sailors, a derelict circus, Irish folk musicians in a Breton castle, and grey-green fields meeting the sea, a frontier between cows and oysters.

It all started with Mme. Papillon, a vigorous and helpful friend of my wife's. It is she who got us to this corner of Brittany that calls itself the Wild Peninsula and is famous for nothing but quiet farms, rocks, coves, and a high, gentle light.

My family had been in Paris less than a year, and already had found that Parisian polish is achieved by a great deal of polishing. It is a fine city but not a peaceful one; a lovely show, and continual backstage nerves. In the summer, Parisians have come to the end of their rope, and they do not so much take a holiday as die out for a month.

We needed a place to die out in, but had left things too late for the normal process of finding a summer house. 'I have found your house,' Mme. Papillon announced, coming over one day, 'at the super-market.' An ad was pinned up in the store, and she had preemptively removed it and brought it to us. It showed a low stone farmhouse behind a white wall.

We did not go to see the house, we went to see the advertiser. M. Arhant is a Breton engineer who lives in Paris; he and his wife and five children received my wife and me and three or four of ours, and in about five minutes we were eating cookies and making shy jokes. We were also quite certain that this house in fields above the sea was what we wanted. Créch Arhant was the name of the house. 'You will find it on the map,' M. Arhant said with satisfaction.

All the country in the north peninsula between Treguier and Pleubian – two small towns – is criss-crossed with tiny roads, each bearing signs for houses or farms or infinitesimal hamlets. Divided by high earth hedges, the small farms are worked hard and held onto hard; every bit of land has a name attached to it, and the fields are ploughed right down to the sea, so that the tractors can reach some of them only at low tide.

It is rolling country, a whole range of brilliant and darker greens. Herds of black-and-white cows graze on it, and on the long inlets below, oystermen set out their frames. All day long there is the gentle, cicadalike sound of small tractors cultivating potatoes and artichokes. The artichokes grow stiff and spiky, each head thrust straight up in the air from a rigid stalk. An artichoke field is a series of exclamations in a difficult language; by moonlight it looks like a gathering of Red Queens from Tenniel's illustrations for *Alice's Adventures in Wonderland*.

Brittany is cool and cloudy despite the efforts of local chambers of commerce that put out statistics picturing it as sunnier than the Riviera. The north coast peninsulas, however, boast a microclimate that does, genuinely, produce a great deal of sunshine. It is in short bursts: In the whole month of July there were only four or five days without a morning or an afternoon of sun.

The local people, who treat visitors with a hospitable solicitude, are genuinely unhappy when the weather misbehaves. Every morning, when I walked a mile into Kerbors – the nearest hamlet – for bread and milk, the shopkeeper would explore the weather on my behalf. 'You see, we had a beautiful sun yesterday,' she would say, as drizzle blurred the shop window. And: 'You will see, by noon it will clear,' Usually it did.

Crèch Arhant is what grey stone French farmhouses are supposed to be and frequently are. Dark beams, red tile floor, huge fireplace, simple but comfortable furniture and the sense of sheltering inside a natural organism like a bear in a hollow tree. It had three small bedrooms, two of them upstairs, a bathroom with a shower, a bright kitchen with a small stove and refrigerator and a doll-size partly automatic washing machine that chugged along cheerfully through the day and only once in a while flooded over. The stove and water heater were fed by butane gas from a white whale of a tank in back.

It stood in a front garden that turned into a field in back, and on top of a hill overlooking the long estuary that runs from Treguier into the English Channel. The sun would set around 10.30 across the estuary, and for an hour afterward a scarlet sky would subside into silver and dark blue, and the green ferns on the far bank would fade to grey and black.

There was walking and swimming and exploring during the day, but the house held the morning and evening, and the value of things done for their own sake. Hanging laundry out to dry: a sea-wind blows it against you, a cloudburst drenches it, and a quick sun bakes in the smell of the country. Washing dishes after a slow breakfast, and listening to BBC's Radio Four, with its sermons, hymn-singing and radio plays.

Our part of Brittany lacks the long sand beaches of the south coast, but for that reason it lacks the big resorts and resort hotels. The coast is hills, crags and islands and pinnacles of rocks, with small sand beaches scattered among them. At Pors-Hir the meadows break into giant rock formations – one enormous boulder has a house literally growing out of it – and below them a perfect semi circle of a sand-and-shingle beach harbours a few German and English picnickers, and many more French. The water, a deep blue-green, bites at the first shock and then braces.

At Ploumanach, down the coast to the west, there is an extraordinary mile-long garden of sculptured rock – boulders as big as three-storey houses, gnarled and shaped fantastically by the waves and sand into animals, fists, faces: They are like stone clouds rolling over the land's edge. At Le Yaudet the woods plunge down to the water from a high hill, on top of which is a chapel in which hang carved wooden ship models, ex-votos from sailors saved from storms.

Inland are castles, ancient ruins and Druidic stones. At La Roche-Jagu, a castle set in a park, we heard four young Irish musicians play jigs and reels and sing folk songs. Brittany is Celtic, and in the summer there is scarcely a village hall or church that does not have an Irish, Scottish or Welsh group making music in it.

There were the towns and the markets. Pleubian, not much more than a village, was three miles away. Three times a week a dusty grey panel truck would pull into its square, and the driver would open the back door to reveal a glittering, twitching array of fresh-caught fish, brown lobsters, long grey eels and oysters. Pleubian has its supermarket, but besides the things you would find anywhere in France there were local products: big jars of Breton honey, round dark loaves of bread and racks of Gros Plant, the pungent white wine of the area that sells for seventy-five cents a bottle.

Treguier, across the estuary, is the jewel of the region. A hillside town with streets of half-timber houses leading down to the port, it is dominated by St. Tugdual's, a Gothic cathedral dating from the thirteenth to the fifteenth century. The cathedral, built of a grey stone that turns biscuit-coloured in the afternoon, with delicately traced arches, contains the tomb of St. Yves, patron saint of lawyers. It forms one side of the tree-shaded central square. Shops and cafés line the other three sides; and every fifteen minutes the bells chime out the St.

Yves Canticle, lopsidedly as if trying to work it out.

When our house overflowed – we had anywhere from three to five children with us at various times, arriving and departing, along with various house guests, on the express between Paris and Brest, thirty miles to the south – we lodged guests in Chez Anny, overlooking the cathedral. It was both extremely simple (no television and no outlets for electric shavers, noisy bar) and inexpensive (about $9 double).

As well as endless cups of coffee in the square, or buckwheat crêpes and cider, Treguier offered **Le Petit Savoyard**. 'One eats well there and lots,' a neighbour told us. Indeed: a huge and splendidly prepared meal – say, tomato salad, quiche, pork chops and roast potatoes, green salad, cheese or dessert for the equivalent of $5. House wine for $2.50 a bottle. A smiling waitress. Bliss.

Other trips were made to village kermesses, or fairs; one, held by the sea, featured a competition in which swimmers raced after a duck whose wings were clipped to keep it in the water. Once we were held up for miles of hairpin curves behind the twenty-seven trucks of the American Circus. One evening in Paimpol we caught up with it: a rackety European company that tours the hinterland and offers, among other things, a first-rate elephant act and a strongman who invites local stalwarts to come out and match him. Its climax is a grand procession to the tune of 'The Battle Hymn of the Republic.' The master of ceremonies emerges as Abraham Lincoln in a false beard and mournful look, and the Gettysburg Address is boomed out in French.

Most of our longer expeditions were by car, but often we would go on five- or six-mile treks. Walking, we discovered that the golden hills were composed of millions of tiny daisies; we found time, on the road and in the cafés where we rested, to talk with people. Kind, generous to strangers – when two of my sons stopped at a farmhouse to ask directions, the farmer invited them in, gave them cider and talked to them at length about America and France – they are Breton-speakers, whose French carries an accent that sounds comically English.

Our friend and guide was Ernestine, a rosy-faced, square-built neighbour who raises rabbits, chickens and flowers. She came by regularly, bursting with talk. She gave us giant lettuces from her garden, took my sons to gather mussels – they came back with more than 8 quarts them – and invited us over for coffee. Mostly she gave us her friendship, her memories and a sense of the country.

She told of the war – 'terrible times.' She told about the old man in the local café who, fed up with the German soldiers boasting about their country's progress, pulled out his glass eye – a souvenir of the previous war – and slapped it down on the counter. 'There's progress for you,' he told them.

She told of her oldest son, a navigator on a merchant vessel, and of her niece, whose husband, a sailor, decided he couldn't stand it anymore. The niece was expecting her second child, and told her husband he had to go: 'How else could they live?' He signed up for another tour, and the third day out he jumped overboard and was lost.

'There is a woman lives near here,' Ernestine said. 'Her husband hated the sea. She wrote him a letter every day to cheer him up. But finally, on one trip, he got so depressed that he stopped eating, and went sick and died. When they opened his trunk it was full of letters: every one she had ever written him.'

Ernestine told her stories with a patient sweetness. She never came over without a present, advice and a disposition to take pleasure in us. She told my wife where to shop, how to prepare mussels, and how to keep an eye on Michael, my oldest boy. 'Steam his letters open,' she said. 'I always did with my boy. I wouldn't read the whole thing; just enough to see what he was about and to be able to give him good advice.'

All these particularities add up to no generality – except that there is no holiday like relinquishing your purposes. And to relinquish them on the Wild Peninsula is to gather a whole assortment of answers that, like the shells on the beach or the daisies on the hill, have no questions at all.

ROME
AND BEYOND

MY ROME

Muriel Spark

I settled in Rome long ago in 1967 because I found myself returning there again and again, staying longer and longer. I think what attracted me most was the immediate touch of antiquity on everyday life. If you live in central Rome you have only to walk down the street and you come to a fountain by Bernini in which children are playing or a Michelangelo embassy or some fine fifteenth century building with today's washing hanging out.

The names Bramante, Raphael and Borromini become like those of friends. One comes into the territory of the Republican ages, the Caesars, the emperors or the medieval popes at any turn in the road, at any bus stop. Here is the Rome of Garibaldi's troops, of Keats and Shelley, of Arthur Hugh Clough (whose narrative poem *Amours de Voyage* contains one of the funniest descriptions of the English in Rome during the troubles of 1848); Byron's Rome, Henry James's Rome and Mussolini's big fat dream Rome with grandiose popular centres and concepts.

The first apartment I occupied was in the Piazza di Tor Sanguigna, not far from the Tiber on the corner of Via dei Coronari, an ancient street of antique furniture shops. I was at that time dazzled by the adjacent Piazza Navona (as indeed I still am), and I greatly desired a permanent home in the piazza. I did find a flat there, with a picturesque view of Bernini's marvellous Four Rivers fountain, but devoid of everything else, including water. The bathroom and the kitchen, explained the landlord, and the plumbing, electricity and other trivialities, were to be laid on by the lucky tenant who succeeded in obtaining from him a contract limited to one year's residence. The rent alone was high, and I knew right away that the project was impossible, but I still enjoy the memory, as I did the experience, of standing in that dark, vaulted, cavelike apartment while the landlord explained in a mixture of Italian, French and English those terms which I discerned, by careful deciphering, were exorbitant.

I fairly egged him on, as far as my powers in Italian permitted, so keen was I to see with my novelist's curiosity how far he would go. The tenant had to be an American, he said. I was a Scot, I informed him, and I doubted that he would find an American to pour capital into his property with a tenure of only one year. He replied that the apartment was in a famous fifteenth century building in which many famous lords had lived, which was true enough. So he went on, while I looked out the window, watching the Baroque fountain playing in the fine October light of Rome. The theatrical figure representing the Nile, his great hand held up as if to ward off some falling masonry, seemed apt to my situation. 'Speak to me,' Michelangelo is said to have challenged his Roman statue of Moses; and indeed, the sculptures of Rome do speak.

At that time I made lifelong friends among the expatriate community of Rome, mostly British and American, almost all of them anxious to put me on the right track as a newcomer. Eugene Walter, a writer and actor, enormous in girth of physique and heart, held the nearest thing to a salon; he was an unofficial reception committee and all roads led to him. With Eugene I did my first round of the sights and heard all the thousand legends he kept in his head attaching to various monuments, and in his favourite restaurants and trattorie I learned the mysteries of what best to order where. I was still living in the Tor Sanguigna, and that first year I began to learn Italian and wrote a novel with a Roman background.

The memories I retain of that first year have imprinted themselves on all subsequent experience. I recall summer evenings at Galeassi's restaurant in the Piazza Santa Maria in Trastevere, where the golden frieze of the twelfth century church gleamed in its floodlight. On the opposite side of the square is a former cardinal's palace. 'Every night at midnight,' said Eugene in one of his apocryphal moments, 'a hand comes out of that door and pulls in the first living thing that passes.'

I moved to an apartment full of history in the Palazzo Taverna, and I radiated out from there. The palazzo was at the top of the Via dei Coronari, overlooking Castel Sant'Angelo. The main room was enormous, a Renaissance Cardinal Orsini's library, and the upper walls and the ceilings were painted with classical scenes and Orsini emblems. I didn't try to furnish it, but made a sitting room in a remote corner while the rest of the room, with its polished Roman tiles, was for going for walks. (It would have made a good skating rink.) In one of the corridors a Roman pillar had been let into the wall.

By this time I was getting used to permanent residence in historic Rome – part of the excitement of visiting one's friends was to see what portion of history their living space occupied. The Palazzo Taverna, with its fountain in the great courtyard, its arches and small courtyards, was fun to live in, and my echoing cardinal's room was to many of my friends one of the wonders of the world. My cats used to love to sit on a rug while we whizzed them round the vast floor. After dinner everyone in the palazzo would go down to the courtyard to take the air with the neighbours. One of the fascinations of Old Rome is that there are no exclusive neighbourhoods. Rich and poor live on top of each other.

The wives of ambassadors to Rome are hard put to seat their guests according to protocol; there are several different hierarchies. In the first place, Italy is a republic, but the Vatican cardinals and ambassadors top the cake. Then there is the Old Aristocracy, whose ancestors were Popes; they stood, up to the early 1970's, very much on ceremony if they deigned to go outside their palace walls at all. The New Aristocracy comprise the hurly-burly of princes and counts who have sprung up since the time of Napoleon – Bourbon descendants fall somewhere among this category, but I know neither where nor who does know. And ex-monarchs usually find their way to Rome, which is another headache for the embassies. (Fortunately these were not my problems, for whenever I throw a party, high and low as it may include, I make it a buffet.)

Nowadays there are fewer ex-royals. But I remember once having stopped by the office of Jim Bell, then in charge of the Rome bureau of an American news magazine, who often played golf with exiled Constantine of Greece. Before we left for lunch a secretary put her head round the door.

'The king wants to speak to you,' she said.

'The king of what?' Jim Bell wanted to know.

I always go to the Rome Opera in the winter. Each year on the night the opera opens there is a great embracing and greeting of fellow ticketholders and '*Bentornato*' ('Welcome back') all round. One never sees these people anywhere else; they are one's opera friends.

On one special evening, when Montserrat Caballé was singing in a Bellini opera, the rain started coming through the roof. Now, a well-known Roman of that time was the late Mario Praz, a critic and scholar of English literature (he wrote *The Romantic Agony*). He was said to have the Evil Eye and was known as the Malocchio. This nickname wasn't attributed with any repugnance, but rather as an affectionately recorded and realistic fact (for such people are regarded as carriers rather than operators of the Evil Eye). Naturally, everyone noticed when Mario Praz was present at a party, and waited for the disaster. There was usually a stolen car at the end of the evening, or someone called away because his uncle had died. Well, when I saw the rain coming in the roof at the Opera, and heard the commotion behind me, I looked round instinctively for Mario Praz. Sure enough, there was our dear Malocchio sitting under the afflicted spot. He died recently and was mourned on a national scale. (The Italians put their artists and people of letters on a higher level than anywhere else I have known.) Before his house could be unsealed for his heirs, robbers got in and looted his lifetime collection of museum pieces and memorabilia.

In the summer I always try to see the open-air performance of *Aïda* at the Baths of Caracalla. These mighty ruins are extremely well adapted to the mammoth spectacle with its superabundance of camels and cavalry, its luxurious scenery and massed troops. The ancient Romans, for whom the Baths were built as a social and cultural centre, would have loved it. But I think it is a great blessing to us that the Baths have fallen into ruin, nature's magnificent sculptures that they are. The originals must have been of decidedly totalitarian dimensions. Against a late afternoon light all Rome looks sublime, and especially the ruins of Caracalla. They are floodlit at night; the environs used to be a favourite night walk, but nobody takes lonely walks in Rome any more. The footpads are rife. Even the girls of the night, with their picturesque roadside bonfires, have deserted the vicinity of the Baths, and the nightingales sing to the ghosts.

My stay at the Palazzo Taverna came to an end after three years, when the landlady wanted the flat 'for her daughter.' My next flat looked out on the Tiber at the front, and at the back on the rooftops and winding alleys of ancient Trastevere. Here again I had one big room surrounded by a few small rooms. The best thing about it was the view of the river at night with a moving bracelet of traffic on either side of the Tiber and over the bridges; and if I was working very late at night I loved to go for a walk in my big room and look out at the three floodlit monuments of my view: the clocktower of Santa Maria in Trastevere; up on the Gianicolo the Fontana Paola; and behind it the church of San Pietro in Montorio. Eventually my landlady wanted this apartment, too, 'for her daughter.'

Tired of landladies' daughters, I acquired for my own the apartment I live in now, a small but very exciting place just emerging from slumdom. It is in a little street between Piazza Farnese, where Michelangelo added a floor to what is now the French Embassy, and the great Campo dei Fiori, the colourful flower and fruit market. This is deep in the Rome of the Renaissance. My apartment dates from the fourteenth century at the back and the fifteenth at the front. It belonged to an inn called La Vacca owned by La Vanozza, mistress of Pope Alexander Borgia and mother of Cesare Borgia. Her coat of arms, those of her husband and those of the Pope, all three joined, are set in the outside wall near my windows. When the workmen were getting this apartment ready for me they tore down some paper that covered the ceilings to reveal beautiful woodwork. A window was found in a wall leading to the main part of La Vanozza's property. Embedded in the old tiles of the floor they found the remains of a speaking tube that communicated with the street door. Whether or not this was used by La Vanozza's fifteenth century call girls, I will never know.

Wherever I live I am in the writer's condition: Work is pleasure and pleasure is work. I find Rome a good place to work. The ordinary Roman is nearly always a 'character,' which is to say there are no ordinary Romans and therefore life among them, although it may be exasperating at times, is never boring. The extraordinary, Byzantine bureaucracy of Italian living and the usual bothers of life are always present, but if I can get, say, a glimpse of the Pantheon – even passing in a taxi on my way to fulfil some banal commission – I find the journey worthwhile. At night, if I go to dine near the Pantheon, I love to walk around with friends in the great, solid portico for a while. It is sheer harmony; the bulk is practically airborne.

LUIGI BARZINI'S ITALY

Luigi Barzini

Veteran foreign travellers usually bring their own Italy with them; they stubbornly see, taste, experience and remember uniquely the country of their wishes. There is therefore almost no point in giving them any advice or illustrating the multiform possibilities of the voyage.

There are no apparent limits to the Italys available. There is, to begin with, an ultramodern country, ahead of many others in fashion, design, architecture and racing cars; there is also a very old one, thousands of years old, where the past is still alive, rich with experience, enchantment and scepticism. You can find there singular art masterpieces, an uncanny sense of liberation from dull constrictions and boredom, childishly simple but excellent food, good wines, world-famous landscapes celebrated by poets, a pagan country where many of the beautiful laughing girls have, as the French say, *'la cuisse légère'*; and the headquarters of the Roman Catholic Church, the sacred land of St. Francis and St. Catherine of Siena. The enumeration could contine ad infinitum.

Italy is the snows of the Alps, the parching heat of Sicily, the mysterious Mafia, Fellini and Mastroianni, picturesque poverty, picturesque new wealth, archaic crafts, robot-run modern factories – but above all, its people: friendly, shrewd, good-humoured and resigned to the worst.

Advice could only be offered to those who have never been to Italy. On their first visit they should see all the obvious, obligatory, celebrated, postcard sights. They should do this without shame, as one examines samples before buying. Later they can come again and seek the Italy of their choice. After a few trips they will find themselves trying to avoid the notorious landmarks and the gaping crowds. They will want to discover the country that travel agencies and group tourists ignore. It is only there that Italians are still allowed (for a few years at least) to live their own genuine life, and where their life preserves its charm and tastes almost intact.

It is, of course, my Italy. Years ago I used to spend my summers in

Ravello. It is an ancient town, high on a mountain overlooking the stupendous Gulf of Salerno, surrounded by chestnut woods and cooled by singing brooks. It is by no means unknown; in fact, it is very famous. English lords owned historic villas and spent their holidays there. Greta Garbo stayed there with Stokowski; Gore Vidal lives there part of the year. Nevertheless, the steep, narrow road, which does not allow herds of tourists to come for the day, and the proud stubbornness of the inhabitants have somehow preserved its character.

What attracted me was both the echo of the past (the bronze cathedral doors were cast in Constantinople nine centuries ago) and the intense life around me. I followed the town's current developments with the passionate interest of a soap-opera fan. I knew the local legends. I knew that the Whitman-like, saintly white-whiskered patriarch sunning himself on a marble seat on the piazza was a Swiss oenologist who practically invented and made famous the Ravello rosé wine at the beginning of the century, married a local girl and begat a large number of legitimate children and an equivalent number of illegitimate ones.

I knew the bell ringer, the potter, the carpenters, the tailor, the blacksmiths. In other words what fascinated me, gave me peace and rested me was not really the contemplation of natural beauty in a vacuum, as one would get in an isolated modern geometrical beehive hotel on a deserted tropical beach – a hotel built by a chain, identical to a hundred others – but the ancient life of the people, their passions, feuds, recipes, vices, skills, ideas, lore – and the yearly feast of the patron saint (St. Pantaleo, who indirectly gave his name to pants), with the band, the fireworks and the solemn procession escorted by carabinieri in their Napoleonic dress uniforms.

I allow myself to describe Ravello because it is already celebrated. I am reluctant to mention some of the less-known fascinating towns or obscure trattorie. It is dangerous. I once invited some American journalists to dinner in an excellent but absolutely unknown restaurant in Rome. Inevitably its name later appeared in newspaper articles, guidebooks and, finally, in airline lists of recommended eating places. The food gradually became uneatable and the service slow and arrogant. The deterioration during my lifetime of Capri and Positano, which progressed proportionately with the increase of their international fame and the wealth of local entrepreneurs and venal politicians, is appalling.

Perhaps the decay of Italy's little-known paradises is inevitable. Perhaps I am exaggerating the power of the press. Such places would probably deteriorate spontaneously even if no journalist described them, go down the drain of their own free will, turn themselves, at best, like Vence in France, from genuine arcadias to self-conscious, cute, theatrical representations of the real thing.

I will therefore indicate a few – not too many – unspoiled places to blasé travellers tired of the same old sights. There are, for instance, little towns of the Venetian terra firma in the Friuli region, which few people visit. In an arc surrounding Venice, as far east as Gorizia, south of Udine, there are literally hundreds of obscure cities, towns and villages each worth a short stay. There are a few where the traveller would want to stay the rest of his life. They are all not many miles, a few minutes' drive, from each other. There are medieval walls, Romanesque or Gothic churches, rococo palazzi, Longobard castles, comfortable little hotels, cheap trattorie where the food and wines are as good as in Burgundy (*prosciutto di San Daniele* comes from there) and where the customer finds himself adopted as a member of the family after a couple of meals.

The craftsmen are as ingenious as the Chinese. You can order (and get within days) splendid suits and shirts – and shoes, antique reproduction furniture, wrought-iron works, marble statuary or whatever strikes your fancy, and you can still get your books bound in vellum or limp leather with gold lettering. There are centuries-old parks, Palladian villas that mirror themselves in lazy canals. To be sure, the main towns are well known and frequently visited, but to find solitude all you have to do is drive to the next village a few minutes down the road.

Or take Apulia, also known as Puglia, the heel of Italy. Along the Adriatic coast there is a rosary of little towns. They are all obscure, all different, all fascinating. Stupendous Romanesque cathedrals (one for each town), about eight or nine centuries old, are built in an opaque white stone, somewhat like the Istrian 'stones of Venice.'

Other ancient towns, just as attractive, are inland, perched on hilltops. Don't miss Castellaneta, where Rudolph Valentino was born, the son of a veterinarian attached to a smart cavalry regiment. Don't miss Lecce, either, a Baroque city intricately carved out of red-gold stone. Worth the trip to Apulia is the mosaic floor of the cathedral at Otranto. It was made nine hundred years ago by a mad monk. He depicted everything he knew: Greek mythology, the Old and New Testaments, fishes, animals, the sea, the sky, the labours of man, Norman knights, Moslem warriors and many other things in an intricate pattern reminding you of Picasso.

The roads of Apulia are in excellent condition. The wines are among the best in Italy, after the Tuscan and the Piemontese. The food, particularly the fish, is as good as and often better than anywhere else in Italy. Curiously, Apulia is the only place where pasta is sometimes cooked with its sauce like risotto. Try *pasta con le rape* at

Otranto, where the rape (the green tops of beets, a kind of broccoli) has a unique taste.

Or visit the little Baroque towns of southeast Sicily, Noto, Comiso, Ragusa, Vittoria, known only to Sicilians. They were built under Spanish domination and resemble some of the more elaborately decorated Latin American towns of the seventeenth century.

The Veneto, Puglia and southeast Sicily should suffice for the time being for the most exigent traveller. I'm keeping other places secret in the vain hope that nobody will discover them, describe them in the mass media, put them on airlines' suggested itineraries and ruin them forever.

FROM THE POPE'S WINDOW

Malachi Martin

Even with all the wonders and marvels and spells of Rome to pull the visitor in this direction or that, there is one magnet that draws nearly everyone. Whatever takes you to Rome, business, pleasure or lifelong dream, you will find yourself in a Vatican-centred – a Pope-centred – city. 'Did you see the Pope?' strangers ask each other, gazing upward from St. Peter's Square to a window where a moment before, at noon, a white-clad figure smiled and raised a hand in universal blessing.

At other times of day that window is unremarkable, one of ten on the third floor of a fifteenth century Vatican building that stands looking in a southeasterly direction over Rome, over its river, the Tiber, out to the distant hills and beyond. That building is part of the Apostolic Palace, a jumble of buildings begun six centuries ago and on which construction is still in progress. Nothing is done hastily in the Vatican. Indeed, that window is only one out of a total of 12,523 windows in the palace – which, in addition, houses more than 10,000 rooms, suites, halls, cellars and passages and two or three lifts, as well as 997 flights of stairs. The Pope's window is one in the papal study. His living quarters are on the fourth floor. But his daily work is done on the third, in that study.

If you or I, tourist or pilgrim, could stand for a moment beside him at that window, we would receive mainly two impressions: of shimmering expanse and of mysterious detail. We would see Rome as it lies in the small province of Latio, with the sky seemingly lifting away from the city and countryside in a fashion that suggests some invisible highway joining Rome with the distant high country far beyond the Campagna plain, the mountains and the sea. The world of man and something of the mystic country above the world of man rushes in to greet you through that window. It becomes a transom opening on the infinite and the eternal.

Then details crowd in on us. The gaze falls over Rome to find a hundred hooded domes glinting in the sun and a myriad of spires, towers, monuments, hemmed in with palazzi, parks, supermarkets, shops, simple houses, all connected by streets of every kind, long, straight, curving, short, narrow, broad. And, night and day, even from that Vatican window, the ear picks up the unceasing hum of Rome. For the city sits on top of hardened, echoing volcanic ash, the tufa. Even a visitor, versed in the rolling syllables of the Roman dialect, can converse in the quiet of an early morning with a friend five streets away, if he has learned to throw his voice à la Romana. These are the things about which we might chat afterward, if we could stand beside the Pope at his window for a minute or two.

But when the Pope looks out of that window, he has none of our ease or fascination. Every detail he sees fits into the template of his duty. What he sees first is not that wide expanse, the city and its monuments. It is, directly beneath the window, the piazza or square of St. Peter's. We, his momentary visitors, would have noted from our guidebooks that it measures 215 yards in its greatest breadth, is flanked on two sides by the colonnade of Bernini, itself a complex of 284 columns and 80 buttresses surmounted by 162 statues, each 12 feet high. In the centre of the piazza, a 132-foot Egyptian obelisk weighing 320 tons.

The Pope would remember, rather, that over 1,900 years ago they ran chariot races below in that ellipse. And, one night after the races, in a narrow street running across the Vatican hill, they killed an ageing Jewish fisherman called Simon Peter, in order to delight an emperor called Nero and his girlfriend, Poppaea. Peter's friends hurriedly buried his body in a shallow grave at the top of the hill, because at that time Roman eagles were screaming victoriously all over the world, the hobnailed boots of Rome's legionnaires were beating out a firm imperial tramp on Roman roads that ran all throughout the empire and civilized Rome had absolutely no use for one miserable fisherman. Not yet.

With a shift of your gaze to the right, but in a direct line of about 1,200 feet from that third-floor window, you can see Michelangelo's dome. Under it, that shallow grave of the fisherman lies beneath the high altar of St. Peter's Basilica, where the Pope says mass.

We, standing at that window, will marvel at that basilica, at its proportions – 651 feet long, our guidebook tells us, 435 feet high, with 777 columns, 44 altars, 395 statues and a bronze ball on top of its dome in which 16 persons can fit comfortably. But the Pope will not forget that, even when the Roman Empire ceased to be, and Peter became the Great Fisherman, still it took over 1,000 years for his successors, each one of them wearing the Fisherman's Ring, to create this basilica as the focal point of a new empire, Christianity; and that it was scarcely finished when that Christian heartland was torn irreparably to shreds by wars, hate, animosity and self-perpetuating divisions.

We can see much from that window – the American College on the

Janiculum Hill, the roof of the Sistine Chapel, in which the Pope was elected by the Cardinals, the round red-brick Castel Sant'Angelo, built by the emperor Hadrian. But the Pope sees chiefly the robust reminders of the principal elements of his Roman organization, with which he must govern his church and perhaps reduce the hate, eliminate the animosity, heal the divisions.

Nearest him is his Secretariat of State – in fact, it is all around him in the Apostolic Palace. This is the oldest and most practised chancellery in our world, peopled with the usual upper-, middle- and lower-grade officials, mainly clerics, and manned by a swarm of secretaries, typists, filing clerks, stenographers, cryptographers, specialists, linguists, researchers – also mainly clerics. The secretariat is headed by the Cardinal Secretary of State, normally the closest adviser and collaborator of the Pope.

The secretariat maintains its own diplomatic representatives in over a hundred countries. Representatives from about the same number of states are accredited to the Holy See. On any given day the secretariat's offices and corridors and conference rooms are full of activity. A huge mass of information flows in from the four quarters of the globe, policies and plans and 'reactions' are hammered out. The quintessence of it all is brought up early each morning to the man in that study on that third floor. And Vatican Radio, call letters HJV, faithfully broadcasts the encoded messages awaited by Vatican representatives and emissaries in all five continents.

Directly across from the Apostolic Palace, on the south side of St. Peter's Basilica, are two other principal elements of papal government. The more important one is concerned with the preservation of Roman Catholic belief and the correct observance of the Church's moral law. Formerly called the Holy Office, it is now known as the Congregation for the Faith (congregation is the Roman term for what we call a government ministry or department). It is housed in a centuries-old building, a former monastery, enclosing an inner courtyard entered by an arched portal. More than any other component of the Vatican, this is a quiet place, full of discreet silences and memories of ancient disputes and struggles stirring in every room and throughout its austere corridors.

Within a stone's throw of the Congregation for the Faith stands the Vatican bank in a relatively modern building, complete with all that makes for a bank – managers, vice-presidents, tellers, messengers, investment experts, accountants, vaults. Here all financial transactions of the Vatican and the Roman Catholic Church as a worldly institution are performed. It would be crass to think that the only raison d'être the bank has is to make money. For one thing, the over $20 million annual budget of the Vatican must be met regularly. For another, the Vatican directly supports hundreds of colleges, schools, orphanages, universities, clinics, leprosaria, philanthropic institutions and some thousands of bishops and priests and nuns all over the world.

But, as with the Secretariat of State, there is a nice calculation to be made by the Pope, as he gazes across at the Vatican bank: in managing its material wealth, his Vatican must not allow spirit to suffer nor faith to be diminished. For the only wealth brought to Rome by the Great Fisherman consisted of spirit and faith planted with his blood on this same ancient Vatican hill one night long ago. 'When I step away from that window,' Pope John XXIII said, 'and sit at my desk, I need consolation. I need strength at my back.' It is symbolically significant that behind the Apostolic Palace, behind the Pope's back as he sits at his desk, lie most of the great treasures the Vatican has preserved from the past, its irreplaceable library and archives, its fantastically rich museums, its long galleries of ancient, medieval, Renaissance and modern art, its vast, vast storage rooms, its collection of paintings and frescoes. And, also, some of the Vatican's more mysterious parts that are unknown, to most people – the Tower of the Winds, for example, and the Room of the Meridian with its zodiac mosaics and ancient frescoes and sunchinks.

Before you leave that papal window, glance out one more time. Let your eye travel. Past the sluggish grey-green waters of the Tiber. Past the nearest of Rome's seven hills, the Capitoline. Past that pile of brilliantly white Brescian marble, the Victor Emmanuel Monument, nicknamed *il peccato mortale* by the Italians and 'the wedding cake' by generations of English-speakers. Out over the other six hills of Rome, northwards to the Pantheon and southwards to the opening of the old Appian Way. Over all the monumental fountains, massive churches, towering columns, monasteries with flaming frescoes, palatial houses and gardens. Over all the staircases by which you can climb and view this Rome. Feel the indefinable – and, at first, puzzling – pull this Rome of the Popes can exert on you.

But do not be afraid of it. Everywhere you can look from this window, great and renowned men and women have been before you and have felt that same mysteriously gentle attraction of Rome and its Pope. John Keats died in a house at the foot of the Spanish Steps. James Joyce spent one winter of his discontent on the banks of the Tiber. Rome's streets and Vatican have been trod by Robert Adams, Elizabeth Barrett Browning, Thackeray, Hans Christian Andersen, Liszt, Buffalo Bill, Queen Christina of Sweden, Nathaniel Hawthorne, Rubens, Stendhal, Angelica Kauffmann, even the pope-baiting poet John Milton (he attended theatrical performances in the palace of the Barberini popes surrounded by red-robed cardinals). And the sad-faced Sigmund Freud, for many of his last years, wrote about 'going home to Rome . . .' Romans can better explain what he meant than most Freudians can! The truth is that all these people, as you, could feel at home in Rome. For Rome is not Italian. It is uniquely itself. And universal.

May is the month to be here. It is the month when Rome blossoms anew and welcomes. Winter bitterness and spring uncertainty are no more. The choking sirocco wind which, Lord Byron said, affects mostly mad dogs and Englishmen, rarely blows over from the eastern deserts. There is scarcely one *temporale*, that sudden downpour of sheet-rain bringing with it a fine red tufa dust. The sky of Latio smiles with that singular luminosity – an amalgam of loveliest blue and transparent light and the white fleece of shapely cloud – that poets and painters swear can be found nowhere else on earth, and that Raphael described as 'the casement of Heaven itself.'

Rome is filled with flowers and sparkling fountains in May. Restaurant tables and chairs are moved out onto every pavement. The marble statues and the earth-brown palazzi bask in the caressing warmth of the new sun. And every soft evening, above the Spanish Steps, around the fountains and colonnades of St. Peter's Square, up on the ancient Capitol and out around the tombs and ruins lining the old Appian Way, the swallows have arrived from North Africa; they dive and soar and bank in the chase of invisible mayflies. Miami may be for December, Sydney for January, Cortina and Gstaad for March, Galilee for September. But Rome is for May. Never will any other place welcome you so at that moment.

Before you leave that window in this May of your mind's eye and your desiring, before you leave Rome – if you really must leave – remember to toss a coin in the Trevi Fountain, a short mile from here. It ensures that you will come back.

And take one more thought with you. Like many of their visitors, great and ordinary, the Romans may not go to mass very often. They regularly elect a Communist mayor nowadays (who does go to mass, by the way). There is a vicious turmoil sometimes in their streets. And, like all the Italians, they are surviving and flourishing in the middle of the worst chaos seen for a long time in a European country.

But Romans have long memories; and they well remember that once before when popes deserted Rome, this city became the refuge of robbers preying on a few dirt farmers and gypsies, its monuments overgrown, with weeds and grass, and that it earned the nickname 'cowpatch' all over Europe, so dank and smelly and dangerous did it become. And so Romans reckon that one major reason why Rome persists and will persist is the charismatic man up at that window who parleys with the Kremlin and with God, the man present-day Romans refer to as '*il nostro polacco romano*,' 'our Roman Pole,' much as they speak familiarly of Julius Caesar as '*il nostro Garibaldi*.' They, and he, know with surety Rome will always house the Great Fisherman. Or cease to be Rome.

STRATEGIES FOR THE VATICAN MUSEUMS

James McGregor

There is no Vatican museum, but a host of Vatican Museums. Through their heart runs a pedestrian expressway to the Sistine Chapel, and along its right of way, dazed groups pursue the tattered banners of their glibly multilingual guides. With an area of over forty thousand square yards and wall space extending to almost five miles, the Vatican Museums are not for the faint-hearted.

Most are gathered under one roof in the Apostolic Palace complex to the right of St. Peter's Basilica; but two collections, the Treasury of St. Peter's and the Necropolis, have separate entrances in the church itself. The visitor to the Apostolic Palace complex can choose from four itineraries, shown on a sign at the entrance. The longest, 'D,' lets a visitor see all the rooms open on any given day. (The shorter itineraries offer a selection of rooms, but bypass much of interest.)

Following the 'D' route, the Gregorian-Egyptian Museum has little of interest and can be passed through quickly. Beyond it lies the Courtyard of the Pigna, named for a gigantic bronze pine cone, a genial but puzzling Roman antiquity. A door in an angle of the courtyard opens into the first of the great early nineteenth century installations, the Chiaramonte Museum – actually a single gallery designed by the neoclassical sculptor Antonio Canova. The gallery is decorated with painted lunettes that celebrate the restoration of important Roman antiquities by Pius VII and filled with long ranks of Roman sculpture and shelf upon shelf of busts and other small works. There are nearly a thousand objects in all.

An installation like Canova's – and there are more to come – completely contradicts modern ideas of how works of art should be shown. Modern museums create neutral spaces and let individual works speak for themselves. Canova, and the architects of the generations before his, liked to mass works of art. They thought of museums as ensembles of architecture, painting and sculpture.

Beyond the Chiaramonte Museum lies the Pio-Clementine Museum, named for Pius VI and Clement XIV, the popes responsible for its reorganization in the mid-eighteenth century. Its smaller rooms are as densely packed with objects as the later Chiaramonte, and its walls and ceilings are even more intensely decorated. Like the Chiaramonte, they should be enjoyed as ensembles first, after which individual objects should be sampled. In this way, their deliberate excess becomes refreshing rather than oppressive. Surprisingly, individual pieces in these rooms stand out as masterpieces: among these are the statue known as the Apoxyomenos, the severe and sparingly decorated tomb of Lucius Cornelius Scipio, and the Belvedere Torso.

In the centre of the Pio-Clementine Museum is the Octagonal Courtyard, an eighteenth century reworking of a sixteenth century statue garden. It has fountains, trees and benches in its centre, and 'cabinets' at its edges that hold some of the cornerstones of the papal collections. The most celebrated of these is the Apollo Belvedere, a Roman sculpture of considerable originality, known since the fourteenth century and brought to this courtyard by Pope Julius II. Of only slight less celebrity is the Laocoön group, buried in late antiquity and excavated in 1506. The Apollo has long stood for the rationalistic side of the classical heritage, with its emphasis on self-control; the Laocoön, with its active surface and Baroque torsion, is at the opposite, expressionist, pole.

The Gregorian-Etruscan Museum on the second floor is a collection gathered in the nineteenth century and housed in sixteenth century rooms. There are some nice fragments from the Parthenon and a fine collection of Greek vases, but the majority of artifacts are, as might be expected, Etruscan. The seventh century BC gold fibula from the Regolini-Galassi tomb shows the Etruscan love for detail and their technical ability. The visitor can also see this in the care with which the veins, tendons and skin texture of the Mars of Todi were rendered. The same statue shows the typically Etruscan disregard for the sense of the whole, expressed in broad rhythms and symmetries, that so concerned the Greeks. The Greek vases, most found in Etruscan tombs, include the well-known mid-sixth century BC amphora by Exekias.

A very long corridor joins these collections to the Raphael Rooms and the Sistine Chapel. Along the way, there are window embrasures from which to admire the gardens, statues and sarcophagi in the Gallery of the Candelabras; sixteenth century frescoed maps of Italy, and a collection of tapestries.

The four rooms painted by Raphael and his assistants in the sixteenth century were the public rooms of the papal apartments in the time of Julius II. Here, working in fresco, Raphael celebrated the fusion of painting, architecture and sculpture. His rooms are at once a statement of the unity of the arts and an assertion of the primacy of painting, which alone can represent all the others.

The Room of the Fire, the first on the itinerary of the Raphael Rooms, was actually the last to be decorated. The frescoes were designed by Raphael, but almost all were painted by his assistants. The second room, the first undertaken by Raphael for Julius II, contains, among other frescoes, the *School of Athens,* Raphael's allegory of classical philosophy that exemplifies the role Julius imagined for the classics in the Church and life of the High Renaissance. Tucked away in a corner of Julius's apartments is the exquisite little Chapel of Nicholas V. Painted in fresco by Fra Angelico, it is a triumph of Quattrocento art, a period otherwise poorly represented in Rome. The route then doubles back through the Raphael Rooms and descends to the Borgia Apartments and the Collection of Modern Religious Art.

Many of these rooms were decorated by Pinturicchio, but his work was severely damaged by nineteenth century restoration; the installation of the modern collection has not helped. In an effort to create contemporary museum spaces, the walls have been covered with burlap. The apartments are dreary and the collection poor. It is better to take the direct route to the Sistine Chapel and bypass this collection entirely

Michelangelo and his Sistine Chapel are known to people who know nothing else about art. They come in busloads to see it, and their numbers make the chapel a noisy and distracting place. But even so, it is a magical place. After the Raphael Rooms, the ceiling is particularly exciting to see, since Raphael and Michelangelo were up to the same thing, creating a fictive architecture and filling it with figures that have the look of sculpture and painting simultaneously.

This is Michelangelo's triumphant statement of the power of painting. Like Raphael, he has expressed a vast and complex Christian story in classical language. But his figures have a grandeur – what his contemporaries called *terribilita* – that Raphael in the more intimate spaces in which he worked did not achieve.

One can ask to be let out of the door at the back left corner of the Sistine Chapel that leads to St. Peter's, or continue to follow the itinerary, which leads back on the second floor and terminates at the museum entrance. The crowd is miraculously diminished and quieted here, and along the way there are delightful discoveries, including a room of Roman frescoes named for its prize, *The Aldobrandini Wedding.* This is where the Vatican Library, which has its own exhibition space, begins.

Two galleries of interest, not on the itinerary, remain. The Pinacoteca (Picture Gallery) houses a small collection of paintings arranged in chronological order, beginning with works of the thirteenth century. Painting before the High Renaissance is hard to find in Rome, so the collection's fine Gentile da Fabriano of a ship and angel in a swirling sea and a pair of magically real *Miracles of St. Nicholas* by Fra Angelico are worth noting. The Pinacoteca's largest room is occupied by three Raphaels, two from the early years of his career and a *Transfiguration,* completed soon before his death in 1520. All have recently been restored. There are also fine Domenichino, Guido Reni and Caravaggio paintings – the rich staples of the Roman diet – as well.

The Gregorian Profane and Pio-Christian Museums contain a striking collection of Roman art and a more modest sampling of Early Christian material. They were formerly housed in the Lateran Palace, and the new (1971) installation provided them is the only truly modern museum of art in the Vatican.

The manifold nature of Roman art is well represented in the Gregorian Profane. Some important examples of Roman 'official' art are also here: the colossal statue of the Emperor Claudius portrayed as Jupiter and the Cancelleria Reliefs, in which the Emperors Vespasian and Domitian pose with assorted deities and personifications. The bulk of the collection could be called 'private' art, made for individuals, the splendid first century AD tomb of the Haterii, for example, and the many portraits and sarcophagi.

Beyond the floor mosaics from the Baths of Caracalla, with their brutal portraits of athletic plug-uglies, the Pio-Christian Museum begins. Suddenly we are in a world of emerging spirituality as the world of classical myth gives way to Christian representations of Old and New Testament scenes. (The same new complex houses the Ethnological Missionary and Historical Museums, which are often closed and contain little of artistic interest.)

The Vatican Treasury is entered through the end of the left aisle of St. Peter's Basilica. It contains, among a host of gaudy baroque reliquaries, a few objects of real beauty. The chief of these is Pollaiuolo's tomb of Sixtus IV. The sarcophagus of Junius Bassus, almost the last object in the collection, is a masterpiece of Early Christian sculpture.

The Pre-Constantinian Necropolis beneath St. Peter's Basilica can be visited only by special permission. The Vatican began excavating the area beneath its high altar soon after World War II in an effort to discover just why Constantine had placed the original St. Peter's there. The archaeologists soon came across an ancient cemetery that ran under the nave. They believe it contains the tomb of St. Peter. A visitor here walks among ancient tombs, their interiors largely intact and their outside walls shining and unweathered. The impression of being in an ancient city is as strong here as in Pompeii or Ostia.

GETTING AROUND

Wear comfortable shoes and eat a hearty breakfast – you are going to do a lot of walking. Even the shortest itinerary – 'A,' directly to the Sistine Chapel and back – takes an hour and a half. The 'B' and 'C' routes each take three hours, and the 'D' about five.

From downtown Rome the most direct route to the Vatican is the No. 64 bus or the metro, line A. From the information office in the left-hand colonnade of St. Peter's Square, a yellow bus for the museums leaves every twenty minutes.

HOURS AND ADMISSIONS

The museums are open from 9 am to 2 pm during the cooler months, from 9 am to 5 pm between July 1 and October 31. They are closed holidays and Sundays, except the last Sunday of every month, when they are open free. Admission prices are about $3.60 a person, $2 for students. At the admissions level are a post office, foreign exchange, cloakroom and a sales desk where the very useful *Guide to the Vatican Museums* ($3.60) may be purchased.

The Treasury of St. Peter's is open from 9 am to 12.30 pm and from 3 pm to 4.30 pm (6.30 pm in summer). Admission is about $2. To visit the Pre-Constantinian Necropolis, write to the Reverenda Fabbrica de San Pietro, Ufficio Scavi, 00120 Citta del Vaticano, giving names of visitors and address and telephone number in Rome.

CHECKING INTO HOTEL DINING

Luigi Barzini

Most restaurant guides for the city of Rome published two or more years ago are inevitably out of date. Likewise, lists of eating places recommended by airlines or international tourist organizations are laughably untrustworthy. The Roman restaurant situation has changed – and is still changing – so radically and constantly that only the viva voce advice of a good friend, who has eaten there recently and knows what he is talking about, can be trusted.

The reasons for this mutability are many. For one thing the number of trattorie in the capital has multiplied prodigiously. (Many of them are good or pretending to be good, and a few are excellent.) It will be discovered that this phenomenon, in Italy as in other countries, is linked to the monstrous growth of bureaucracy in the modern world, government's minute interference in the economy and the disappearance of servants.

All big deals and their financing must be approved, in Italy, by some bureaucrat or other. Laws must be passed, modified, or abrogated under the pressure of interested parties from the provinces. As a result there is in Rome at all times a floating population of men who spend more time in hotels, restaurants, trattorie, nightclubs, ministries' waiting rooms and the private studies of politicians than in their own provincial offices. To them one must add hundreds of members of parliament from out of town, the foreign bishops and high prelates visiting the Vatican and the foreign film actors always present in Rome. They all go to swell the number of Romans without servants who now eat out as often as they can afford to. It is not surprising, therefore, that new restaurants with cute names are opened practically every day, old ones fold up or change hands and cooks move continuously from one job to a better-paid one. All this happens so often and so fast that no guidebook can keep up with it.

Years ago nobody used to eat in hotel restaurants. The menu was always in misspelled French, the cuisine was without surprises – mostly a pallid version of genteel international cooking. The versions of local specialities provided for foreign tourists were almost as tasteless as the meals served to the sick in clinics. Everybody therefore preferred to eat in the lowest inns, *osterie* or trattorie, where the genuine plebeian taste of the food was preserved. All this has changed with the success of these establishments. Now there are only a few real plebeian eating places left.

The names of the restaurants that used to be good have been publicized all over the world. No Italian goes near them. Japanese, Americans, Arabs and Germans fill the tables. Nobody protests if a dish is badly done because foreign tourists are timid by nature and nobody knows what the stuff should really taste like. Most owners have become multimillionaires, at least in lire. The rooms have been redecorated to look like stage versions of a Roman trattoria.

There was, a few years ago, no longer room in Rome for the Italian version of haute cuisine, the best examples of which could be found before World War II on the famous Italian liners, the *Conte di Savoia* and the *Rex* on the Genoa-New York run, and the *Victoria,* on the Venice-Shanghai run. Did those great chefs leave no disciples? Did the suave maîtres d'hôtel, who made each customer feel he was not just a customer but a unique personage, vanish, taking their secrets with them to the grave?

The gradual deterioration of most of the lowly trattorie has somehow brought about a renaissance in hotel dining rooms as well as a few very soigné and smart restaurants. And this is my advice: Forget for once the folklore, the smell of garlic, the picturesque, the loud-voiced *padrone,* the bizarre recipes allegedly handed down by a peasant grandmother. Such things still exist but few of them are genuine.

Travellers do not have the time and the expertise to distinguish the excellent wheat from the fraudulent chaff. Guides are unreliable. Try, for a change, the restaurants of the few hotels where the new pride in the hotelier's craft is visible and tasteable. The table is once again beautifully laid with gleaming crystal, shining silver, impeccable linen and flowers. The maître d'hôtel is once again what his grandfather was before 1914. The waiters are well dressed, attentive, quick and efficient. And the food is usually imaginative: new versions of traditional dishes, variations of old themes and novelties that arouse your curiosity and appetite. Everything is unmistakably fresh, since the chef himself has bought the very best ingredients in the market at dawn and nothing is out of season. (Italians eat peas or grapes or peaches or anything else only during the few weeks in the year when they are at their best.)

Which hotels and restaurants? Try **Le Jardin dell'Hotel Lord Byron,** Via De Notris 5 (phone 360 9541), to begin with. (Do not be surprised by the mixture of Italian, French and English words in the name. Italian hotel owners have always used foreign words as decoys, sometimes clumsily. One of them built a new hotel for the American bishops who were to convene in Rome for the Vatican Council and proudly called it 'The Sporting House.' It should be evident that no American bishop chose to stay in it.) The Hotel Lord Byron is small, elegant, surrounded by the greenery and silence of Villa Borghese. The cooks and maître d'hôtel come from Italian embassies abroad, foreign embassies in Rome or great households. The menu varies a little every day and greatly from year to year. The choice of wines is excellent.

The restaurant on the roof of the Hotel Eden, Via Ludovisi 49 (phone 474 2401), now called **Charles** after the maître Giancarlo Castrucci, has a spendid view and is as good as the dining room of the Umberto Biancamano in the old days. Also highly recommended is **Le Rallye** at the Grand Hotel, Via del Corso 126 (phone 678 3364), **La Cupola** at the Hotel Excelsior, Via Veneto 125 (phone 493 448) and the **Roof Garden Restaurant** at the Hassler-Villa Medici, Piazza Trinita' Monte 6 (phone 678 2651). Finally, an unusual recommendation: a good restaurant in a setting where no finicky gourmet would seek it. It is called **La Pergola** and it is at the Cavalieri Hilton, Via Cadlolo 101 (phone 344 341). It would be worth the gourmet's while to overcome his snobbish diffidence and try it. It is one of the four or five best restaurants in Rome and possibly Europe.

SMALL HOTELS OF CHARACTER

Paul Hofmann

The round brass sign on the door of the graceful neoclassical building on top of the Spanish Steps reads YOUR HOME IN ROME. Visitors who value the panorama of the Eternal City's cupolas, obelisks, pine trees and roofscape more highly than colour television and a well-stocked pantry in their rooms or a nightclub downstairs couldn't do much better.

Reservations are of the essence, since the **Scalinata di Spagna**, Piazza Trinità dei Monti 17 (telephone: 679 30 06 or 679 95 82), is one of the city's smallest hotels. Its fourteen rooms on two floors are spoken for most of the time.

'Either you make a reservation two or three months ahead, or you take a chance,' says Giuseppe Bellia, the genial manager. 'Some would-be guests book a room half a year ahead, and then at the last minute cancel because they had to change plans. Whenever we have a free room unexpectedly it goes to whoever comes first.'

Scalinata di Spagna, which means Spanish stairway, has a large terrace with lots of greenery, small tables and plenty of chairs that invite one to linger and enjoy the glorious view, which can be seen from many of its rooms as well. There is also a parrot, Cacao, which often sits on the head of a winged alabaster maiden, greets visitors with 'Hello' or '*Ciao,*' is madly jealous of the black hotel poodle, Sally, and has a yen for uncooked spaghetti.

The rooms are simply furnished, each with a private bath or shower. Doubles cost $48 to $50 a day, including Continental breakfast. (**The Hassler-Villa Medici** across the little piazza, one of Rome's finest hotels, charges more than three times as much. It is more opulent than the homey Scalinata di Spagna, but the vistas are the same.) No other meals are served, but there is a small house bar. Good restaurants abound in the neighbourhood.

Mr. Bellia, a Venetian, and his German-born wife, Gisella, managed two pensions before they bought into the Scalinata di Spagna a few years ago. The informal way in which the place functions is epitomized by a bookshelf in the corridor outside room Nos. 1 and 2. It is loaded with English-language paperbacks that guests have left behind; current guests may read them on the spot and even carry them off if they have not reached the last page during their stay.

Well-heeled and discriminating visitors who require luxury might consider the **Lord Byron**, Via dei Notaris 5 (360 95 41, 360 95 42), the most sophisticated of the city's many small hotels. The white Riviera-style building is set in a garden at the highest point of a sloping, quiet one-way street near the Borghese Gardens and the Villa Giulia Museum. It is a showpiece of interior design and smooth service. Corridors are in lacquered white and tobacco shades; rooms are immaculate, with a profusion of soft lights, fine linen and draperies, hidden refrigerators filled with small bottles of Champagne and other drinks, remote control colour television sets and sumptuous marble baths.

The Lord Byron used to have fifty-five room and suites; now there are only forty-two, because some have been sacrificed to enlarge the remaining ones. (Work is still going on in parts of the building.) A double room with breakfast costs about $124 a day, a single $101. Its small, smart basement restaurant, Le Jardin, is open to the public.

Because of their lower overhead, the small hotels are usually less expensive than bigger houses in the same official categories. True, service may not be what it is in the larger establishments, especially in the traditionally slack period from November to Easter. In the afternoons and evenings, for example, the desk clerk in some hotels may be the only employee in the house, answering the telephone and doing other chores; guests arriving late may have to carry their own bags up to their rooms. (In the high season, on the other hand, relatives of the owner or manager may help out, and guests speaking no Italian may have a hard time making themselves understood – although the manager himself almost always knows at least a smattering of English.)

But the reasons why many visitors prefer a smaller place often have nothing to do with money. The little mavericks in the hotel industry often cater to a faithful clientele from the Italian provinces and usually steep their guests in rich Roman atmosphere and personal attention.

These places may be tucked away in old, picturesque corners of the city, on some downtown piazza or on a twisting street without sidewalks, and many evoke historical reminiscences.

One example is **Albergo del Sole al Pantheon**, Piazza della Rotonda 63 (679 33 29, 679 34 90). Two marble plaques on the reddish building proclaim that it was once known as the Albergo del Montone (Inn of the Ram), and that among its guests were the sixteenth century poet Ludovico Ariosto and, in our century, the composer Pietro Mascagni, who stayed there when he was preparing the Rome performance of his opera *Cavalleria Rusticana*.

Behind the Renaissance façade there is a lobby with a fountain, ceramics and modern décor. A comfortable double room, with private bath, looking out on the portico and the Corinthian columns of the Pantheon costs $38 a day; other doubles with bath cost $33.50. Breakfast, if desired, is $3.20 a person extra.

A scholarly friend of mine who visits Rome periodically to do research, and who detests the chain hotels with their tourist groups and banquet crowds, always checks in at the quaint little **Albergo dei Portoghesi**, Via dei Portoghesi 1 (654 51 33, 656 42 31), near the Tiber embankment and the Piazza Navona. Close to a Portuguese church and ecclesiastical college, the entrance to the twenty-nine-room house on a narrow street is inconspicuous and looks musty. Inside, the place is neat and cosy. Some of the rooms have been done over recently. A double with bath costs $41.50, breakfast included. If you are lucky, you may get No. 20, which has a small sitting room and is really a little suite, for the same rate.

The Nettuno, Via del Lavatore 95 (679 43 22, 679 63 18), is less expensive: a large double room with private bath can be had for as little as $17.50 a night. The twenty-eight rooms have stone floors, as do many Roman homes, and are clean. The furniture is Spartan; there is no lift and guests have to be either imperturbable sleepers or early risers, for the Nettuno faces an outdoor fruit-and-vegetable market where the bustle starts around 7 am Monday through Saturday.

But the old, solidly built hotel is at the very centre of the city, at the foot of the Quirinal Hill, with the Trevi Fountain only a few steps away. The neighbourhood, with the exuberant colours and sounds of the market and its many eating places and shops, displays a quintessential slice of Roman life. The Nettuno serves no meals – not even breakfast, which in many hotels is either obligatory or included in the price of the room. This, too, can be an advantage, since breakfast in Roman hotels, small or big, is all too often meagre (undistinguished coffee, a couple of rolls, a little butter of dubious freshness and a tiny plastic container of jam) and overpriced ($3 and up). The alternative offered by a stand-up espresso bar – two of the crisp rolls called *cornetti* and a cup of good cappuccino for about $1 – is attractive. There are half a dozen such espresso shops in the neighbourhood.

Here are a few other favourites among scores of small Roman hotels, grouped according to their location. Unless otherwise noted, breakfast, the only meal served, is included in the price of the room.

NEAR THE SPANISH SQUARE

Carriage, Via delle Carrozze 32/36 (679 31 52, 679 33 12), twenty-four rooms, all with private baths. Modern, looking out on two narrow downtown streets, double rooms at $51.

Margutta, Via Laurina 34 (360 95 41), twenty-three rooms, in a neighbourhood dotted with art galleries and antiques stores. Doubles with bath, $32.

Mozart, Via dei Greci 23 (678 74 22), thirty-one rooms (all air-conditioned), on a narrow road opposite the Music Academy of St. Cecilia. Doubles with private bath at $42.

Gregoriana, Via Gregoriana 18 (679 42 69, 679 79 88), nineteen rooms, on a quiet, distinguished street that the poet and novelist Gabriele d'Annunzio made famous. Doubles with bath at $62.

Homs, Via della Vita 71/72 (678 04 82, 679 29 76), thirty-two rooms, plain. Doubles with bath at $38, without bath $28.

NEAR THE VIA VENETO

La Residenza, Via Emilia 22 (474 44 80), twenty-seven large chintz-filled rooms and a small garden. Doubles with bath at $56.

Sitea, Via Vittorio Emanuele Orlando 90 (474 36 47), thirty- seven rooms, opposite the top-rated Grand Hotel. An elegant place. Doubles with bath at $65.

NEAR THE VATICAN

Sant'Anna, Borgo Pio 134 (654 16 02), eighteen rooms, in the earthy Borghi section just outside Vatican City. Doubles with bath, $39.

Prati, Via Crescenzio 89 (65 53 57), twenty-five rooms, on a broad, tree-lined street, plain. Doubles with bath, $23.50, doubles with shower, $22, other doubles, $17.50, all rates without breakfast.

Finally, another hostelry in one of the quietest spots in Rome, on top of the Aventine Hill, is actually a cluster of three small houses set in a lush garden with palms and other trees. They are the **Sant'Anselmo**, Piazza Sant'Anselmo 2 (57 35 47, 57 28 31, 578 13 25), with twenty-three rooms; the **Aventino** with nineteen rooms; and the **Villa San Pio**, with twenty-four rooms; lobbies and rooms are well appointed. The Colosseum, the Palatine Hill, the Circus Maximus and other ancient Roman monuments are nearby. The Sant'Anselmo takes reservations for the Aventino and the Villa San Pio. A double room at any of them is about $38.

FOR STROLLERS,
ROME IS A TIME MACHINE

William Weaver

Like everybody else, I learned about Rome in school; and for me the ancient city lived in the old Alinari photographs, standard in every Latin classroom at the time – Colosseum, Forum, Pantheon – suggesting that the once-great capital's buildings all resembled the Lincoln Memorial or, closer at hand, the Bank of Warren on Main Street in Front Royal, Virginia. In other words, I pictured a city in black-and-white, austere, unpopulated, frozen. Years later, when I finally arrived in modern Rome and saw those quasi-familiar monuments, I received an unpleasant shock. The buildings had none of the pristine sparkle of the District of Columbia; Rome's landmarks were grey or yellow or a deep burnt umber. And weeds sprouted from the cornices. From the same cornices irreverent pigeons left their mark on passers-by. An army of cats – some sleek, some scrawny, all antihuman – paraded through the ruins with the arrogant mien of possession that suggested the Republic's senators.

This was not the tidy, sober city I had anticipated, but I quickly learned to accept it, then love it. The cats gave me a clue. Rome does not belong to them entirely; it belongs also to the Romans (and, I venture to hope, also to appreciative visitors). Rome is not some scholar's reconstruction, not a Latin-grammar illustration. It is a dynamic place, where past – or rather, pasts – mingle with present, where people and cats and dogs live and move. After watching those cats, I began to observe, with pleasure and envy, the way Romans handle their city: not with institutional respect, but with familiar affection. A delivery boy will prop his bicycle against a stretch of Servian wall; a labourer stretches out under a tree on the Palatine for a postprandial snooze, casually draping his jacket over a marble fragment. Children play hide-and-seek among truncated columns while their nurses knit and gossip, perched on the remains of a rostrum.

Rome is a city of layers. Literally, the ancient stratum underlies the medieval city, the Baroque city, the modern city. But layers can also be vertical; they can interlock, intersect. As you walk along a downtown street, you can see a Roman column incorporated into the façade of a Baroque palazzo, or a fragment of ancient wall preserved in the atrium of a glass-and-steel apartment house. Some of the ruins were inhabited in the Middle Ages, and some are today. Most of the poor squatters who, until a few years ago, had constructed makeshift dwellings in the arches of the aqueducts, have now moved to more sanitary and conventional housing; but there are some highly prized artists' studios discreetly inserted into the Aurelian Wall, near the Via Veneto. And if you walk down the Via Teatro di Marcello from the Capitoline, you will see on your right the great bulk of the Theatre of Marcellus, the most elegant collection of flats in the city (the writer Iris Origo's spacious apartment includes a hanging garden complete with fruit-bearing orange trees). Continuing your walk down the same street, you encounter a typical Roman variegation of buildings: government offices dating from the Fascist era, the little Renaissance church of San Nicola in Carcere, constructed from (and in) the remains of three ancient temples, then some actual temples, then, at the curve, on your left, the four-way arch that marked the ancient city's cattle market, and – to the left of that – a sober early Renaissance building now converted into a classy and pricey residence-hotel.

Wherever you walk in the old city, you sense the past beneath your feet: a skeleton, a pedestal, an armature of the Rome you are living in. Builders hate it. If they start digging the foundations for a new construction, they are certain to uncover a patch of Roman pavement or part of a house or perhaps some potsherds; if they are law-abiding, they will inform the Fine Arts authorities; and, Roman bureaucracy being what it is (and apparently was, even a millennium ago), construction will be delayed for weeks and months. Rome's subway, still not entirely completed, has been interrupted over and over again by such troublesome discoveries.

If you want to flesh out that imagined skeleton of the city and form a precise idea of the layout of ancient Rome, you could profitably pay a visit to one of the city's least-known and, to me, most satisfying museums. This is the Museum of Roman Civilization, in one of the frigid, Mussolini-Roman buildings in the EUR quarter (a convenient subway ride from the centre of Rome). This vast museum houses not one genuine work of art; it contains endless plaster casts, models, reproductions, arranged to give a comprehensive notion of what ancient Roman civilization was like: its architecture, its commerce, its army, its family and social life, its art. There you can actually see the reliefs of Trajan's column 'unrolled' like a comic strip, so you can study the carving in a way that would be impossible with the original. In one room of the museum there is also a scale model of the city of Rome in Trajan's time. This really does look stark white, and the buildings do resemble a series of First National Banks (surely even in the days of Trajan there must have been a few scattered weeds). But it is fun to pick out the built-up lump of the Capitoline, the hulking Colosseum, the dish-shaped Circus of Domitian.

The Circus of Domitian is now Piazza Navona, where you probably sat and had ice cream yesterday or the day before. And the slit-like street you can see in the model, running northward from the Capitoline, the Via Lata, is now known as the Corso and is, as it was then, a main artery in Rome's commercial bustle. You can pick out the ancient gates, most of them still punctuating the girdle of the inner city, under new names. The Porta Flaminia is now the Porta del Popolo (refashioned in part by Michelangelo); the Porta Tiburtina – which welcomed arrivals from Tibur (Tivoli) – is now the Porta San Lorenzo. The Porta Appia was renamed San Sebastiano after the saint martyred in the vicinity; and the Porta Aurelia, leading to the sea and the coast road, dominates the Janiculum, two blocks from the American Academy, as Porta San Pancrazio.

The Via Aurelia is only one of the famous Roman roads – all of which, as we know, led to Rome – that are still in operation. Next to the history-laden Appian Way, a favourite walk for the less footsore tourists, there is the Via Appia Moderna, a major thoroughfare. The Flaminia, the Cassia, the Nomentana, the Prenestina, still stretch from the city like spokes. And inside Rome you can follow on twentieth century pavements the same itinerary that the Caesars and their fellow citizens once took. East of the Corso, the busy Via Nazionale, with its hotels and cheap shops, is the former Vicus Longus, the Long Alley, which connected with the Vicus Patricius. As its name suggests, this 'Patrician Alley' was once a fashionable address; now, as the Via Urbana, it is largely a noisy slum street, though the church of Santa Pudenziana remains as testimony to its former status, since – according to tradition – the handsome building stands on the site of the house of the wealthy Roman Pudens, who received Saint Peter there as a guest.

In the late 1920's and '30's Mussolini must have felt the same sensation of ancient grandeur under the pavements, only he was in a position to do something about it. So, with a team of archaeological advisers (and fawning yes-men), aiming at reminding the decadent modern Italians of their glorious imperial past, he made extensive excavations, ruthlessly tearing down time-hallowed medieval streets, heedlessly shifting buildings (the little church at the entrance to the Piazza Campitelli, just before the Theatre of Marcellus, originally stood much closer to the Capitoline), and exposed some ancient monuments. The largest of these is the Tomb of Augustus, a great mound encircled by cypresses, which stands in the midst of the Piazza Augusto Imperatore, between the Corso and the Tiber. Elderly Romans today lament this boring reconstruction because, to uncover it, Mussolini sanctioned the destruction of the Augusteo, the city's best symphony hall, where generations of great musicians had played.

Actually, Mussolini's excavations seem to diminish Rome's dynamism, arresting the interplay between old and new. The static Augustan tomb looks somehow fake, as bogus as the surrounding, pompous Fascist structures, with their big but ungainly arcades, their chill marble.

More impressive is the partly excavated Domus Aurea, the half-buried remains of Nero's great palace, erected on the Oppian Hill (not far from the church of San Pietro in Vincoli, where you go to admire the Michelangelo Moses). Nero's successors buried his vast construction and built over it; time and damp have destroyed or damaged much of the elaborate decoration. But there is still a magic sense of discovery when you visit the dim, dank grottoes, much as many sixteenth century painters visited them and were inspired (some – including Giulio Romano – left their names scratched on the walls). Unfortunately – or fortunately, depending on how romantic your attitude is – archaeologists plan large-scale further excavation of the Domus Aurea, so in the fairly near future its wonders will be brought to light and more scientifically, if less charmingly, displayed and preserved.

Modern Rome also has a literary patina. It is hard to sit in the Colosseum without thinking of Henry James and Daisy Miller. For that matter it is hard to look at any monument, ruin, square, without recalling what previous articulate visitors – from Stendhal and Augustus Hare to Eleanor Clark and Anthony Burgess – have observed and described. At times the weight of the past becomes almost unbearable, and a few years ago, when a brilliant American painter of my acquaintance fled Rome after his first twenty-four hours, I understood him, though I could not have followed his example.

Curiously enough, one of my favourite escapes from Rome is into the past: I go to the ruins of Ostia Antica (another easy subway ride). Though excavation of this one-time port for Rome began in the early 1800's, the real shape of this ancient city has emerged only in this century, and very recent work has uncovered some significant areas and monuments (including a synagogue, indicating the presence of a considerable Jewish colony much earlier than historians had realized). Here the past is not buried. There is only one layer – the surface – and you can walk the grassy streets, feeling you are in a real city, with apartment blocks (the large, stark *insulae*), shops and squares. In good weather I recommend taking a picnic basket into the ruins. Select a roofless, walled yard, spread your bread and cheese, open the wine and have a meal where some Roman family used to have theirs in, say, AD 100.

I find that a visit to Ostia makes Rome – ancient Rome – more distinct in my mind, and as I rush along the Via Lata toward my dentist's office or an appointment at Rosati's Café near the Porta Flaminia, the clatter of a chariot echoes in my inner ear, or the subtle rustle of a toga.

CITY OF SECRETS AND SURPRISES

Shirley Hazzard

Those who love Naples are continually challenged to defend the city by visitors who have spent a harrowing day or two there, on their way to Sorrento or Positano, Amalfi or Ravello, or to the islands of the Neapolitan gulf. Travellers who have lost wallet and temper in the Naples crush, been cheated by taxi drivers, felled by an aberrant clam and bedevilled by chaotic traffic, have stood in that great scene of anarchy and poverty and wondered at the city's fame.

They do not take kindly to the devotion Naples inspires in all who know it well. Most galling perhaps is our very acquiescence in the charges: Yes, quite true, the streets are dirty, the museums inconvenient, the services strangled by corruption. Worse still, the twin foundations on which modern tourism rests – restaurants and shopping – are not a prominent feature. Yes, indeed, Naples is indefensible.

It is also an incomparable civilization in itself; the only city of the classical world, as a Neapolitan writer has said, to survive into our times. 'A Pompeii that was never buried.' As Venice differs from other Italian cities in having no Rome in its origins, so Naples is distinct for incorporating its Greek past – the northernmost colony of Greater Greece in Italy. What remains of that ancient Greece at Naples is not, however, the elevated calm usually invoked as 'classical,' but rather the temperament execrated by Juvenal in the Greeks of the first century after Christ:

> *Quick of wit and of unbounded impudence, as ready of speech as any orator and more torrential, carrying in themselves any character you please from geometrician to rope-dancer . . . Experts in flattery – and yet believed. If you smile, they split with laughter; if you shed tears, they weep . . . They always have the best of it, at any moment taking their expression from another's face . . . And nothing is sacred to their passions.*

Those passions also add much that is sombre and tender to the resilient denizens of Il Cratere, as the arena setting of the city is sometimes called in invocation of its presiding genius – the Vesuvius to which thoughts and glances ever turn at Naples, as though to a point of reference, or a sun. Through a phenomenal continuity of recorded experience here, we know, in some measure, how Neapolitans have felt in their successive incarnations of nearly three thousand years, dominated by their unpredictable volcano, looking out at their beautiful bay – where, in Byron's phrase, 'Fame is a spectral resident.'

Naples requires time. Goethe, on his first visit, apologized for the absurdity of a mere four weeks' stay. To travellers who offer the insult of a few hours or days, the city returns its own harsh indifference, plunging them into misadventures and dismissing them. 'Covering distance' is meaningless anywhere on the Italian peninsula – where a radius of fifty miles drawn around almost any city can provide delight and interest for a lifetime; it is utter folly at Naples, where revelations are not instantaneous as at Florence or Rome and need a state of mind that settles on the outsider only gradually, as a revelation in itself. 'I tell myself, either you were mad before, or you are mad now,' said Goethe under the spell of the Neapolitan siren Parthenope, legendary spirit of the city that grew up around her tomb. 'To be enabled to dream like this is worth all difficulties.'

What is the mystery into which we are initiated at Naples – this sense of life profoundly informed by awareness of death that values the smallest pleasure as god-given, fatalistically attributing misfortune to the gods' sterner associate, Il Destino? For all its scenic display, Naples is a city of secrets.

If you come to Naples and stay at one of the good hotels on the waterfront you will enjoy a view of the harbour from windows which, if you're lucky, look over the Castel dell'Ovo – a medieval construction rising on a fragmentary villa of Lucullus and open to visitors. The small yacht basin below the castle is busy with private boats in summer, and with contraband traffic all year round. Outside the hotel, however, the surroundings are lifeless and decayed; pleasant shops are few, litter blows, traffic trundles. The vacant sensation of this quarter of Naples – the once-celebrated Santa Lucia – derives from two relatively recent obliterations: demolition following the catastrophic cholera epidemic of 1884, and the bombardments of 1943. In fact, Naples always has something of an air of having just survived calamity; it is one theme of her story.

At the top of Via Santa Lucia you will come to the royal palace, on a vast piazza laid out, with magnificent intention, for the Bourbon kings. But the piazza is intersected by traffic, and has become a car park; the palace is dingy, the arcades of the basilica opposite are befouled. In the best laid plans of mice and men, at Naples, the mice tend to win.

Persisting, you will soon discover the opera house, the seedy Galleria and the huge Castel Nuovo that dominates the port. Even so, the city eludes the search for its centre. The truth is that there are many centres at Naples, each vital to its own city quarter. And Naples is rifest perhaps at its oldest point, the district of Spacca-Napoli, where the city splits along its Greco-Roman *decumanus*. If – leaving anything snatchable safely at your hotel – you had simply taken the 140 bus from Santa Lucia to its city terminus, you would have found yourself in Naples indeed. The bus leaves you in the shadow of the church of Gesù Nuovo and its gem-cut fifteenth century façade. In mid-piazza, the Baroque runs riot in an ornate *guglia*, the Neapolitan obelisk. Before you lies a labyrinth of Gothic churches, Baroque and eighteenth century palaces, classical and early Christian fragments, medieval passages and sunlit cloister-gardens.

An itinerary can be proposed – if you wish – beginning with the heavenly beauty of the ceramic cloister behind Santa Chiara; continuing to the little Via San Gregorio Armeno, street of the *presepi*-makers – craftsmen of the celebrated Neapolitan Christmas crèches – where the church of wildest rococo has a tranquil garden upstairs, and the adjacent Gothic glory of San Lorenzo, where Boccaccio first saw Fiammetta, and where Petrarch spent a rainy night in prayer. Rising on Greek ruins, San Lorenzo also offers a Roman excavation in its adjoining cloister. Nearby, the Duomo and its ancient lower church embody the story of Naples. Such suggestions might be endless; but their meaning is inseparable from the area itself, animated with the unquenchable life of numberless shopkeepers, artisans, booksellers, pedlars and other artists of survival who live along the teeming thoroughfares of Via Benedetto Croce, San Biagio dei Librai, or Via Tribunali.

Here, modern classifications fall away, and we are restored to a world of unregulated, eccentric personality, to an outlook that encompasses all human possibilites, to faces and graces – and an intelligence – formed by a longer story than our own. In this scene of dilapidation and magnificence, Neapolitans move among their extraordinary architecture as in a natural element: Even the grandest edifices are not 'monuments' but expressions of living temperament in their nobility, their strangeness or sweetness, their theatricality. The simplicity with which, in all Italy, citizens will treat some great shrine as a familiar is almost reciprocal at Naples – where the very buildings draw vitality from the populace, who in turn seem nourished on colour, form and line.

A New York art critic, exuberantly greeting the arrival in America of the exhibition dealing with eighteenth century Naples, tells us that 'Naples is poor in mementoes of the Renaissance.' While definitions of mementoes may vary, there can be few cities, after Florence and Rome, with grander Renaissance monuments than Naples – the immense gateway of reliefs at the Castel Nuovo; the out-pouring of

Renaissance sculpture at Sant'Anna dei Lombardi; Giuliano da Maiano's triumphal arch at Porta Capuana; the stern harmony of Palazzo Penna. Many such examples come to mind. Yet more often the Renaissance at Naples merges, submerges or re-emerges, like all other periods, in a thousand unannounced details – the mighty entrance of a crumbling palazzo; a fine frieze or doorway in a scruffy lane; Pontano's exquisite academy, now a storehouse for coffins (a development that would not have been lost on the great humanist); or the lofty tomb, by Donatello and Michelozzo, recessed beyond the altar at Sant'Angelo à Nilo and accessible only at Sunday mass. A city of secrets is a city of surprises.

In fact, paradox has as much to do with the outsider's first unease at Naples as with the city's eventual claim on his affection. Time is long here, but a town with a volcano is no place to forget mortality. For a people who see existence as a synthesis, there are no conflicting elements, and Naples offers no neutral zone where tourists can be spared the worst. (On a recent chilly evening, among the fashionable shops that cluster round Piazza dei Martiri, a crowd of earthquake victims waited at a doorway for their meagre official stipend.) The puritan view that a sense of pleasure cannot be justified amid so much affliction is meaningless to Neapolitans – who know that pleasure cannot be deferred for ideal circumstances. For connoisseurs of survival, triumph and tragedy are indivisible.

Though modern suburbs offend the sight, the setting of Naples has not changed: from the lovely garden at San Martino, on the city's height, we see the prospect the ancients saw. To the right lies Posillipo – the headland the Greeks called Pausilypon, 'a rest from care.' To the left, where Vesuvius rises, the coast curves past Herculaneum and Pompeii, and the newly excavated Oplonti. The indentation of Sorrento gives place to an unspoiled countryside of olive groves and villages, on the cape where once a temple of Athena looked across to Capri. And, at the horizon, the outline of Capri itself – its lesser peak, still sacred to Tiberius, and its greater. Even in a land where *bello* is every infant's third articulate word, this beauty is unrivalled.

If the 'region of Naples' may be extended, at its southern extreme, beyond Salerno to the Greek temples at Paestum, its northern limit is defined, less than ten miles from Naples, by the ruins of Greek Cuma – one of the supreme monuments of the ancient world, little visited on its silent shore. Between Cuma and Naples lie Cape Misenum, Baia and the Phlagrean Fields – the volcanic 'Fields of Fire,' a Virgilian landscape of antiquities – and Lake Avernus, entrance to the legendary underworld. For centuries here the now shabby little town of Pozzuoli held sway – as Puteoli – as the foremost port of Europe and a resort of fabled luxury for the powerful of Rome. Puteoli was the ancient city, Neapolis the new. Now Pozzuoli looks over its 'sea of marble' – which holds the wreck of a thousand monuments and palaces that lined this coast long ago – to the volcanic cone of Ischia and the lemon groves of low-lying Procida.

The modern eye will scarcely focus here. Every promontory and overgrown declivity holds fateful associations; and the eye of imagination prevails.

From Misenum, in AD 79, the polymath Pliny set out with quadriremes to rescue the victims of Vesuvius, and died in the attempt. Watching the great eruption, on that same August day, his adolescent nephew, the younger Pliny, gathered the impressions he would later record for Tacitus. At Agrippa's naval yard, still visible beside Avernus, ships were made ready for the battle of Actium. All around the Cratere stand remnants of the lavish villas praised by Statius and decried by Horace, scenes of leisure, thought and art – and of imperial murders. From this shore Seneca watched an approaching fleet, and identified the Alexandrian mail-packets by the trim of their topsails. Here Virgil lived, the poet of this region – who, born a Mantuan, declared: 'Parthenope holds me.'

'Naples has never been worse,' says the pained observer. Really? – not under Fascism, or in the degradation and malnutrition of the postwar decade? Certainly, if you come to know Naples you will never cease to rail at its woes – joined in your laments by Neapolitans too courteous perhaps to inquire how other societies are likely to look by their third millennium. Glimpses of the arcane, the grotesque, the diabolical will never fail to startle and estrange – compounded, as in most great cities, by modern violence and disaffection. But few days will pass without some fresh discovery of dignity, delicacy and endurance; when you are not humbled and exalted by actions of human fellowship and inexpressible grace. For myself, each arrival on this shore is a rejoicing. And I wonder at the stroke of fortune that first brought me here to live in intimacy with this civilized spirit and to share its long adventure.

LIVELY BIRTHPLACE OF A
FATEFUL WORD

Jan Morris

A perpetually busy pedestrian thoroughfare, starting as the Lista di Spagna but changing its name repeatedly along the way, leads rumbustiously from the railway station at Venice into the heart of the city. Six or seven hundred yards along it, I suppose, beyond the great canal called Canareggio, a smaller street takes off to the north; and if you follow this one, the Rio Terra Farsetti, after a few minutes you will find yourself standing upon a wooden bridge before the looming back-quarters of a monumental row of buildings.

They are six, seven or eight stories high, very high for Venice, and they look from this side distinctly forbidding, for not only are their serried windows small and dark, but a canal runs all the way round them like a moat. Lines of washing flap cheerfully enough, it is true; there are canaries in cages and geraniums in pots, somebody's basket hangs on its long string waiting for the morning mail and here and there you may glimpse the movements of housewives in high kitchens. The tunnel-like entrance in front of you, though, looks grimly unwelcoming, and the sockets in its stonework, evidently meant for iron bars, make it look disturbingly like a prison gate.

Be bold. The tunnel is dark and dank indeed, but when you have passed through its shadows, and emerge through the doorway at the other end, you find yourself astonishingly in a very large, stony, airy kind of piazza, with a few young plane trees, three stone wellheads and marble benches dotted round about, and the fronts of those tall houses, not quite so cheerless from this side, towering high above it all.

It feels quite different from any other Venetian square. It feels indeed only half-Venetian, with a particular tang or perhaps muffle in the air. And this is not surprising: for you are standing in a very particular part of Venice, the Ghetto – the first of all the world's enclaves to bear that fateful name, and physically perhaps the best preserved of them to this day. Put away your guidebooks. Your instincts will be enough.

Jews were often powerful, rich, influential and admired in the Republic of Venice, but like Jews everywhere in Europe they were frequently harassed, too, and in the sixteenth century they were all obliged to move themselves lock, stock and barrel into this place. It had been an area of iron foundries, and was called 'Geto Novo' – 'New Foundry' in the Venetian dialect – and so a harmless and necessary word went into all our vocabularies as a synonym for cruelty and intolerance. Its inhabitants were never physically harmed, but they were made to wear identifying badges and were confined to the Ghetto at night: Sentries in boats patrolled the canal that completely surrounded the quarter, and barriers were placed at sunset in those ominous doorway sockets.

The Jews of Venice flourished and proliferated all the same, their situation being much happier here than in most cities, and one's first instinctive impression of this remarkable place is not one of subjection – confinement, certainly, but confinement rather in the New York manner, cramped but opportunist. Like Manhattan's sky scrapers, these tall buildings were designed to make the best use of limited space, and with the wide open square in front of them – one of the few *campi* in Venice, incidentally, to have café tables in it – they possess a dour but undeniable excitement. One could hardly have sneered at the people who lived in this stern enclave, and indeed the life of the Venetian Ghetto in its best years was lively, varied and creative.

Look up above your head now, and on the lintel there you will see the words BANCO ROSSO. It is a private house now, but once it was one of the three Jewish banks that prospered here, and contributed largely to the financial stability of the Republic itself. The Jews were not allowed to own land, but they were indispensable as bankers and pawnbrokers, as ships' suppliers, as furnishers to diplomatic missions, as agents of many sorts. Though they were officially un-Venetians, and though this Ghetto was established in a part of the city largely reserved for aliens, still they often stood paradoxically close to the founts of power in the Republic.

So we must not imagine this square, as we stroll over its somewhat bumpy flagstones, to have been a sullen or even a particularly introverted place. From the beginning of the Ghetto until its abolition at the fall of the Venetian Republic in 1797 it was a place more often than not full of vitality: Merchants discussing deals or exchange rates, learned rabbis passing here and there, visitors, no doubt from the adjoining foreign missions – scholars calling on the great publisher Daniel Bomberg, fashionable Venetians on their way to the salon of the poet Sara Copio Sullam or the consulting rooms of the famous ghetto physicians – sea captains organizing their provisions, poor folk come to hock their heirlooms, craftsmen of many kinds hammering and chiselling and sawing in ground-floor workshops all around.

The Ghetto soon expanded, and spread beyond the moat first to the south, to the area of an older iron foundry (Ghetto Vecchio), and then to the east, where it absorbed some handsome patrician mansions to form the Ghetto Nuovissimo. This was its limit until the end, and you may trace its presence exactly still, just as it was, untouched by war or pogrom.

High on the rooftops, among the bulbous Venetian chimneys, you may notice a couple of wooden cupolas, rather rickety and toppled now, but still elegant, like grace notes above the massive composition of the square below. Shortage of space made the first Jews of the Ghetto build their synagogues eyrie-like above their houses, shops and offices, nearer to God indeed than any other houses of worship in the city.

They built five in all during the first century of their segregation, three above the original square, two in the Ghetto Vecchio. All are still there, and even in this half-Eastern metropolis of the seas they are wonderfully exotic buildings to discover – so gilded still, so hung with elaborate lamps, so rich in memorial slabs, so mellow with woodwork, so grave with hanging textiles. In the Venetian manner they are called Scuole (Schools) and they remember in their names the particular communities that built them: the German School, the Italian School, the Spanish School, the Levantine School and the Canton School, which was named for the Canton family of bankers.

Though all have been rebuilt at one time or another, each remains different in style as in origin. The German School, for instance, the oldest of them all, is like a little opera house, trapezoidal in shape, surrounded by a delicately latticed women's gallery, and with a *bimah* or pulpit of light and spindly gilt, like a sedan chair. The Spanish School on the other hand is tremendously imposing: It is said to have been rebuilt in the seventeenth century by Baldassare Longhena, the architect of the great Salute church at the head of the Grand Canal, and is a showpiece of Baroque solemnity, marbled, classically de-tailed, heavy with brass candlesticks and hugely pendant chandeliers.

These structures were, of course, the foci of the Ghetto, around which all else revolved, and while some fell into decay in later years, some have never ceased to function. I went to Saturday service recently in the Levantine School, founded in 1538 in the Ghetto Vecchio, and marvellously moving I found it. There were perhaps a couple of dozen of us in the old building – a few women in the gallery, a handful of men below – but thrilling it was to think, as the ancient words sounded, as the cantor and his assistants huddled around their sacred scrolls like seers or navigators, that through all the miseries of exile and prejudice, through all the rise and fall of the very idea of Ghetto, that ancient sanctity had triumphed.

Though the Jews of Italy were guaranteed full civic equality by

King Vittorio Emanuele II in 1866, a large community of Venetian Jews lived in the Ghetto until the precarious days of Fascism and Nazism in the 1930's when many of them left. During the Second World War, in two terrible episodes, two hundred were deported to Germany and never seen again. Today only some twenty Jewish families live within the Ghetto area, but scattered through the municipality of Venice there are nearly seven hundred Jews in all, and their headquarters remain here within the old confines. The community council and the rabbinate have offices in the Ghetto Vecchio; the House of Rest for elderly Jews is in a corner of the Ghetto Nuovo; services are held every Sabbath in the Levantine School, and on special occasions in the Spanish School, too.

During the last few years the Ghetto has been noticeably reviving. I remember the place, thirty years ago, as melancholy indeed, its tall buildings crumbling, its great square rubbish-strewn and deserted, its Jewishness apparently hidden away behind locked doors – only an eighteenth century stone slab of rules and regulations, and a sombre twentieth century memorial to the dead of the concentration camps honoured the history of the first of all the ghettos. Today things are very different. There is a new and more assertive memorial to the victims of the holocaust, a series of bronze slabs by the sculptor Arbit Blatas, but there is also a burgeoning of Jewish consciousness in a more hopeful kind.

For one thing, those old synagogues are being restored one by one to glory, and are already becoming a tourist attraction fascinating even by Venetian standards. For another, there is now a lively museum of Jewish art, beneath the German School. And for a third, the Ghetto at large has found a new pride in itself, and attracts to its purlieus many kinds of craftsmen and their families – not to speak of Jewish visitors from abroad. The old square rings again to the sound of saw and hammer, children kick footballs about the wellheads, and cheer up with their laughter the old people of the House of Rest, which has its own little oratory, by the way, besides an excellent kosher dining room that is, I am told, very hospitable to visitors.

Jewish shops show themselves again. 'Shalom!' is heard across the square. On one corner of the Ghetto Nuovo, Gianfranco Penzo produces and sells works of art, in glass and enamel, that are an innovative blend of Jewish and Venetian forms – a union of styles, it seems, never achieved before. On another corner, until he emigrated recently to the United States, was the shop of the glassworker Gianni Toso; one of his chess sets, in which a team of rabbis is matched against a team of Christian priests, was bought by the Corning Glass Museum, the ultimate accolade for craftsmen in glass.

Then there are a couple of shops selling specifically Jewish souvenirs, candelabra, ornaments, postcards; and some Jewish furniture-restorers, following one of the oldest traditions of the Ghetto; and in the Calle del Forno, Oven Lane, a bakery still makes unleavened bread and Jewish sweetmeats. Sometimes there is a wedding in the Spanish School, and into the little square outside seep the wheezy strains of its venerable hand-pumped organ; and almost any day of the year, at about 10 o'clock in the morning, tourists from all over the world come trailing down the alleyways on their guided tour of the synagogues, exchanging old Jewish jokes in Italian, Hebrew or Brooklynese. The Ghetto, a place of sad suggestion, has lost is sadness for now.

Well, almost lost it. We entered the Ghetto at its northern end, where the silhouette of the square is an excitement in itself. We will leave it at the south, down the long narrow street of the Ghetto Vecchio, and there we may still feel some gentle emanations, wistful perhaps rather than tragic, of sorrows long ago.

The deportation memorial is sad, of course, and the list of names, on the wall of the Levantine School, of those Venetian Jews who died in the First World War – Aboaf, Boralevi, Foa. But it is something less tangible, something suggestive in the atmosphere or in the old grey walls that makes this thoroughfare a little dispiriting still. It feels so very tight, so shut-in, so introspective. Faces look pale down here in the shadowy light, eyes seem to look out a little suspiciously from the doors of workshops or the windows of houses up above. It feels, in short, just a little, just a tremor, like a living ghetto still.

Of course it is all imagination – the past is gone, the gates are open, the Jews of Venice are free as air: but still I think you may experience, as you pass through the southern gateway of the Ghetto on to the sunlit quayside of Canareggio, where the fish stalls are a babel of commerce and the espresso machines hiss hospitably in the cafés – I think you may experience, all the same, some faint sense of unease or even unreality: as though you have passed through a chamber of time, or wandered down that alley from one sensibility to another.

ALL THE FACTS (SOME TRUE)
ABOUT GONDOLAS

MacDonald Harris

We have Venetian friends who live in the sixteenth century palazzo near Campo San Cassan, in a quiet part of the city out of the ordinary tourist track. We have borrowed their apartment occasionally and have lived in it for two long stays. In this way I have had the opportunity to become familiar with the more remote parts of the city, have struck up friendships with all kinds of ordinary people and have even learned a few words of the Venetian dialect, which in some ways is more like Spanish than Italian. A street is a *calle*, pronounced exactly like the Spanish, and a small canal is a *rio*. A number of words from Venetian have passed into English – *ghetto*, *lagoon*, *canal* and *arsenal*, for example. And of course *gondola*.

Like practically every other writer who has lived in Venice, I was eventually seized with the idea of writing a book about it. As I imagined it, it was to be a historical novel set in 1797, at the time of the fall of the Venetian Republic to the Bonapartist armies. The climax of the novel was to take place in the Arsenal – but the trouble was that the Arsenal was still being used by the Italian navy and was a military reservation off limits to all civilians, especially foreigners.

I soon made what seemed to me a remarkable discovery. A certain *motoscafo* – one of the small water-buses that ply around through the canals, like buses in any other city – went directly down a *rio* through the centre of the Arsenal, exposing all of its military secrets, such as the huge covered bays in which war-galleys were constructed in the sixteenth century. It is as though, for some unexplained reason, an American bus line went directly through the centre of Fort Knox. Anyone can take this *motoscafo*; it is line No. 5, called Circolare Sinistra because it circles around the city to the left, and you can board it at San Zaccaria near San Marco.

I went through the Arsenal countless times on No. 5 and took a lot of photos. I liked the idea of doing my work on a floating bus. Venice, entrancing for anyone, is all the more so if you love water, and if you love ships and boats, as I do. In Venice everything that is done by trucks and motor vehicles in other cities is done by boats. Refrigerators, grand pianos and stage sets for the opera at the Fenice are delivered in boats and criminals are taken to jail in floating Black Marias. The hearses that carry the dead to the cemetery at San Michele are boats. And for taxis, there are gondolas.

I was fascinated by the gondola the first time I ever saw one. Like the Micronesian *prua*, the clipper ship and the Indian birchbark canoe, the gondola is one of the great naval designs of all time. Its lines are perfect and its proportions are graceful. It is exactly suited to its function, and in addition to this – or perhaps because of this – it is exquisitely beautiful. The secret of its design – but I anticipate.

Since the research on my novel was going rather slowly, I decided that first I should perhaps write a small nonfiction book about gondolas, with pictures and technical details. I started off on this job full of confidence. I was certainly qualified; I knew Venice, I understood boats and I knew how to write. I discovered that, although a great deal has been written about gondolas, there was almost nothing about their technical aspects, including their design and construction. The thing that intrigued me – the thing that would intrigue anyone who took the slightest interest in boats – was the secret of how the gondolier made the thing go straight even though he rowed only on one side. He could make turns to the right or left, he could stop it, back it up and start out again in a straight line, all with nothing but the long oar sticking out over the water to the right. There was a mystery here that I was determined to clear up. Either the gondoliers were enchanters who had learned how to transgress the laws of physics, or they were doing something with the oar I couldn't grasp. I made friends with a gondolier.

His name was Alvise, which is simply the Venetian form of Louis, and he was a very helpful and friendly young man. The trouble was that much of his explanation involved Venetian terms, such as *stali* and *premi*, and my Venetian was still imperfect. I did gather that there was a sort of feathering motion at the end of the stroke, the sort of thing you do when paddling a canoe on one side. The trick couldn't be explained by analogies from canoes, however. (For one thing, in a canoe you paddle close to the hull and you don't have a long unwieldy oar sticking out ten feet over the water on the right-hand side.)

I examined Alvise's gondola a little more carefully and learned the names of some of its parts. It was out of season and he had nothing much to do but chatter to me about these matters. The most curious and beautiful part of the gondola, it seemed to me, was the elaborately carved hardwood oarlock, the post against which the oar was set to make the stroke. It had all sorts of notches and convexities in it to hold the oar for different manoeuvres. It was called the *forcola*. When I got the idea of buying one to take home as a souvenir, Alvise offered to sell me his own for a million lire, then about $1,600. I was beginning to see that he had a nice sense of humour. Later, prowling about the various antique shops in the city, I found you could get one a good deal cheaper; they ranged from $50 to $300. In fact, I found a shop near Campo Santo Stefano where workmen could be seen making *forcole* in the rear, amid a mounting pile of chips on the floor. A kindly antiquarian explained to me that scores of these were manufactured every day to sell to tourists. They never got near a gondola. A real *forcola*, he told me, was carved from a natural crook of a tree, and no two were the same; gondolas were custom-made for their owners and each gondolier had a slightly different notion of where the notches and convexities were to go. He had an authentic *forcola*, from a real gondola, which he offered to sell me. The price was a million lire.

Back to the nomenclature: The elaborately worked iron halberd at the bow of the gondola was called the *ferro*, which was straightforward enough; it simply means iron. Alvise had several explanations, all of them contradictory, as to why there were six projecting blades on the *ferro* plus a broader one at the top. The best story was that the small blades represented the six precincts, or *sestieri*, of Venice, and the large one represented the whole city. As to why the *ferro* was on the bow of the gondola at all, there were also several stories. Perhaps it was so that the patricians in the old days – sharpening their halberds – could warn other craft out of their path. Perhaps it was to catch weeds in case the gondola went out into the marshes. Or perhaps it was on account of the *felze*.

Felze? The *felze*, Alvise explained, was the cabin that fitted over the passengers in cold weather. All gondolas used to have them *poco fa*, a while back. (I discovered later that he meant in the eighteenth century). The *ferro*, you see, *Sior Capitan* (since I knew so much about boats he had decided by this time I was a captain), is just the same height as the *felze*; so, if you want to go under a low bridge, if the *ferro* will go through, then the *felze* will go through too. Like a cat's whiskers, the *ferro* was a feeler for testing small openings.

So far so good. In order to see what a *felze* really looked like, I went to inspect an authentic eighteenth century gondola in the museum of the Ca' Rezzonico. As far as I could tell, it was exactly like the gondolas in use today, except for the *felze*. The *felze* looked something like one of those removable hard-tops you can get for your Mercedes-Benz or other sports car, except that it was taller in its proportions and it was black. When I examined it more closely, however, I found out finally what a Venetian blind was. This was something that had puzzled me for years. There are no Venetian blinds in Venice, just as there is no French toast in France. The high windows of the older palazzi are closed with solid wooden shutters, and you must remember to latch them when there is a thunderstorm or they will swing around wildly, like loose cannons on a warship, and smash the windows. Most Venetian houses are so close together that the sun never comes in anyhow, so there is no need for Venetian blinds. But there, on the *felze* of the gondola in Ca' Rezzonico, I saw them – thin black narrow slats, hinged at the ends and held together with another slat you could push to open and shut them. Some ingenious American, no doubt, who saw them on his travels, was caught by the idea and went back to his own country to found the first Venetian blind factory. I was really pleased with this discovery.

There was another mystery I had been pondering over for years, and it was a rather delicate one. How did people manage to carry out these romances-in-gondolas that we were always reading about in stories? The largest of the three seats, black like everything else, was a kind of double armchair called the *poltrona*, and the back of it was bolt upright. With my limited knowledge of anatomy, and of romance, I didn't see how it could be done. But, inspecting this antique gondola more carefully, I found a cunning latch at the rear of the seat, where a hand could reach around and feel for it. Turn the latch and the back of the *poltrona* fell flat. The gondolier, presumably, was a discreet fellow, and besides he could't see anything through the *felze*. Of course gondolas didn't have *felzi* anymore. It was true, I thought, that the quality of life had declined in the twentieth century.

Well, all of these discoveries, proper and improper, had still not explained how you made a gondola go straight by rowing only on one side. I asked Alvise if he would give me a lesson. *Certo*, he said, mentioning an astronomical price, which I agreed to pay. When we got out on the water, however, I discovered that he had no intention whatsoever of letting me stand up there on the stern and take hold of the oar. What he had in mind was a demonstration. It was probably only a problem in translation. Very well, I would pay the astronomical price for a demonstration. It was all research, and perhaps the gondola book would make some money. He demonstrated several different oar-strokes. It was something like paddling a canoe – *premi* meant a stroke with a little outward swish at the end that corrected the tendency to curve to the left, and *stali* was a stroke in which you held water at the end, in order to – well, I still didn't quite understand it.

I crawled far out on the end of the gondola, past the place where Alvise was standing, in order to photograph the swirls of water around the oar-blade as it went through its various strokes. I thought that if I studied the photos later I could figure out how the various strokes differed and how they made the gondola turn to left or right. This was successful; the trouble was that when I leaned out for the last shot I fell off the gondola into the lagoon. Perhaps 'fell off' is too violent a term.

What happened was simply that I lost my balance on the stern, found that I had nothing to hang on to and slid, limb by limb, with as much dignity as I could muster, into the lagoon. I had plenty of time to hand my Pentax to Alvise.

Alvise, who was really a friendly fellow, didn't jeer at me at all on account of this mishap. Instead he advised me to go for information to the local office of the gondoliers' guild, which is called the Cooperativa Daniele Manin fra Gondolieri di Venezia. There I found another friendly person, the director of the guild, Commendatore Ugo Palmarin. When I explained to him what I wanted – I had dry clothes on by this time and was very plausible, casually dropping terms like *forcola* and *premi* – Commendatore Palmarin was quite helpful. He not only provided me with a photocopy of the hull lines of a typical gondola – exactly what I had been looking for – but he gave me a note to the proprietor of the *squero,* or gondola boatyard, in San Trovaso, an out-of-the-way corner of Venice seldom visited by tourists, even though it is not far from the Accademia. I should have gone to him in the first place.

With the help of Commendatore Palmarin's plans and explanations – he demonstrated for me, using a teaspoon as an oar and an ashtray as a gondola – and what I learned by visiting the *squero,* I soon felt I had solved the mysteries about gondolas and their design. At the *squero* a dozen or more of them were hauled out, upside down or on their sides, in various stages of repair. The chief secret was that the bottom of the gondola was not straight. One side of the hull was more deeply curved and the other was flatter, like a bow and its bowstring. An empty gondola, therefore, set into the water and given a push, would describe a long and gentle curve to the right – thus counteracting the tendency to turn to the left caused by rowing on only one side. And that wasn't all. The flat bottom of the craft was tilted, so that as it sat in the water empty it heeled to one side. When the gondolier stepped onto it, he stood with his weight on one side, so that he brought it level again. This forced the asymmetrical hull farther down into the water, and increased the built-in tendency of the hull to curve to the right. The gondolier could steer the craft, I now saw, simply by moving his weight a few inches to the right or left on the piece of rug where he stood behind the passengers. This incidentally solved another mystery – why gondoliers are so particular about exactly where the passengers sit and how they distribute their weight.

I took some pictures at the *squero* and shook hands with everybody, including the workmen, whose hands were covered with pitch – I saw now how they made the lightly built wooden boat watertight. But, for one reason or another, I never did write the technical book about gondolas. Perhaps I was so awed by the mysteries I had solved that I foresaw, or feared, there would be many more – too many for any mere foreigner to grasp. Why, for example, are all gondolas painted black? I had never thought about that.

I did, however, write my novel; *Pandora's Galley* was published a couple of years later. Coming back to Venice after the book was published, I took a trip through the Arsenal on *motoscafo* No. 5 just for old time's sake. As soon as I saw the gondolas in the *rio,* I got excited again and thought that perhaps I could do the gondola book after all. I knew all about rowing them, which nobody else did. If there were other mysteries, I would get to the bottom of them. What if they were painted black! I could ask Alvise why it was; he would give me some explanation or other, even though it might not be the right one.

I got off the *motoscafo* at San Zaccaria and soon found him near the Molo. He was manoeuvring his gondola to get it between the big mooring stakes stuck into the mud along the quay, and in some way he was making it go sideways. There is absolutely no way that you can make a gondola go sideways by doing anything whatsoever with an oar while standing far back on the narrow stern of the thing. He pretended not to recognize me and stopped making the gondola go sideways as soon as he saw I had noticed what he was doing.

AFOOT AND UNHURRIED IN LUCCA

A. Alvarez

In northern Tuscany the tourist trade route runs west along the autostrada from Florence to Pisa, missing Lucca by less than a mile. No doubt this arrangement satisfies Lucca and its citizens perfectly well, since it is a conservative town in a conservative area – one of the few in Tuscany where the Communists have yet to make significant inroads in local politics. The place is elegant, unhurried and spectacularly self-enclosed: It lies behind a dry moat and vast slanting ramparts of mellow brick, their tops thickly wooded and wide enough for a good road and shaded picnic area.

The ramparts, which took a hundred years to build and were finished in 1650, are pierced by arched gateways ornamented with marble figures and coats of arms. Originally the gates were defended by drawbridges, double iron doors and heavy portcullises, all of which have now gone. Yet driving in under the great dark archways still feels like entering a castle – a separate, private world where you have to watch your manners.

Within the walls, of course, the din is like that of any other Italian town. George Orwell pointed out that the Italians can't do anything without making a terrible noise, and the Lucchese are no exceptions. Pedestrians and automobiles and motorbikes jostle each other in the narrow streets and the racket echoes back from the looming buildings. Yet even the noise is intimate, like family chatter. The battalions of booming foreigners who patrol Florence and Pisa, cameras at the ready, are nowhere to be seen.

They ignore Lucca, I suppose, because the place is blessed by having no three-star Grand Tour masterpieces, nor even an art gallery worth mentioning. There is a museum in the Palazzo Guinigi, a fifteenth century brick palace with what looks like a barn for drying hay on its roof and a tall brick tower crowned, incongruously, with trees. But the paintings and historical bric-a-brac on display are mostly second-rate. To the masterpiece addict, the best Lucca can offer is three or four beautiful churches containing three or four beautiful pieces of sculpture – which is not much, in Italy, for a provincial capital with an archbishop and fifty thousand inhabitants. Lucca's real attraction – apart from its olive oil, which is the best and most famous in the world – is its atmosphere, an intricate distillation of that curiously Italian historical richness in which the present and the past are inextricably mingled, and ancient buildings are adapted unselfconsciously to modern uses and modern lives.

It once was, for example, an important Roman city; Lucca commanded the junction of the Cassia, Clodia and Aurelia roads and was the site of a summit conference between Julius Caesar, Pompey and Crassus in 56 BC But the great amphitheatre it boasted at that time was first destroyed by the barbarians, then had its columns and marble quarried for churches. Later still, during the Middle Ages, houses were built on the ruins, using the foundations and what remained of the original Roman structure.

Today the perfect oval of the amphitheatre has become a kind of imperial frame for tenement housing: There are shops in the dark cellarage where the gladiators and wild animals once waited; the arena is cluttered with Fiats and sleeping cats; in place of the spectators' stalls are narrow, ramshackle houses, their windows festooned with lines of drying clothes.

Lucca's moment of glory came early, in the twelfth and thirteenth centuries, when its power was almost as great as that of Florence, and Lucchese silks, exported all over Europe, brought in considerable wealth. Architecturally this was a boon, for it means that the style of the three main churches is basically Romanesque – simple, harmonious, Early Christian – and even the specifically Lucchese additions – the tiers of carved saints and sinners and animals – are formal and ingenuous, like Douanier Rousseau paintings turned to stone.

The earliest and most perfect of the town's three major churches is the Basilica San Frediano, just inside the city walls. Its chaste white façade, blank except for three doors and four small round windows, rises to a huge thirteenth century mosaic, vividly coloured but very stylized, of a great blue Christ flanked by two great blue angels ascending majestically above a row of glum apostles. The interior is dark, spacious and solemn, the three tall naves separated by unadorned columns. There is also a Romanesque font, elaborately carved with a comic strip of Egyptians pursuing Israelites, all of them in medieval armour and cassocks, some riding two to a horse. Just inside the door is a statue of a lady with a face and flowing robes as pure as a snowdrop. It is probably the work of the great Sienese sculptor Jacobo della Guercia.

His other masterpiece is the tomb of Ilaria in the Cathedral San Martino. Ilaria was the wife of Paolo Guinigi, the despotic ruler of fifteenth century Lucca. But she died young and her tomb, an act of devotion by her otherwise unspeakable husband, is a work of extraordinary tenderness. Her serene head lies on two plump cushions, and where her feet protrude from the sweep of her robes a little pug dog – the symbol of domestic fidelity – is curled up asleep. Her dress is high-waisted and high-necked, her chin is firm, her mouth peaceful. Ruskin called the statue 'a lesson of love as no coldness could refuse, no fatuity forget and no insolence disobey.' Except, that is, for the dancing cherubs on the tomb below, whose faces are peculiarly dissolute and knowing.

The Cathedral also houses the Volto Santo, or Holy Countenance, to which pilgrims came in the thousands during the Middle Ages and by which generations of French kings swore their oath. According to legend, the Volto Santo was carved by Nicodemus, who helped bury Jesus, then was hidden for centuries in a cave. An Italian bishop learned of its whereabouts in a vision and put it on a ship without a crew that found its way miraculously to the Ligurian coast at Luni, near Genoa. There it floated while the Bishop of Luni and the Genoese tried unsuccessfully to get aboard.

But the ship, apparently, had a will of her own and kept out of their reach until Giovanni, Bishop of Lucca, arrived with his followers. Giovanni knelt down on the sand, prayed and 'stretched out his arms with great devotion toward the ship, and with his hand drew her to earth as though she had been a feather.' The carving was then put on a wagon drawn by two unbroken steers, which headed immediately for Lucca and stopped of their own accord outside San Martino.

It is easy to understand why the Volto Santo should come equipped with a legend. The crucified, blue-robed figure is large, primitive, forbidding and unearthly. The head, with its black hair and beard and chocolate-coloured face, leans forward accusingly, eyes wide, grieving mouth downturned. It is a figure of terrible agony and no forgiveness at all, a looming presence that puts to shame the jewelled knick-knacks that surround it and makes the frivolous little octagonal chapel in which it is housed seem like a bird cage for a panther.

Both the Cathedral and Lucca's third major church, San Michele, have exteriors that start Romanesque and solemn but fail helplessly to sustain the mood, becoming more and more fanciful with each new story. San Michele, in fact, is built on the principle of a saloon in the Old West: Its pokey interior is three stories shorter than the façade that rises, like the final triumph of a deranged pastry cook, in ascending tiers of marble columns, each different from its neighbour – twisted, carved, lozenged, white, brown, green. Crowning it all is St. Michael himself, an orb in one hand, a spear in the other, feet placed firmly on a lively but defeated dragon. On either side of him two angels blow their trumpets to proclaim the victory. It is an architectural form of grand opera that would have appealed to Puccini, who was born just opposite at Via di Pioggio 30.

Three churches and four pieces of sculpture: Even the most dutiful culture vulture can get through them in a morning, leaving the rest of the day to enjoy the pleasures of the town itself.

Lunch, for example, in Lucca's one downtown restaurant to be awarded a star by Michelin. Michelin's Italian choices are usually more interesting for the places left out than for those included, as though the boisterous style of Italian cooking were beyond the exquisite French palate. But in Lucca, for once, they have got it right. The **Buca di San Antonio** is fastidious and quiet, despite the collection of dented brass instruments that hang from the ceiling among the smoked hams. The linen is crisp, the glasses and cutlery glitter and the house speciality, baby goat roasted on a spit, is unfailingly delicious. In late summer, after the rains have come, they also serve the regional speciality of giant fungi roasted in the oven with oil and garlic, like a joint of lamb. The house *digestif* is Grappa di Barola, which is as different from the ordinary rotgut grappa as Napoleon brandy is from three-star.

After lunch, while the rest of the town is taking its afternoon nap, is the time to wander the web of narrow streets and little squares where all the styles of architecture for the last seven hundred years are jumbled together – Romanesque churches, diminutive medieval palazzi, Renaissance window-cages, monumental eighteenth century doors, nineteenth century lodging houses with wooden balconies and protruding ironwork lamps. The sour green strip of canal in the Via del Fosso leads out to the city walls, where you can walk on the grass in the shade of giant chestnuts and plane trees and enjoy the cool breeze from the Apennines to the north. It seems a long way from Florence, baking in its basin of hills, or the sweating crowds in Pisa's Piazza del Duomo.

If you leave the walls at San Frediano and cross the square, past the coppersmiths with their pots piled up on the sidewalk, you come to the bottom of the Via Fillungo, Lucca's answer to London's Jermyn Street, where the shopfronts are as elegant as the clothes and leather goods and jewellery on display: windows framed in art nouveau glass, gold lettering on glossy black above the doors, a jeweller's shop with carved wooden window frames like choir stalls.

In the late afternoon there is an endless *passeggiata* along the Via Fillungo, as though the whole town, young and old, working and idle, had the duty to wander, window-shopping and gossiping, at least once a day, down the curving length of the street.

At its midpoint is the Antico Cafe Caselli, now called Di Simo, the unofficial cultural centre of Lucca since the early years of the century.

Puccini, Mascagni and the local major poet Giovanni Pascoli were friends of the original owner Caselli, and after Puccini's death he celebrated their memory by awarding annually a Caselli Prize for Literature, the Figurative Arts and Music. The tradition was revived after World War II by the Gruppo Renato Serra, which met weekly from 1947 to 1954. The names of those who attended the meetings are carved on a marble plaque on the rear wall; they include Salvatore Quasimodo, Giuseppe Ungaretti, Mario Praz and the '*poeta Americano*' Robert Lowell.

The literary gatherings no longer take place, but the atmosphere remains: the turn of the century preserved in lavish mahogany and glass. It is a long room with covered glass counters running half its length, one displaying savoury snacks, the other cakes, chocolates and candies. Behind the savoury counter is a bar with an extraordinary display of malt whiskies, behind the other a wallful of imported teas and biscuits and Tiptree jams. There is also the usual extravagant showcase of home-made ice creams. At the back of the main café is a smaller, darker room, opening onto a square, where a handful of silent customers sip coffee and play chess. It is like a London club without the pomp and snobbery: solid, comfortable and somehow out of time, as though its values had a life and harmony beyond fashion. In other words, it is like Lucca itself, the perfect town for those who love Italy and its way of life but dread the occupational hazards of sightseeing – the crowds and what Robert Benchley once called 'museum feet.'

ATHENS
AND BEYOND

PUZZLE OF THE PARTHENON

John Russell

One of the oddest, oldest and most controversial facts about European travel is that if you want to understand the Parthenon in Athens you simply have to stop off in London on the way.

The reason for this is that the Parthenon – the temple of Athena that stands on top of the Acropolis Hill that dominates Athens – is a sculptural achievement as much as an architectural one, and that since the beginning of the nineteenth century many of the most important sculptures from the Parthenon have been in the British Museum in London. They have never looked quite comfortable there. The light is wrong, the rooms are wrong. But there they are; and whereas many of the sculptures that stayed on in Athens have suffered . terribly from neglect, from wind and weather, and more recently from industrial pollution, the Elgin Marbles – to give then the name by which they are universally known – are relatively in very good shape.

How they got to be in London is a tale often told but not so often understood. The Seventh Earl of Elgin was British Minister to Turkey in the first years of the nineteenth century, when Athens was a Turkish fief. Unlike many of the people who had been picking away at the Parthenon for years, he was neither a vandal nor a crook. He was an experienced diplomat and a man of taste and good judgement. In 1801 he got permission from the Turks to remove a certain number of sculptures from the Parthenon and take them to England. He paid for them with his own money, he got them back to London and he sold them (not at a profit) to the British Museum. It is therefore in London, as well as in Athens, that one of the supreme achievements of Greece in the fifth century BC must be studied. It is almost, though not quite, as if anyone who wanted to see Shakespeare's *Hamlet* had to see the first three acts in England and the rest in Albania.

There was nothing new about removal of the sculptures. People had been taking down sculptures from the Parthenon since the early Christian era. Isolated pieces can be found to this day in French and German museums. Nor had the Athenians been above taking a piece or two to ornament their own houses. It was not until the second decade of the nineteenth century, when the Greeks finally won their independence, that the Parthenon became a matter for serious scientific study, as distinct from a seductive junkyard from which every man felt free to help himself.

Even so, Lord Elgin's actions were very badly regarded – not least, by his own countrymen. One traveller claimed that the huge rectangular slabs had been so clumsily cut away that large pieces of the surrounding masonry came away with them. Another said that the removal of the sculptures has been 'conducted with an eager spirit of insensate outrage, and an ardour of insatiate rapacity, in opposition not only to every feeling of taste, but to every sentiment of justice and humanity.' The name of Elgin was mud. *Elginism* and *Elginist* are fighting words to this day.

Meanwhile the sculptures quietly settled in as an accepted part of the British Museum. The huge building – itself a masterpiece of Greek Revival architecture – became known as a place in which classical Greek sculpture could be examined at leisure. Philhellenes padded through the palatial forecourt, looked their fill, and went off to restore themselves at the Museum Tavern, which still stands across the way. Artists came from all over, too, as they still do, to examine what was accepted as the all-time high point of naturalism in sculpture. (Henry Moore, for one, took from the Elgin Marbles when he first began to work on the theme of the reclining figure.)

The visitor saw them then, as he sees them now, in close-up. He saw them in a way he could never have seen them in Athens, where they were shown high above his head. He saw that fabled creature the centaur in the heat of action. He saw horsemen in full career. He saw long- horned cattle. He saw gods and heroes, and he saw the people of Athens streaming by in solemn procession. He was a very lucky fellow, and yet the experience was incomplete.

Impressive as they were in London, there was – and there is still – something unsatisfactory about the Elgin Marbles. They were not carved as 'museum pieces.' Nor were they meant to be studied more or less at eye level. They were meant to stand way above our heads. Many of them were part of a narrative frieze that went on and on for ever and ever. Quite apart from all that, they belonged with the architecture. Their proportions were dictated by the architecture, and it was only in the context of the architecture that they made complete sense.

Furthermore, it wasn't just any old architecture. The Parthenon in Athens is by universal consent one of the most remarkable sights that this earth has to show. No matter how we rate the surviving monuments of antiquity, the Parthenon has to come very high among them. In point of accessibility, moreover, it is the unquestioned Number

One. Unlike the marvels of Peru, it does not leave us breathless from high altitude in a land where all is strange to us. Unlike Persepolis in Iran, and Angkor Wat in Cambodia, it is not off-limits today. Unlike the labyrinthine temples of Karnak, it is finite and compact.

Besides, no one ever got lost looking for the Parthenon. What site could be more conspicuous than the Acropolis, a metropolitan mountaintop within minutes of a major airport? No visitor to Athens can lose sight of the Parthenon for long. And when we go to see it at close quarters the climb still has an element of initiation about it. No matter how many others may be treading the same steps, the primal awe remains intact. There are experiences that simply cannot be devalued, and this is one of them. Even in ruined state, the Parthenon speaks for a style of building that in majesty, lucidity and serenity has never been surpassed.

When I first saw it, as a schoolboy, the Parthenon was still freely accessible. Visitors were few, out of season. You could walk up and down, and in and out, as you pleased. You could get to feel its proportions in your very bones, and you could ask your friends to pose for a photograph the way Isadora Duncan preferred – in profile, with the incomparable columns as a frame and the clean blue Aegean skies overhead. Nobody bothered you. The shepherds and the goatherds had gone, as had the wolves and foxes that once infested the area, but fundamentally you stood where Byron had stood, and Chateaubriand and Ernest Renan (whose 'Prayer on the Acropolis' is to this day in every anthology of French prose).

What we had, in other words, was a nineteenth century experience in an environment initiated in the fifth century BC. We did not complain. What was our view of classical Greece, after all, if not a nineteenth century view? The great nineteenth century scholars, translators, commentators, historians and archaeologists had had their way with us. We read as they read, saw as they saw, felt as they felt. Plato and Socrates spoke, for us, in the accents of Benjamin Jowett, the Master of Balliol College, Oxford, in Victorian times. Greek drama on the English stage had got nowhere since the turn of the century. Homer came to us by courtesy of Butcher & Lang, a long-running Victorian team. (If sometimes it occurred to us that Butcher was well named, we had to stay in after school for saying so.)

There was no getting away from those eminent Victorians. The Parthenon, the Acropolis as a whole and indeed every classical site in Greece had been edited by them. If there had ever been a Byzantine era in Greece, they were not going to tell us about it. If the long Turkish domination had brought mosque and minaret even into the interior of the Parthenon itself, they took them out and saw to it that they were never mentioned again. Even our opinions about everyday life in classical Greece were formed by oleaginous late-Victorian subject paintings; and when we took that novelty of the day, a Hellenic cruise, we were guided here, thither and yon by a genuine unreconstructed Victorian clergyman.

It was not as bad as it sounds, either. We got to know the Parthenon in our own time and at our own pace. In particular, we took in the surviving sculptures at all times of day. We saw them in monochrome, of course, and in battered state. But we were not roped off, as visitors are today. Nor could we foresee the industrial pollution that has done irrevocable damage not only to the Parthenon but to the Acropolis as a whole. (When the famous caryatids were taken down from the Erechtheum, not so long ago, they were in a state of filth and decay that wrenched the heart.)

What we didn't do, and what nobody has managed to do satisfactorily, is to imagine what the Parthenon looked like when it was first completed. In this matter we were, and are, and always shall be, in a no-win situation. Reared to think of classical sculpture in terms of cool white marble, we resent the idea that the Parthenon was once high and strong in colour. Once we have learned to fill out the fragmentary signals that come to us both in Athens and in the British Museum, we should almost begrudge beginning all over again if we saw them as they originally were – complete, and with bronze accoutrements.

In other words we know what the Victorians saw, more or less, when a newly independent Greece encouraged foreign scholars to study its ancient monuments. We know, more or less, what the great explosion was like that wrecked the Parthenon once and for all in the year 1687. (Athens at the time was being attacked by the Venetian armies. The Turks used the Parthenon as a powder magazine. The Venetians scored a direct hit, and that was the end of the Parthenon in anything like its original form.) And we know, more or less, the informal tumbledown look that the Parthenon had for the next century and more. The eighteenth century Acropolis was like a Turkish market town that had got itself some disproportionately impressive ruins.

But if we go backward in time there are long centuries that we cannot decipher at all. We like to imagine the Parthenon in the fifth century BC, when Pericles the statesman, Pheidias the sculptor, Aeschylus and Sophocles the dramatists and Plato and Aristotle the philosophers could have walked in to see the forty-foot-high statue of the virgin goddess Athena that was at that time the culminating feature of the Parthenon. But the great age of Athens was brief. And what is not so easy for us is the period only a century or two later when someone wrote that 'Athens is now famous only for its beekeepers.'

So the Parthenon sets us problems of entanglement that have never quite been solved, and perhaps never will be. It belongs to the history of art, but it also belongs to the history of society. It would be hard to cite any other single collective effort, pressed through at top speed over a single generation, that produced such remarkable results. Pericles thought of everything, when he planned the new Acropolis, and he thought of everyone. There can hardly have been a single Athenian who did not in some way contribute directly to the Parthenon, and to its neighbours on that mountaintop. Plutarch the historian tells us how Pericles itemized everyone, from the pilot at sea to the rope-maker on land, and from the goldsmith, the coppersmith and the stonemason to the horse-breeder, and he made them all feel important.

It is for firsthand evidence of that astonishing episode in human history that we scan the sculptures in the British Museum, and press against the barriers that now keep us away from the Parthenon.

FROM ACROPOLIS TO ZAPPION

David Plante

Getting out of the plane into the warm air, I find myself facing Mount Hymettus, wide and high and purple against the deep blue sky, all along its base apartment houses, and tears come to my eyes. I think: I love this place.

Then an hour-long wait in line for a taxi. The line is regulated by a policeman. My turn comes and the policeman leaves for a moment. The taxi driver asks if anyone else is going to Pangrati, the area in Athens where I am staying in a friend's apartment. Most drivers will stop to pick up extra passengers going in the same direction as you. I only mind that my driver asks for other passengers because the person who steps forward is an enormous woman with an enormous suitcase and two enormous daughters. The policeman comes back and he and the driver shout at one another. I am taken alone by the angry driver. He covers the meter with a cloth.

In Athens, he goes in and out of small streets, lost, for many of the drivers are from the provinces and do not know their way around. I try to speak Greek to him to let him know I'm not unfamiliar with the city, and he speaks Greek back, most of which I don't understand. The radio is on loud, playing Greek popular music, which, with twanging strings and high, wailing voices, puts me immediately into a Middle Eastern city; and from the rearview mirror dangles a *komboloi* with a tassel (every time I see these worry beads, I am reminded of Islamic prayer beads), a blue glass medallion emblazoned with a white eye to ward off the evil eye, and a Byzantine crucifix made of a coloured reproduction pasted on wood. There is a sign below the covered meter, MH KAPNIZETE, NO SMOKING, and he is smoking up a cloud as dense as the cloud of city pollution – called, in fact, '*to nefos*' the cloud – we are driving through.

When, finally, he finds the apartment house, we both get out and he says in English, 'Five hundred drachmas.' I know the fare can be no more than half that, and I say I want to see the meter. 'Broken,' he says. I insist on seeing the meter. 'Three hundred,' he says. Again I insist, and he slaps his hands together and holds them up as though to push me over and shouts, 'Tipote, tipote.' ('Nothing, nothing.') I say, 'Two hundred.' I want to thrust the two hundred drachmas at him and stride away, but I don't have less than a five-hundred-drachma note, which he has to change, and throwing the drachmas at me he turns away. I think: This bloody place.

The apartment house is on a hill, above the First Cemetery of Athens, and every time I walk down the hill I see, over the flat tops of cement buildings, the rocky Acropolis and the high Parthenon.

For a long while, all my perceptions of Athens were, I now realize, odd. Last Easter, at a Holy Friday service, I left the church for a while to wander around the back, among the trees blossoming in the garden, and in a little window I saw a young man, an acolyte, blowing on an ember to ignite it enough to burn incense, and, though I had never witnessed such a scene, I stared as if at a picture that was familiar to me. And then it occurred to me: so many of the images of Athens, of all of Greece, *are* familiar, especially from vivid photographs in books. What was odd was that the real world here reminded me of images of it I had come with, and the real world was given vitality by those images.

We believe we know Greece before we come. We know the place by looking at photographs of it, and we know it from its music, and we know it profoundly from its literature and architecture and sculpture. And we know it, too, from our grammar-school history books, in which different forms of government were illustrated by one man standing above many men (Tyranny), a few men standing above many men (Oligarchy), and many men standing together (Democracy), all the men, above or below, wearing short mantles and sandals; we know it from Doric, Ionic, and Corinthian capitals on the fronts of our libraries, city halls and banks. It is a familiar place.

And yet, it is all unfamiliar.

Modern Athens will finally reduce to ruins any idea you have of it before you come. When Greece won its independence from Turkey in 1827, Athens was so reduced in importance that the seaside city of Nafplion in the Peloponnese was chosen as the country's capital before it. A European, Otto of Bavaria, was made the first King of Greece, and with him came an entourage of architects. Athens, in the nineteenth century, was built largely by these architects in their 'neoclassical' style, a style that came more from a Romantic idea of Greece than from the Athens centuries gone. The new city was as invented as the official language, Katharevoussa; this formal language was devised by the European-educated grammarians who based it on the ancient language, or what they believed was the ancient. It is now virtually defunct, as nineteenth century Athens is defunct, except in our continuing, 'neoclassical' notion of the marble city. Cement apartment buildings replace the neoclassical houses.

I have come to love this city as it is. I love it for many reasons, not least of which is the friends I have here; and I love it for the images it supplies, beyond any I once had of it as the ideal city.

The first day I start at the Olympic Stadium, modern, a deep, sharp, marble curve on the side of a wooded hill, and one of my favourite sites in Athens. I cross over the highway. There are four or five main highways running through Athens, and they are like wide, roaring rivers of motorbikes, cars, trucks, buses, all in the blue haze of their exhaust.

Then I go into the Zappion Gardens and past the neoclassical Hall of Congress, its double row of Corinthian columns standing out against a yellow porch, and, through the doors, you see into a large atrium, at the back of which are columns flanked against a red wall.

And then into the National Gardens, along red earthen paths under densely growing palms and orange trees. Stone troughs in the tangled vegetation run with cool water, and the hot sun flares in the shadows.

Out of the garden, across another highway, I climb to Kolonaki Square and sit at a café. The awnings above the cafés cast a deep shade in which people lounge in a kind of stillness, while outside, in the heavy sunlight, there is frantic movement. At the table next to me, three middle-aged Athenian women, with tinted eyeglasses and gold bracelets, eat croissants with the tips of their fingers, and switch from Greek to English and back with every other sentence.

These cafés, fashionable, appear stark, the plastic upholstery of the chairs often split and revealing the foam rubber beneath, and cigarette butts everywhere. (Greeks seem to smoke more than the people of any other country.) Then, an ordinary coffee house, or *kafenion*, can strike you as one of the most elegant places you've ever seen: the simplest tables and chairs in a square space, neon-lit, pegs on one wall for hanging coats, and on another wall one shelf, high up, with three bottles, and that is all.

Like cafés, you never quite know in Athens, unless you're told, what is a special *taverna* or not. A sheet of paper is spread over the flower-patterned plastic sheet on your table, and on the paper is placed a plastic bread basket with the knives and forks along with the bread, the napkins tucked underneath. The floor usually has a flower-patterned covering. The small tables and chairs are always rickety. At the back of the room is a door with a curtain, of yet a different pattern of flowers, and beyond that is the kitchen. The only difference between a *taverna* I happen to stop at when I'm hungry and eat indifferently and one I'm taken to is the quality of the food; in both the menu will be the same, but in the good one the food will be 'light, light,' which is, I think, the highest compliment that can be paid to food by an Athenian.

After my coffee I go down to Constitution Square, or Syntagma, overlooked by the flat, wide Parliament building, once the palace of

King Otto. Against the wall between its double flights of marble stairs is the Tomb of the Unknown Soldier with, above, a large bas-relief of an ancient Greek soldier, dead, but still armed. It occurs to me that, whereas I look at sculpture in museums with a studied reverence, I hardly notice sculpture in public places. This bas-relief is, I think with a sense of revelation, beautiful.

Down the south side of the square is Ermou Street; after a few fancy fashion shops come the more typical narrow ones, not far from being stalls, selling bolts of cloth and shoes and electrical parts, all displayed outside on the uneven sidewalk. In a stark pastry-shop window I see trays of dry rusks, toasted bread slices, *koulouria*, a kind of pretzel, covered with sesame seeds. Shop windows frame a culture. All the soaps, shampoos, vitamins in a pharmacist's window are from other European countries and America, and in a grocery-shop window most of the products are labelled in English.

A little farther on is Monastiraki Square, overlooked by a large mosque; at its base are small shops with sandals, sweaters made from goats' wool, Coca-Cola and cheese pies. There is no indication on my map of the mosque, which, outside, looks derelict. Inside, it is being converted into a museum.

And now I go round the ancient Agora, along the metro tracks, and up past a pine-wooded knoll, and not knowing where I am quite, I turn at a street called Smith, and farther up I leave the paved street for a dirt road, and this takes me through pine trees up onto a hill of bare, white rock, from where I can no longer see the city below. The still air smells of resin. I wander, and come across an open gate in a chain-link fence. There is no one around. I go in, toward the Athens observatory, and beyond, I stop and, alone, hear myself say, 'My God!' I did not expect to see the Parthenon, confronting me above a hillside of pines.

The next day I start my walk at Hadrian's Gate, and visit the ruins of the temple of Olympian Zeus. The few, high Corinthian columns stand in a bare field, one column fallen, its great, fluted drums separated and leaning on one another, the capital of worn acanthus leaves tipped on its side.

Climbing toward the Acropolis, I glimpse through gates the great blocks of corroded stone among cypresses of the Theatre of Dionysius. Just over the steep walls of the Acropolis appears the side of the Parthenon against the blue sky. The traffic roars by me on the left as I walk past olives, cypresses, oleanders on my right. I ascend a flight of deep steps to the Roman arches of the Theatre of Herodes Atticus, which appear white and floating, one row above another, and, above them all, the pediment of the Parthenon.

I go round the base of the Acropolis to the Panathenaic Way, the ancient road that once connected the market place below to the temples above. I walk for a while on the thick, black paving stones, those remaining, and into the Agora, to the site of the daily life of ancient Athens. All about, on the bare earth, are marble fragments. Some are stored on shelves behind wire mesh. They are numbered, and you think that if you could only sort them out and connect them in the right way, you would reconstruct the entire site, as American archaeologists used parts to reconstruct the Stoa of Attalus (wrongly, many say). The *stoa* is a museum and, inside, I go from glass case to glass case, studying the objects of life: pots, stone buttons, a razor, a wine cooler, a holy-water basin, standard weights of bronze and lead, an official liquid measure, jurors' ballots, a water clock for timing speeches in law courts, and a peculiar machine, now only a broken marble slab with fine slots, for choosing Athenian officials by lot.

Back along the Panathenaic Way, I leave the Agora, cross the bridge over the metro tracks, and enter Monastiraki, the junk market of Athens. On my walks, I, an inveterate junk man, always seem to end up in Monastiraki. In Abyssinia Square I look at the brass pots, the door knockers and glass lamp shades and old straight razors in the stalls. I see battered dentist's equipment, hammers and planes, stoves, folding beds, old coins and paper currency, bells and flat irons, and scales with round weights.

All of these objects, these images, are separated out from one another in museums, but not in the streets. It is in the streets that you find history uncategorized, bits and pieces heaped together as a heap of marble fragments I once studied in the Roman Agora, against a back wall, of Classical, Hellenistic, Roman, Byzantine capitals, cornices, architraves, and the shafts and turbans of Ottoman gravestones, too. Out in the streets, you see a woman carrying a round pan of stuffed tomatoes. You see a crumbling neoclassical house, the narrow balcony held up by scrolled marble supports, and along its front the black and red, overlapping letters of a political slogan. You see everything as an icon, and all your wonder is iconology.

On Saturday morning two friends, Michael and Etta, take me to Plaka. They, Athenians, have not been there in years. Plaka is the old village around the Acropolis that used to be Athens during the four centuries of Turkish occupation. Many of its narrow streets are now pedestrian, and about the old buildings is the scaffolding of restoration work. Athenians are rediscovering Plaka.

We stop at a churchyard to listen to the singing of nuns. One nun comes out and asks us if we want to see inside the church, which she unlocks. (All churches are locked now because the icons are stolen.) The icons are decorated with sprigs of basil, and there are pots of basil on the floor. Michael asks the nun if she approves of the changes in Plaka. She is animated, wearing a grey apron, a black cloth tied around her grey hair. She says a nightclub across from the church has been closed; while it was functioning, the nuns couldn't sleep all night. We light candles, kiss the icons (Michael tells me this is done by pressing the tip of your nose to the surface and kissing the air), and the nun gives us sprigs of basil to take away.

We climb higher, up to Anaphiotica, just under the back wall of the Acropolis. It is a village. We are in another Athens, where small white houses have blue shutters and doors, and cats lie in the middle of the streets, only wide enough for one person to pass at a time.

The times spent with friends in Athens become, in themselves, icons when I think back on them and try to describe them.

A friend takes me on the Athens metro, from Monastiraki Square to Omonia, to see the old wooden carriages. We wait on the platform for the new trains to pass, and get into one with wooden shutters and rattan seats. At Omonia Square he takes me to the turn-of-the-century café, Neon, with its high ceiling with patches from where the plaster has fallen, dusty plaster sphinxes holding up torn paintings, so dark you can't make them out. On cracked marble tables rough men play chess and backgammon. The marble of our table is marked in pencil with a score. We drink ouzo and eat cucumber slices.

Another day I am invited to see the new offices of an insurance company: they take up two floors of a cleanly cut modern building, on the outskirts of Athens, where many such buildings are set, and from the double glazed windows I see, in the harsh sunlight below, scruffy yards where huge terracotta pots, used marble sinks and the marble decorative parts of destroyed neoclassical houses are sold. I see cypresses and highways. The offices are air-conditioned; the walls are hung with prints and paintings of modern Greek artists. The young director, with whom I have coffee, plays with tiny silver worry beads.

In a car, I am driving with friends over Turkovounia, a rock of a hill, like the jagged rocks in Byzantine paintings, which fifteen years ago was considered outside Athens, and is now built up with the city's apartment houses high up its rocky sides. We pass a group of people in a crag below, standing close together and still, with blue-and-white Greek flags among them, and I am told that during the German occupation Greeks were taken to that desolate spot and shot. One of the people in the car, a journalist, recalls coming to Turkovounia when no one lived there but the poorest, in stone shacks, and how he, a young Communist during a time when it was illegal to be one, talked them into joining the party.

A fashion show is held in the new shop of Natalia Hatgis, who is Greek-American. A pomegranate is broken on the marble floor. The thin, blonde, foreign mannequins stride up and down the platforms in clothes of international design. No one can understand how a twenty-two-year-old can be so professional. Some Athenians say, 'It is because she was brought up in America. If she were from Athens . . .!'

On Sunday morning I am with a friend's family at a cemetery for the memorial service of his mother. It is windy, and the flames of the thin candles stuck in the flower-strewn sand on the grave blow while the priest intones a prayer, the black sleeves of his robe billowing. Then a box on the marble curb of the narrow plot is opened, and *koliva* is spooned into little white bags with black crosses. The *koliva* is boiled wheat kernels mixed with nuts, sugar and cinnamon, and it is eaten at the graveside. It symbolizes the flesh of the dead person. I ask, but no-one knows, what the origin is.

In the living room of an elderly, prominent writer, I am served *gliko*, a preserved apricot, on a little cut-glass dish, and a glass of cold water. All about are piles of books. She is from Constantinople (Istanbul), and came to Athens in 1922 with the exchange of population between the Greeks and the Turks, which brought thousands of refugees to Greece with their culture, a distinct culture that is not always given proper credit. She is voluble about the Fanariots, Greeks who continued to live in Istanbul after its fall to the Ottomans. She speaks in French. Before I leave, she gives me a copy of an anthology of Black poetry translated by her late husband. She dreams of visiting the Mississippi River.

An Athenian friend and I are showing a former student of mine around the Archaeological Museum. The student is from the American Midwest. Nikos is giving him a lecture. My student does not know what Mycenean is, however. Nikos asks questions, but the student can't answer. Finally, Nikos asks, 'Well, do you know what the Parthenon is?' 'No,' the student says. I am embarrassed, because I am not sure if, at eighteen, I knew. 'But didn't you learn anything about Greece at school?' Nikos asks. 'No,' answers the student, 'we learned about Egypt.'

Shortly before I am to leave, I make my visit to the Parthenon. Perhaps I should go with friends, but I am still Western Romantic enough to feel at moments that the deepest experiences are solitary. The fact is, Greece disproves this, because I know, beyond these moments, that my deepest, my most lasting experiences, have been with others, with Greeks. But I go alone, up the wonderful walkway, designed by the recently dead architect Pikionis, who assembled it out of fragments, some with odd architectural details, from the Acropolis. I am among hundreds of pilgrims, visiting the greatest shrine to, the greatest icon of, Western Civilization. As I climb, I look around at modern Athens, which fades out into a distant haze of pollution. I pay for my ticket and go through a gateway. The stone is as smooth as a holy image kissed by centuries of worshippers.

INSIDER'S GUIDE TO GREEK CUISINE

Nicholas and Joan Gage

Compared to the cuisine of Greece, the gastronomic arts of every other country in Europe, including France, are a mere flash in the pan. Centuries before Christ, while neighbours to the north were gnawing on thigh bones, the Greeks were savouring roast lamb with capers, saffron rice, honey cakes, persian peaches, and perfumed wines. Plato gravely discussed such questions as which kinds of fish should be baked and which boiled. During the Middle Ages, Greek monks donned white versions of their black caps while perfecting their cuisine, giving us the chef's toque.

A visit to Athens offers both unexpected pleasures and pitfalls to those who would sample the best of Greek cooking. Throughout the country, especially in hotels and restaurants catering to the tourist trade, the visitor is confronted with menus labelled Continental, a term that translates as an overcooked and underseasoned attempt to satisfy all national palates at once.

He would be better advised to walk into the humblest working-class *taverna*, where, for a few dollars, he could assemble a meal of boiled mountain herbs, huge kidney-shaped beans called *gigantes* in a vinaigrette sauce, a Greek salad, a dish of chicken in tomato sauce with rice pilaf, and a plate of fried squid, accompanied by the house retsina wine. Ordering in such a *taverna* is no challenge, even for those without a word of Greek, for it is customary to go right into the kitchen, peek into the simmering pots and point to what you want.

The Greek *taverna* spans the entire spectrum of price and elegance. At one end is the working-class *taverna* found in every neighbourhood, comprising bare wooden tables, walls lined with wine casks, and the wife of the owner labouring over a large stove. At the other extreme are restaurants like **Mirtia** (The Myrtle Tree) on the hill above the Stadium, and **Steki Tou Yianni,** 1 Troias St. (phone 821 2953), in the quarter of Athens called Kipseli. Mirtia, 35 Markou Mousourou (phone 701 2276), is a favourite of diners with well padded wallets or expense accounts. The décor features village handicrafts and wine kegs, strolling musicians provide passionate renditions of old Greek tunes while the diners join in, and there is no need to decide what to order – the courses follow each other, on and on – tiny fried squid; salty *taramasalata* made of cod roe; seafood wrapped in flaky pastry; pies of cheese, spinach or seafood; rice-stuffed grape leaves in an egg-lemon sauce. Finally, when the point of satiety is long past, there will be a main course such as roast lamb or stuffed capon, followed by fruit and Greek coffee. Eating in these two restaurants is an excellent introduction to Greek cuisine. But they tend to close for long periods in July and August, so it's essential to check before going, and to book a table. Dinner will come to about $20 a person, including wine and tip.

Every Greek has his own favourite *taverna*. Here are two of ours.

Taverna Anna, at the corner of Perikou and Gregoriou No. 10 streets in the suburb of Nea Filothei (phone 692 8435), is a short taxi ride out of Athens. Anna is moderate in price (about $8 a person with wine) and offers such specialities as snails, peppers with sausages, duck with olives, rabbit stew, and, if you're lucky, wild boar.

A second favourite is the venerable *taverna* **Xynou,** 4 Angelou Yeronda, in the bustling Plaka area. A rabbit warren of winding streets and crumbling neoclassical buildings just below the Acropolis, Plaka was once all there was of Athens. Now it's a noisy Latin Quarter section where warm weather brings the tables out onto the rooftops, shills attempt to entice passers by inside, and those few brave souls who have bought the old mansions and restored them to their former glory try to pass legislation to remove the undesirables from their neighbourhood.

It's necessary to exercise caution when entering a restaurant in Plaka, for no matter how glowingly the food, belly dancers, and musicians are described, these are often tourist traps. If you want to skip the belly dancers and glossy décor and concentrate on good food and authentic old Plaka atmosphere, go straight to Xynou. Head for the kitchen and choose from among the pots. (The veal and courgettes is excellent.) Then sit down to enjoy the food, intimate rooms, wall murals of old Athens, strolling musicians, and a pleasant outdoor garden that from some tables offers a glimpse of the Acropolis. Dinner will come to about $8 a person.

Hardly a humble *taverna* but an excellent and expensive restaurant featuring carefully researched cuisine and décor of the Greek islands is the **Taverna Ta Nissia** on the lower floor of the Athens Hilton, 46 Vas Sofias Blvd. (phone 722 0201), which draws as many Greeks as foreigners. Its enterprising chefs periodically present gastronomic festivals such as the game festival in the autumn. Dinner with wine will cost about $25 a person.

Perhaps the most charming *tavernas* are those by the seaside. In the port of Pireaus, a $2.50 taxi ride from town, is the curving yacht habour of Tourkolimano (which many patriotic Greeks now call Mikrolimano – small harbour – instead of Turkish harbour). It's hard to imagine a more romantic spot for enjoying the sunset while sitting at the water's edge as small yachts bob nearby. The harbour is lined with restaurants so close together that even the waiters have trouble telling where one restaurant ends and another begins. All the establishments in Tourkolimano provide the same fresh seafood, but the cognoscenti prefer **Kanaris,** 50 Akti Alexandrou Koumoundourou (phone 417 5190), where dinner with wine can come to $25 a person.

This is the technique for eating at Tourkolimano: Choose a table belonging to the restaurant of your choice (ignoring the entreaties of waiters from nearby establishments). Sit down and order salad and hors d'oeuvre, then make your way across the road to the kitchen of the restaurant, where you will select the seafood or fish you want, usually still flopping in the ice-lined drawers. The portions of fish are weighed and the customers are charged by the weight of their dinner. While awaiting your meal, you return to the waterside to enjoy the view, as pedlars offer pistachio nuts, cooked shellfish, and corsages of gardenias and star jasmine, and sleek, overfed cats gather hopefully at your feet.

The sea exerts a siren call to all Greeks,. Athenians often drive to the seaside suburb of Glyfada for an evening of seafood and music. Two of the best fish restaurants are there: **Psaropoulos** (phone 894 5677) and **Antonopoulos** (phone 894 5636), where the only drawback is the ear-splitting sound of planes landing and departing from the Athens airport. Prices are high; dinner will come to about $25 a person with wine and tip.

The coastal road that leads through Glyfada, Voula, Vouliagmeni, and Varkiza contains a seaside *taverna* at every bend. Here, too, are the large, noisy, crowded and expensive bouzouki nightclubs where the most popular Greek singers perform and, for a price, customers can break plates, dance on the tables and consume liquor and mediocre food until dawn. The Greeks love it, but unless one enjoys spending up to $100 for a $5 bottle of wine and listening to music amplified to a degree that endangers the eardrums, these establishments are best avoided.

Greek cuisine is essentially Eastern, made up of many small courses called *mezedakia* (singular: *mezes*) and built on such cornerstones as lamb, olive oil, rice, figs, yogurt, coarse wholemeal bread, shish kebab (called *souvlaki*), and complicated dishes of ground meat with herbs, spices and rice, often stuffed into vegetables or wrapped in leaves.

The best place to find true Anatolian-style Greek cooking, and the favourite restaurant of all knowledgeable Athenians, is **Gerofinikas,** 10 Pindarou Street (phone 362 2719). One enters through a long, rather squalid-looking alley lined with cubicles that once housed a thriving brothel. At the end of the alley, doors open into a vision of gleaming copper braziers, linen-draped tables and the old pine tree that gives the restaurant its name, growing right through the roof. The Oriental Greek specialities are displayed like works of art in the spotless glass showcases, and elegant pyramids of flowers, seasonal fruits and elaborate sweets tempt the eye. Gerofinikas is presided over by Monsieur Bernard, a jovial Greek from Constantinople who speaks half a dozen languages fluently (he's currently polishing his Japanese) and unerringly greets each incoming guest in his or her native language.

The problem of choosing what to eat there is formidable, but one speciality not to be missed is an appetizer of rice orientale, studded with currants, spices and bits of chopped liver. The seafood is excellent, and it's worth the trip to sample the calorific caramel-and-whipped-cream dessert called *ekmek kataif.* While it's sometimes possible to walk in off the street and find a table at Gerofinikas at lunchtime, reservations are essential and hard to get for dinner. A meal with wine will come to about $15 a person.

Despite our caveat against food labelled Continental, there is a restaurant called **Dionysos,** 43 Gali St. (phone 923 3182), on Philopappou Hill, in the very shadow of the Acropolis, which is extremely popular with the expense-account crowd. Its Continental cuisine is adequate, though both food and service have declined recently. Its main attraction is a matchless view, from the second-floor dining rooms, of the Parthenon overhead, which at night glows with a constantly changing play of colour, thanks to the nightly sound and light performance.

When making dinner plans, keep in mind that Greeks dine late, refreshed by the long afternoon siesta. The most popular time for reservations is 10 pm, and those who arrive before 9 may find themselves eating alone or waiting for the restaurant to open. Also, although the dinner bill includes a 15 per cent service charge, if the dinner and service have been adequate it is customary to leave a 5 to 10 per cent tip – half on the plate for the waiter and half on the table for the busboy.

To find a quick, inexpensive but tasty lunch during a break from shopping, try **Corfu** (phone 361 3011) at 6 Kriezotou (about $8 a person with wine). It is close to Voukourestiou Street, now a pedestrian mall and one of the most pleasant areas for shopping for jewellery, clothing, or native handicrafts.

It's not necessary to order a full restaurant meal to enjoy Greek food and atmosphere. Greeks punctuate their day with pauses for refreshment. Some of the nicest moments are those spent whiling away spare time at an outdoor café sipping ouzo or tiny cups of thick Greek coffee, which can be prepared in thirty-seven degrees of sweetness, from *sketos* (unsweetened) through *metrios* (medium) to *glykos* (sweet).

The *zacharoplasteion,* or sweet shop, fulfils an important function in Greek life as a centre for socializing, people-watching, and meeting members of the opposite sex. The traditional pastries, made from many layers of paper-thin dough called *filo,* filled with chopped nuts and drenched in honey, are not meant to be served with a meal, but to be savoured on special occasions or as afternoon or late-night snacks. Sweet shops are found everywhere, and on warm summer nights it seems that the entire population is sitting outdoors at a *zacharoplasteion,* enjoying the scene while eating *baklava* and sipping tiny cups of thick black coffee.

Just off Constitution Square are **Zonar's** and **Floka,** two landmark sweet shops, shoulder to shoulder on Panepistimiou Street. In addition to pastries, they provide food (such as Zonar's hot chicken pie) and a variety of fanciful ice-cream concoctions. The most stylish Athenians do their café-sitting around Kolonaki Square, where the fashion parade is as important as the menu.

Wealthy shipowners, government ministers, publishers and power brokers congregate at the doyenne of Greek hotels, the **Grande Bretagne** (322 8361), on Constitution Square. Fortunes and reputations are made and lost daily within its elegant, antiques-filled foyer, the intimate bar, and the very English G.B. Corner – the Athens version of the Plaza's Oak Room.

The major religious and seasonal holidays play an important part in Greek eating habits. Christmas is the time for *patcha,* a delicate soup made of tripe in an egg-lemon sauce; *kourabiedes,* sweet, buttery shortbread cookies; and *Christopsomo* (Christmas bread), decorated with walnuts, sesame seeds and a cross of dough . On January 1 every family exchanges gifts and cuts the *Vasilopeta* – Saint Basil's cake – in which a coin is embedded. Whoever gets the coin will, of course, have good luck for the coming year.

One traveller of our acquaintance arrived in Greece ready to gorge himself on lamb, only to discover that it was the time of the Lenten fast; nowhere was red meat to be had. Easter is the religious and culinary apex of the Greek year. The last week before Lent is carnival, or *apokreas.* Children in elaborate, often rented, costumes fill the parks and attend parties. The seven-week fast begins with Catheri Deftera – Clean Monday – when houses are scrubbed, along with the pots and pans that have been used to cook now forbidden foods (all dairy products and the flesh of anything that has blood). The Greeks buy loaves of the unleavened bread called *lagana* and head for the seashore, where families fly handmade kites and dine on seafood and such permissible Lenten dishes as mussels, shrimp, sea urchins, squid, octopus and *taramasalata,* made of red carp eggs. Holy Week, before Easter, is a time of the strictest fasting. Even wine and olive oil are forbidden. After communion on Holy Saturday the faithful wait for midnight mass.

After dark, virtually everyone in Greece hurries to the nearest church, holding unlit candles. At the stroke of midnight the priest emerges with a flickering candle and announces, 'Christ is risen!' The light he holds spreads from candle to candle, through the church, to the crowds waiting outside, until every square in Greece is illuminated. Fireworks are set off as the people walk home, protecting their candles from the wind, and all of Athens glows with streams of candlelight. The Greeks break the fast after midnight with bowls of lemon-scented *mageritsa,* made of the entrails of the lamb in an egg-lemon-dill sauce. The next day, Easter Sunday, even the poorest Greek feasts on spring lamb roasted over a spit and spicy kebabs made of the intestines, washed down with ouzo and retsina. In every neighbourhood of Athens the odour of roasting lamb and the sounds of singing and dancing fill the air.

Late summer and autumn bring wild game, the harvest festivals, and the high season for the peerless Greek fruits – grapes, figs, melons, pomegranates, and tomatoes, which will spoil one forever for their tasteless American counterparts. Mid-July begins the annual wine festival at Daphne, a monastery just outside Athens built on the site of an ancient shrine to Apollo. For a small entrance fee one may stroll around the grounds, glass in hand, sampling hundreds of Greek wines from huge casks and imagining oneself part of an old-fashioned pagan bacchanal.

Greece has many excellent native wines. Porto Carras, Boutari, and Elissar are good unresinated whites; Naoussa is a full-bodied red; and Monte Nero is an outstanding smooth red wine never found outside the country. Mavrodaphne is a sweet dessert wine, and ouzo, a strong Pernod-like spirit distilled from the residue of the grape after the wine-making process, is the fiery national beverage.

The resinated white wines, retsina, are the *vins du pays,* generally considered an acquired taste because of the sharp tang of resin. Many *tavernas* have their own retsina on tap, and somehow, on a hot summer day near the seashore, nothing but retsina seems to go as well with a platter of freshly cooked fish.

That is, after all, the quintessential Greek dining experience and the one easiest to enjoy: oilcloth-covered tables under woven thatched awnings at a seaside *taverna*; on the table: freshly cooked small red mullet (*barbounia*), a plate of tiny fried squid (*kalamarakia*), a loaf of coarse country bread, peasant salad with chunks of feta cheese and ambrosial tomatoes, frosty bottles of retsina. Over such a meal, gazing at Homer's wine-dark sea, one feels truly Greek, at one with the ancients, compelled to agree with Henry Miller: 'Greece is the home of the gods; they may have died but their presence still makes itself felt.'

LANDMARKS, LODGING, GETTING AROUND

Marvine Howe

It is said that Athenians of the fifth century BC were outraged with Pericles for pampering and embellishing the capital, as if it were some vain woman, decking it out with costly stones, statues and temples. Pericles would not recognize his city today; her features are weathered and her jewellery somewhat tarnished. But there is still that magic time at sunset when the light softens, spreading a rosy blush over the city's face, and by nightfall Athens has recovered her intense and ageless vitality.

The newcomer may have trouble seeking out Athens's ancient treasures, which risk being submerged and destroyed by the ills of modern life: masses of anonymous concrete, pounding traffic and corrosive air. Planners are struggling desperately to revive the glories of Pericles's day. A major effort is under way to save the Acropolis, that monumental rock in the heart of ancient Athens. The visitor will have to endure scaffolding and fenced-off areas and cement copies of the original statues, with the satisfaction that the masterpieces of classic art, such as the temples of the Parthenon and the Erechtheum, will be preserved for future generations.

The Greek Minister of the Environment has an ambitious plan to save historic Athens by incorporating the city's main monuments and archaeological sites into a vast cultural area of pedestrian walks. Plaka, that quaint nineteenth century neighbourhood that hugs the Acropolis, has already been greatly improved as a pedestrian area. Another effort is to convert discothèques into boîtes or *tavernas* with live music, preferably guitars and bouzouki.

The minister, who predicts that Athens will be a different city in ten years, has a commitment to get rid of the city's old gasworks, a major source of pollution. Other plans include the restoration of once elegant nineteenth century residences that had become warehouses and the conversion of old quarries in the surrounding hills into theatres, cultural centres, parks and athletic fields. There's also a project to fill in the sea at Faliron Bay to make a large park, 'like Grant Park in Chicago.'

Meanwhile the number-one problem for everybody is transport. Buses are overcrowded and confusing for most visitors because their signs are, naturally, in Greek. The cost of a local ride is twenty-two cents and free before 8 am. A suburban train will take you down to the port of Piraeus or up to Kifissia, but unfortunately it doesn't go anywhere else. Taxis are low-priced but generally full or off-duty, especially since private cars are permitted in the city centre only on alternate days. A taxi will take you almost anywhere downtown for just over a dollar, but the driver will invariably stop to pick up other customers going your way.

Athens has two airports: the Olympic, or west, airport (for all Olympic Airways flights, international and domestic) and the International, or east, airport. Both are within city limits, so make sure the taxi meter is running; the fare to town by the direct route comes to about $3.30, with a small extra charge for luggage. In the rush hour the taxi may take you the long way on Kareas Highway on the hills overlooking Athens, which means the meter will run up to about $5. If there's a taxi strike or it's late at night and there are no taxis around, the bus from the International Airport is convenient because it takes you to central Constitution Square for sixty-six cents. It's best to walk around downtown Athens, and pleasanter than waiting fruitlessly for a taxi. Although Athens has a population of 3.5 million, most sights are downtown, which is very accessible on foot.

Pollution is another problem, particularly when there's *to nefos*, as the dark brown cloud of photochemical smoke is called. Athens has been declared one of western Europe's most polluted cities, along with Nice and Milan. It's particularly bad on stifling windless days in midsummer, which is one reason Athenians leave town then. Yet for a New Yorker, used to inversions, smog and depressing humidity, the fuss Athenians make about their climate may seem unfair. Still, Athens is at its best in the autumn or winter on those crisp, clear windy days when everyone breathes freely again.

Another hurdle for visitors to Athens is the hours. They are erratic, unfathomable and often highly annoying, even more outlandish for the average Anglo-Saxon than the hours of Spain or Mexico. Do as the Athenians do; you'll get more out of your stay. Athens is an early-to-rise, late-to-bed city with a long afternoon hiatus that is presumably siesta time, although it is said that's when working couples get the housework done. Shops generally follow this routine, although some evenings they simply don't reopen. Museums and archaeological sites generally close afternoons in winter, as well as one day a week, either Monday or Tuesday. Tourism officials say labour costs make a second shift prohibitive except in the busy summer season.

Eating hours also differ: Lunch can begin at 1pm, but 2 is better and

3 quite acceptable. Some restaurants open for dinner at 8.30 pm, most at 9, and if you prefer to dine when Greeks do then it is 10 pm or later.

Where the visitor will not have problems is in finding a suitable hotel; they exist at every price level. There are three new luxury hotels aimed at the affluent business market. **The Athenaeum Intercontinental Hotel**, 89-93 Syngrou Ave. (phone 902 3666), looks more like a modern art gallery, a kind of Athenian Pompidou Centre with sculptures, murals and canvases by some of Greece's best contemporary artists. It is on Syngrou Avenue, Athens's new business centre, more or less equidistant from the airport and the city centre ($130 double, tax included). Just down the road is the **Ledra Marriott**, 115 Syngrou Ave. (phone 952 5211), with its spectacular rooftop pool just across the way from the Acropolis ($120). It has the only Polynesian restaurant in town, the **Kona Kai**, which is expensive but oozing with status (dinner for two with wine, $50 to $60; phone 952 5211).

The Astir Palace, on Syntagma (Constitution) Square across from Parliament, has doubles for $90. The hotel's **Apokalypsis Restaurant** looks out on a fourth century BC wall discovered by chance during construction. It specializes in Greek cuisine; dinner for two with wine, about $50. (Telephone 364 3112.)

Then there are the old favourites: **The Grande Bretagne**, built in 1842 as a private mansion, has more class than its younger rivals (double, $73 to $92). The hotel's **G.B. Corner**, on the corner of Syntagma Square, offers international and Greek cuisine. (Phone 322 8361.) **The Hilton**, 46 vas Sofias Blvd. (phone 722 0201), the first international hotel that came to town, twenty years ago, is getting a facelift inside and out. Doubles cost $95 to $153. Its rooftop **Galaxy Bar and Supper Club** enjoys one of the best views in town, with the whole sweep from Hymettus Mountain to Lycabettus and including the Acropolis and the sea. **The Caravel Hotel**, 2 vas Alexandrou Ave. (phone 729 0721), around the corner, is clearly catering to the wave of Arab tourists. They have converted the Italian restaurant to the **Kasbah**, serving Middle Eastern cuisine, and built a mini-mosque on the roof, next to the sauna (double $45 to $51).

For the economically minded, there are many smaller hotels. **St. George Lycabettus**, 2 Kleomenous St. (phone 729 0715) has a good view of the Acropolis from the rooftop restaurant bar in the quiet neighbourhood of Lycabettus Mountain (double with breakfast, $38 to $43). Nearby, in fashionable Kolonaki, is the **Athenian Inn**, 22 Haritos St. (phone 723 9552), where writer Lawrence Durrell sometimes stays (doubles, about $26). There are a host of B-class hotels like the **Athens Gate**, 10 Syngrou Ave. (phone 923 8304), with a roof garden overlooking the Acropolis ($26 double).

My suggestion is a minimum of three days for Athens. Spend the first morning at the **Acropolis**; don't miss the **Acropolis Museum** (closed Tuesday) where the caryatids and other sculptures are kept from the polluted air (about $1.50 admission). Then go to the old Agora, just down the hill, and the **Thission temple**, which closes a little later than the Acropolis. Take a late lunch, then stroll the old cobbled streets of Plaka to see the restoration work on the nineteenth century homes, visit the tourist shops or relax in a café.

Visit museums on the second morning. **The National Archaeological Museum** has what is probably the best collection of classic Greek art in the world ($1.65, double for a camera; free on Sunday). There are three other musts: the **Byzantine Museum**, the **Benaki** and, if there's time, the **National Gallery of Modern Greek Art**, all within easy walking distance of the Hilton. Then take a bus tour to **Sounion** to see the lovely coast road and resorts along the Saronic Gulf to the **Temple of Poseidon** at Cape Sounion (about $10).

The third morning can be spent shopping or window-shopping. Souvenir shops in Plaka offer bulky sweaters for about $15, flowing Grecian cotton gowns for about $10, as well as a lot of junk. Uptown, the more elegant shops are found on El. Venizelou Avenue, generally known as Panepistimiou. The Zolotas and Lalaounis jewellery shops reproduce fine gold museum pieces. Another sophisticated area is near Kolonaki Square. Hand-made leather sandals are found in the Monastiraki quarter for $11 or less. John Andy and Haris Kazakos-Moccissino offer casual and elegant footwear for around $30 a pair.

The third afternoon should include lunch at the port of Piraeus, where there's a string of popular restaurants. Then rush back to the city in time to view the sunset over the Acropolis from **St. George's Chapel** on top of Mt. Lycabettus (walk or take the cable car) or just sit in one of the popular cafés on **Syntagma Square** – weather and pollution permitting – and watch the *evzones* (presidential guard) drill in front of Parliament.

Unlike most capitals, Athens's cultural season takes place in summer. That's when the Athens Festival puts on spectacular shows in the ancient **Herodes Atticus Theatre** at the foot of the Acropolis, from June to the end of September. In winter there is theatre at the **Liriki Skini's Olympia Theatre** on Akademias Avenue, interrupted sometimes by musicians' strikes. There's plenty of theatre; it is said that every Greek star has his own troupe. Quality performances are given by the **National Theatre** near Omonia Square ($5). The best folk dances are in the **Dora Stratou** open-air theatre on Philopappas Hill, nightly in summer. But the Lyceum of Greek Women performs at the **Aliki Theatre** from November to March, usually one evening a week.

To find out what's going on, check the English-language daily *Athens News,* the monthly *The Athenian* and *Thirty Days* and a free guide, *This Week in Athens,* available at major hotels. For general information such as museum and shopping hours, the tourist police can be helpful: Phone 171. A centre for tourist information is the **National Bank of Greece**, on Syntagma Square and Stadiou Street (phone 322 2738). It is open daily, including Sunday, **The American Hellenic Chamber of Commerce** is at Valaoritou 17 (phone 361 8385).

OLYMPIA: SACRED WOOD OF THE GAMES

Peter Levi

Olympia, with its vast extent and its enormous pine trees, belongs to the summer. On winter afternoons the yellow sun glitters on snow-capped Arcadian mountains. In spring or in autumn wildflowers grow everywhere and the grass is dense. But the pine trees that cast their shadows on the ruins in summer grow there because a nineteenth century Queen of Greece had them planted. She said they would make all the difference, and so they did.

The ancient Olympic games took place in August, when the sun has a sharp bite to it. Even the dust is hot, and the difference between the feel of the hot dust on the running track and the cool marble of the starting position, which is still in place, says something to the soles of the feet. The athletes sweated in the sun and panted in the shade for weeks before the games started. Olympia was a holy grove, a sacred wood of trees dotted about with monuments. The running track and the practice track ran away out of it, and the racetrack for horses, which is too huge to have been excavated, must have vanished into the hazy distance.

The solemn beauty of Olympia now has something to do with the play of light and shade, the smell of pine trees, and the huge fallen masses of the temple of Zeus. It is a place of powerful sensations, not of vague or picturesque sentiments. The scale of the fallen columns is all the more terrible because of their strength, and the texture of the yellow and white lichen on the charcoal skin of the marble says all that needs saying about age.

When I first saw Olympia, I wandered around it for hours in a daze, and finally fell asleep. The sleep was not a long one, because a guard woke me up; you are not allowed to sleep in ancient places. It was not only the sun that undid me. The ancient athletes used to train mainly on cheese, but Greek cheese and Greek wine and the noon sun in August inspired me just to find a shady place and lie in it.

It is curious how much of the physical sensation of ancient Olympia is still to be had in one transformed way or another. The sun is the same, and the occasional sultriness, since this is earthquake country.

The cone-shaped hill of Kronos, dedicated to the father of Zeus, still rises placidly above the sanctuary. The River Alpheus is still as freezing cold as the plunge-bath of the ancient athletes. No bridge has ever been found on the Alpheus, so that anyone who came from the south, as many did in the early days of the games, must have forded their way through deep water.

Another of the surviving sensations, maybe the strangest of all, is the modesty of the small altars of gods scattered here and there among the trees. They make an interesting contrast with the crowded stone bases of the monuments of human beings. Often if you look at the upper surface where the athlete's statue stood on its base, you can tell how he stood. The boxers have one foot firmly planted, the other on tiptoe. The wrestlers stand somewhat differently. Some of the figures are simply praying, or crowning themselves.

There is something fearfully competitive about the Roman dedications. Most of them, Romans being foreigners, stood outside the limits of the grove, on special ground that later, by a legal fiction, was declared to be part of the holy ground. There the equestrian statue-bases still crowd one another for space. Small wonder that the Romans so envied any simple boy wrestler four or five hundred years dead who had his antique, restrained statue inside among the trees.

Most of the state monuments at Olympia are impressive and even inspiring, but without that Roman sense of a horseman 'arrested in terrific motion,' as Faulkner puts it somewhere. My own guess is that the two splendid figures of heroes recently recovered from the sea off southern Italy, naked heroic warriors of a mature grandeur from the first part of the fifth century BC, must have stood in the semicircle southeast of the temple of Zeus. They are very unlike the smooth realism and erotic frippery of later art. They are as solid as the heavy ear that survives from a bronze bull at Olympia, and as grown-up as the Zeus carrying off Ganymede.

The most important state monument at Olympia was a latecomer. The temple of Zeus itself was built as much or more to be the political expression of a new democracy as for any purely religious reason. It has that in common with the Parthenon. Maybe the ancient world would not ever attach the word *pure* to religion; their feelings were always practical and aesthetic and superstitiously conservative at the same time.

The purity and solemnity of the Olympia we visit today is a product of time and ruination. The buildings look as if they had been as we see them for 2,000 years, although in fact they spent nearly 1,500 years under ten feet of mud. Olympia now is the most beautiful embodied dream that our grandparents dreamed. Its life is the slow breathing of the pine trees.

The modern Olympic games are another dream of the same generation. The nearest actual model for that revival was an athletic festival dreamed up out of a rough, traditional village athletic meeting at Much Wenlock in Shropshire, on the border between Wales and England, in the early nineteenth century. The King of Greece, among other eminent persons, showed great interest in the possibilities. But if you look around you at Olympia, you will see that its origins must once have been similar. This obscure holy place, which when it became famous took its name from the distant mountain of the gods, was a water source by a sheltered spread of flatland under the hills between the upper and lower grazing grounds, a meeting place of shepherds.

The countryside around it is beautiful but not dramatic. It is not typical of Greece, because this is the wet west with its flowers and deep grass and its congregations of trees. But an ancient writer calls it the most beautiful landscape in Greece. It is best seen from the dense delicious, old-fashioned garden of the SPAP Hotel. That is a place to visit for a drink even if you never had the good luck to stay in the room with the best view, the one with the iron balcony. The whole vast glen opens out from it, the Alpheus glitters across the fields, the pillars stalk like ghosts of pillars among the pines. Bees buzz in a tree full of jasmine.

The grandeur of the decorations, the astonishing early chapter in the history of sculpture that you can see in the museum, meets the simplicity of origins in the temple of Zeus. There is still a heavy stone at Olympia inscribed with the name of the man who first, in the sixth century BC, lifted it above his head. The temple itself, when it came, was proportionately heavy and monumental.

Ancient writers record that the statue of Zeus enthroned in it was the Zeus of Homer's sublime verses, shaking his hyacinthine hair so that the earth trembled. They say it added something to the idea of religion. If you can conceive that this enormous and very expensive object was intended to celebrate the end of tyranny and the beginning of democracy then you will have understood something about the Greeks. Maybe one should think also of Washington.

But nothing survives except through a lifetime of lifetimes. When the temple was half ruined it was adapted as the bastion of a small Byzantine fort. The workshop where the gold and ivory statue was built up piece by piece by the sculptor Pheidias became a church, and as a ruined church it still stands, with an inscribed stone or two built into its brick walls.

In the recent excavation of that church they found fragments of moulded glass from the decorations of the flowering sceptre of Zeus, and a small black drinking cup that has 'I belong to Pheidias' scratched on the base. He must have had a drink now and then, if he worked through the Olympic summer. Or was it an old cup in which he stood his small tools, as a workman might do today?

The oddest monument of ancient Olympia has quite disappeared. The river swept it away. It was the altar for sacrifice to Zeus in the open air. It consisted of the compacted, puddled ash and muck of all earlier sacrifices. By the second century AD it stood as high as a tall tree, and you had to approach it by a flight of steps of the same material. It was too holy to be improved with marble; it just piled up. The grove belonged to Zeus, and he had no special stone, though the other gods had. Nothing is left of it except an enormous gap among the crowded monuments.

The modern village of Olympia has a certain phoney sophistication as much in contrast with the grove as the awful architecture of the new museum, and even more regrettably, because the inside of the museum is fine and decorous and blessedly cool. But even the modern village has genuine touches. The older people have the extraordinary charm of their generation, and the true country is not more than a hundred yards away. The last time I was there in winter I used to watch a flock of sheep in the early mornings quietly cropping the flowers from the boxes outside the hotels. I hope no hotel owner has yet got up early enough to have that stopped.

The railway station at Olympia is the end of the line. This is where the river valley narrows and the road begins a businesslike assault on the mountains of Arcadia. The station, where at slack hours the hens wander across the railway lines, is a very pretty one in neoclassic taste. The old yellow museum near the SPAP Hotel is in the same taste. This is rarer in Greece than you might expect. It shows the influence of an old Mayor of Pyrgos, the nearby town, who built much of his own city in the same striking way, but most of that perished long ago. It is just another way in which Olympia is a Victorian dream come true. The SPAP is the only Greek railway hotel that was ever built.

The best guidebook is surely by Pausanias, the second century AD Greek travel writer, and the greatest Olympic poet is Pindar. In more recent times, Olympia was a place that George Seferis greatly loved and often visited. There is something as fresh as a daisy about Olympia even at midsummer, as if the stones were like the sea.

O, GREECE!

Hugh Leonard

There are two sights the traveller in Europe never forgets. One is that first glimpse of Chartres Cathedral from five miles away, solitary and seeming to sail the wheat fields like a leviathan. The other is the Parthenon just after sunrise. Athens is slate grey with dusk and smog; high above it, pricked by first light, the columns soar, dwarfing even the Acropolis itself. No photograph can prepare the visitor for the actuality; it sandbags the senses. The heart is seized. And far off behind the temple and beyond Piraeus, the Aegean is molten silver.

I love Greece for many reasons: for its good manners, for the melancholy that masks its zest for life, for its climate and its islands, each one different from the next. But most of all I love it for the immediacy of the past. To arrive there is a homecoming; at once, and with a certainty as serene as it is absolute, the mystery is solved: This is where one began.

Athens, for all its size, yields its pleasures quickly. And you need no guide for the ninety-minute drive to Cape Sounion, no one to tell you where the land ends, that the sea has blues and violets that never knew an artist's palette, that Byron carved his name into the marble of the Temple of Poseidon. Elsewhere, however, it is good to travel with a Greek as mentor; inevitably, he will treat myth as history, time as an impertinence and antiquity as last week.

On my own first visit to Greece, my guide was the venerable and gaunt Manos Katrakis, an actor who is to Greek theatre as Olivier is to British. We drove on a January morning to the red-brown ruins of Mycenae, guarding an amphitheatre of mountains, and passed through the Lion Gate across the threshold of the House of Atreus.

'There,' Mr. Katrakis declaimed, pointing to a nearby hilltop, 'is where the sentinel saw Agamemnon returning from the Trojan Wars and ran to tell the adulterous Queen Clytemnestra that . . .' Caught up by the rhetoric, I completed his sentence inelegantly: '. . . that the jig was up.'

That afternoon we visited the magnificent theatre at Epidaurus, to which countryfolk still come by donkey cart from a hundred miles away, often sleeping by the roadside. At Mr. Katrakis's bidding, I wheezed up to the topmost row (the theatre can seat 14,000), and he proceeded to demonstrate the acoustics by reciting the prologue from *Prometheus*. Magically – for, as I have said, the month was January – people appeared as if out of the earth, stood, wondered and applauded.

A word about the Greek character. Greece, whatever the maps or the rules of the Common Market may say, is not part of Europe. Least of all is it a part of Asia Minor: Talk to an Athenian about 'the war' and he will assume that you mean the final (1821-27) revolt against the Turks. Bring him further up to date and he will shrug, mention Ohi Day ('Ohi' means 'no' and every year on October 28 the Greeks celebrate dictator Metaxas's 'no' to Mussolini's demand that the Greek-Albanian border be opened to Italian troops) and perhaps relate how an anonymous hero scaled the sheer cliffs of the Acropolis one night to replace the swastika of the occupying Nazis with the Greek flag. Greece, the visitor will discover, is a continent to itself.

Inevitably, there are niceties of behaviour that should be observed. If a Greek is your host, for example, it is bad manners to drain a wine glass to the lees; it implies that he has been remiss by failing to top it up. Neither is it the done thing to wave goodbye with the palm of the hand forward – it is a gesture of rejection, and an accompanying smile only makes it worse.

The real difference between the Greeks and the Others goes deeper. One recent summer in Thasos, I had just left a vast open-air nightclub when there was a power failure. Before candles could be brought, the tourists gleefully flocked out en masse without paying their bills. Only the Greek customers remained. The New Yorker, the Londoner, and the Parisian will discover that even the most illiterate Greek villager still practises the two golden rules of Pericles: Moderation in All Things and Know Thyself.

I am a creature of habit. My hotel in Athens has always been the St. George Lycabettus, high up on a baby mountain and only a five-minute stroll downhill into the heart of the city (for the uphill journey only a Sherpa would disdain the services of a cab). And my restaurant in that city is unfailingly the Gerofinikas, an oasis of elegance at the end of what seems to be a tenement hallway. Outside Athens, I rely on simple accommodations and local specialities or on the ubiquitous and ambrosial 'village salad': tomatoes, cucumber, olives and slices of feta cheese. And wine as light and simple as the meal. Gourmets may wince, but I have never eaten badly in a Greek taverna.

Every year, the same impatience for the islands that has thus far robbed me of the glories of Delphi impels me across the Aegean. Islands are, like music, a matter of taste. Mykonos, for example, has always reminded me of Fire Island with windmills. Thera, or Santorini, which may once have been Atlantis, is too stark; Lemnos, although it boasts a superb hotel is, alone among Greek islands, achingly dull.

The first of my islands was Skiathos, in the Sporades. It boasts one road, a small, lively town (the best taverna is Ilya's, which, let ailurophobes beware, has a garden infested by scores of lean, lap-addicted cats) and the finest beach in all Greece, a half-mile of flawless sand known as Koukounaries. The best hotel, the Skiathos Palace, is yards away. As in the case of many resort hotels, I use the word 'best' in the relative sense. The rooms are a delight, the floors marble and cool to the naked foot; against this, the staff are surly and lunch is a marvel of uninspired frugality.

Apart from the beaches, the only daytime diversion on Skiathos is the boat trip to Kastro, the remains of the island's former capital. The path upward is precipitous, and I remember sitting down, overcome by vertigo and unable to budge, while a local priest skipped by, goatlike in his peasant's boots, with a smiling salutation of 'Kalimera!'

My second island was Crete: a world unto itself where, at Herakleion airport, the arriving visitor is confronted by the world's shortest conveyor belt. The piling of Pelion upon Ossa was as nothing compared to the chaos when a hundred or so suitcases, rucksacks, backpacks and portmanteaus rise into a teetering mountain.

The ruins of Knossus, seat of the Minoan civilization, are a few miles away. These were excavated by Sir Arthur Evans as recently as 1909, and if his reconstructions and recopying of frescoes have caused fury among the purists, the impression of past grandeur disarms all others.

A visit – or, if you like, a pilgrimage – should be paid to the grave of Nikos Kazantzakis, author of *Zorba the Greek,* on a hilltop overlooking Herakleion. A cab driver refused to allow me to leave Crete until I had seen the high, simple cross and the epitaph:

I expect nothing . . .
I fear nothing . . .
I am free.

Crete is intimidating at first sight. The land itself, mountainous and sun-bleached, seems inhospitable; in the villages, the faces are leathery and gaunt, the hands brown and toil-hardened. A very real tradition of kindness to strangers exists, however: A visitor in trouble instantly becomes not a tourist but a guest.

Actually there is a sharp distinction to be made between traveller and tourist. The former will seek out the remotest inland villages, stay for a pittance in simple, white-scrubbed rooms, and allow the hours to creep by over cups of bitter Greek coffee (it is Turkish, really, but nothing good, you are told, ever came out of that place). The latter will inevitably head for the resort town of Hagios Nikolaos.

The place is bustling; syrtaki music jangles the length of every street and alleyway; new high-rise blocks appear yearly. The town is probably unique in that it was ruined by television: A BBC series, *The Lotus Eaters*, exploited its picturesque charm and brought the tourists. Today it is good for souvenirs and restaurants (the best, overlooking the pebble beach, is the Faros) and not much else; for tranquillity one takes the road for Elounda.

The drive – only seven miles – is best undertaken before nightfall: The Greeks have the custom of erecting guard rails along the straight stretches of road and leaving the hairpin turns unprotected. The journey is worth the consternation, however. For one thing, the Elounda Beach Hotel is a joy, with air conditioned stone bungalows jutting over the sea. There is a pool, a sandy beach (rare for Crete) and 'Cretan Night' every Tuesday, a lively cabaret with native foods, ouzo and singing and dancing – as always in Greece, travellers are encouraged to join in. Only dinner is, as always in hotels, to be avoided. A mile away, the village of Elounda itself merits a shrug at first glance, but it has a bedraggled serenity. I remember a twilight supper at the water's edge: As the moon rose, we flicked pellets of bread over the quayside and watched the sea come alive in a scene worthy of a mini *Jaws*.

My favourite island now is Thasos, too far to the north to attract the cruise ships or tourists who use the Cyclades as so many stepping-stones. It is ninety minutes from Kavalla – a delight in itself – and drivers should know that in Greece one boards a ferry in reverse, with a stomach-turning glimpse of oil-slicked water on either side.

Most of Thasos is lush and mountainous; few European islands can surpass it for beauty or the redness of its sunsets. A good road encircles the island (the circuit is sixty miles), and one lingers at tiny, pine-shaded beaches such as Aliki or the sleepy port of Liminaria, a paradise for the idler. The capital, Thasos (also called Limin), has a ruined theatre and excavations; and as the sun goes down there is the *volta*: residents and tourists alike parading on the quayside deriving untold mirth from the sight of each other.

Tavernas abound, but can be noisy. Two rival establishments, next door to one another, have television sets mere inches apart and tuned to different channels. This, compounded by the bouzouki music from a nearby café, impelled us off toward the best restaurant on the island, at the port of Prinos Skala, forty minutes' drive away.

My preferred hotel is the Makryammos Bungalows, just out of Thasos. The beach is idyllic to an unlikely degree, except when the day-trippers swarm in (at a price) by caique and motor launch. The food is Greek and therefore good, and there is about the place an amiable dottiness. The bald headwaiter is Egyptian and frequently homesick; a young donkey is apt to stroll up, seize one's bottle of beer in his teeth and guzzle the contents; and this must be the only hotel in Greece that regularly runs out of lemons and tomatoes.

Not long ago, a friend asked me why I unfailingly return to the Greek islands when there are so many other places to be seen and enjoyed. I could only answer that this is like approaching a man who is happily in love with a beautiful women of intelligence, grace and refinement and asking him why he does not go out on blind dates.

NOTES ON THE CONTRIBUTORS

A. ALVAREZ has homes in London and Lucca. Among his books are *The Biggest Game in Town* and *The Savage God*.

SUSAN HELLER ANDERSON, a reporter for *The New York Times*, has lived in Paris.

R. W. APPLE, JR., is chief of the London bureau of *The New York Times*.

LUIGI BARZINI has been a journalist and a politician. Among his books are *The Italians* and *The Europeans*. He lives in Rome.

QUENTIN BELL, the son of Clive Bell and Vanessa Stephen, is Emeritus Professor of the History and Theory of Art, Sussex University, and the biographer of Virginia Woolf.

SAUL BELLOW, Nobel laureate in literature, has also won the Pulitzer Prize and three National Book Awards.

RONALD BLYTHE is the author of *Akenfield: Portrait of an English Village* and *The View in Winter: Reflections on Old Age*, among other books.

MICHAEL BRENSON, who reports on art for *The New York Times*, lived in Paris for a number of years.

RICHARD EDER was formerly chief of *The New York Times* Paris bureau.

JOAN GAGE, a Massachusetts-based writer, lived in Athens for five years.

NICHOLAS GAGE, formerly chief of *The New York Times* bureau in Athens, was born in Greece. He is the author of *Eleni*.

DONALD GODDARD is the author of *Blimey! Another Book about London* and *Ace of Diamonds*.

PAUL GOLDBERGER is the architecture critic of *The New York Times*. His most recent book is *On the Rise: Architecture and Design in a Postmodern Age*.

MACDONALD HARRIS, whose novels include *Tenth*, *Herma*, and *Screenplay*, lives in Southern California.

SHIRLEY HAZZARD was born in Sydney, Australia. Her novels include *The Transit of Venus*, which won the 1981 National Book Critics Circle Award for fiction, and *The Bay of Noon*.

PAUL HOFMANN, a former *Times* correspondent, lives in Rome. He is the author of *Rome, the Sweet Tempestuous Life* and *O Vatican!*

A. E. HOTCHNER is the author of *Papa Hemingway* and *The Man Who Lived at the Ritz*.

MARVINE HOWE has served as chief of *The New York Times* bureau in Athens.

RONA JAFFE is the author of eleven books, including *Class Reunion* and *Mazes and Monsters*.

HUGH LEONARD, the author of *Da,* is a playwright who lives near Dublin. He is a frequent visitor to Greece.

PETER LEVI is a poet and classical scholar at Oxford. He is also the author of *The Hill of Kronos* and *Atlas of the Greek World*.

MALACHI MARTIN has written widely on matters of faith and morals. His works include *There Is Still Love, The Final Conclave,* and *The Decline and Fall of the Roman Church*.

JAMES MCGREGOR is a member of the American Academy in Rome. He was assisted by Ruth Gais, a classical archaeologist, in the preparation of the article on the Vatican museums in this volume.

BERNADINE MORRIS covers fashion for *The New York Times*.

JAN MORRIS'S books include *The Venetian Empire, Conundrum* and, most recently, *Journeys*.

DAVID PLANTE is an American writer who has lived in London for twenty years. His books include *Difficult Women* and *The Secret*.

FRANK J. PRIAL is the wine columnist for *The New York Times*.

V. S. PRITCHETT was the author of several collections of short stories, in addition to biographies and criticism.

FREDERIC RAPHAEL is the author of film scripts and novels, among them *Darling* and *The Glittering Prizes*, and a biography of Byron.

A. L. ROWSE, emeritus fellow of All Souls College, Oxford, is the author of numerous histories of the Elizabethan age and an authority on Shakespeare.

JOHN RUSSELL, chief art critic of *The New York Times,* is the author, most recently, of *Paris*.

JOHN DE ST. JORRE is a senior associate at the Carnegie Endowment for International Peace in Washington. He is co-author, with Anthony Edgeworth, of *The Guards*.

MURIEL SPARK was born in Scotland, and now lives in Rome. Among her novels are *The Prime of Miss Jean Brodie* and, most recently, *Loitering with Intent*.

D. M. THOMAS, the British poet, translator and novelist, is the author of *The White Hotel* and *Ararat*.

JOHN VINOCUR is chief of the Paris bureau of *The New York Times*.

WILLIAM WEAVER is an American critic and translator who lives in Tuscany. His books include *The Golden Century of Italian Opera* and *Duse*, a biography.

PATRICIA WELLS, restaurant critic of *The International Herald Tribune* in Paris, is the author of *The Food Lover's Guide to Paris*.

CHRISTOPHER S. WREN, chief of the Ottawa bureau of *The New York Times*, studied Chinese at Cambridge University.

JAQUELINE WREN, a writer who lives in Canada, earned an M.A. at Oxford after studying there at St. Hilda's College.

ABOUT THE EDITORS

A. M. ROSENTHAL is the executive editor of *The New York Times* and has been in charge of its news operations for the past fifteen years. He is the recipient of a Pulitzer Prize for his work as a foreign correspondent for *The New York Times*. Mr. Rosenthal is the author of *38 Witnesses* and co-author with Arthur Gelb of *One More Victim*.

ARTHUR GELB is deputy managing editor of *The New York Times* and supervisory editor of the new Sophisticated Traveller magazine. He was formerly chief cultural correspondent of *The Times*. He is co-author with his wife, Barbara, of the Eugene O'Neill biography, *O'Neill*.

MICHAEL J. LEAHY is the editor of *The New York Times* Travel Section, of which NORA KERR is deputy editor.

INDEX